Territories of desire in queer culture

Refiguring contemporary boundaries

edited by

David Alderson and Linda Anderson

Manchester University Press

Manchester and New York

distributed exclusively in the the USA by St. Martin's Press

Published by Manchester University Press
Oxford Road, Manchester M13 9NR, UK
and Room 400, 175 Fifth Avenue, New York, NY 10010, USA
http://www.manchesteruniversitypress.co.uk

Distributed exclusively in the USA by
St. Martin's Press, Inc., 175 Fifth Avenue, New York,
NY 10010, USA

Distributed exclusively in Canada by
UBC Press, University of British Columbia, 2029 West Mall,
Vancouver, BC, Canada V6T 1Z2

British Library Cataloguing-in-Publication Data
A catalogue record for this book is available from the British Library

Library of Congress Cataloging-in-Publication Data applied for

ISBN   0 7190 5760 4   *hardback*
        0 7190 5761 2   *paperback*

First published 2000

07 06 05 04 03 02 01 00   10 9 8 7 6 5 4 3 2 1

Typeset in Minion
by Northern Phototypesetting Co Ltd, Bolton
Printed in Great Britain
by Bell & Bain Ltd, Glasgow

Territories of desire
in queer culture

MANCHESTER
UNIVERSITY PRESS

Contents

Notes on contributors

David Alderson lectures in English Literature at Manchester University. He is author of *Mansex Fine: Religion, Manliness and Imperialism in Nineteenth Century British Culture* (1998) and co-editor of *Ireland in Proximity: History, Gender, Space* (1999).

Linda Anderson is Professor of Modern English and American Literature at the University of Newcastle-upon-Tyne and is the author of *Women and Autobiography in the Twentieth Century* (1997) and *Autobiography* (forthcoming: 2000).

Glyn Davis is a lecturer in Screen history and Theory at Edinburgh College of Art. He is currently writing a doctoral thesis on contemporary queer culture, and has had papers published on lesbian and gay film spectatorship, and mainstream cinematic representation of HIV/AIDS.

Laura Doan is Professor of English at the State University of New York, Geneseo. Most recently she has edited, with Lucy Bland, *Sexology in Culture: Labelling Bodies and Desires* and *Sexology Uncensored: the Documents of Sexual Science.* She is completing a manuscript called *Fashioning Sapphism: the Origins of a Modern English Lesbian Culture* (Columbia University Press) and co-editing with Jay Prosser, *Palatable Poison: New Critical Perspectives on* The Well of Loneliness.

Jonathan Dollimore is Professor of English and Related Literature at the University of York. His books include: *Radical Tragedy* (1984); with Alan Sinfield, *Political Shakespeare* (1985); *Sexual Dissidence* (1991); *Death, Desire and Loss in Western Culture* (1998).

Santiago Fouz Hernández is a lecturer in Spanish in the Department of European Studies at Durham University (Stockton campus). He studied at the University of Santiago de Compostela (Spain) and then

completed an MA at the University of Newcastle-upon-Tyne where he
is writing a PhD on the representations of masculinity in contemporary Spanish and British cinema. His most recent publication is an
article on Spanish actor Javier Bardem for *Spanish Cinema: Calling the
Shots* (Leeds Iberian Papers series).

Deborah Hunn has taught at the University of Adelaide and at the
Flinders University of South Australia. She is currently teaching in the
English Department at the University of Western Australia where she
is completing a PhD in queer theory and modernist narrative. Her
publications include articles on Australian lesbian pulp fiction, queer
theory and Virginia Woolf.

James Knowles lectures in the Department of English Studies, University
of Stirling. He has written extensively on Renaissance literature,
especially masculinity and the masque, and has edited *Shakespeare's
Late Plays* (1999) with Jenny Richards. He is currently editing the
masques and entertainments for the New Cambridge Works of Ben
Jonson and is completing his monograph, *The Theatrical Closet.*

Bill Marshall is Professor of Modern French Studies at Glasgow University. He is the author of books on Victor Serge and Guy Hocquenghem,
and of a forthcoming book on Quebec National Cinema. He has
written widely on French film and media culture.

Andrew Moor completed his PhD research on the films of Michael Powell
and Emeric Pressburger at the University of Newcastle. He has recently
written on Anton Walbrook for *British Stars and Stardom,* ed. Bruce
Babington (Manchester University Press, forthcoming), and is
working on a full length study of Powell and Pressburger. He teaches
Film Studies at the University of Wales, Bangor.

Chris Perriam is Professor of Hispanic Studies at the University of
Newcastle-upon-Tyne. His main research interests are in contempo-
rary Spanish cinema and Spanish-language poetry in the contexts of
cultural and gay/queer studies. His publications include: *Desire and
Dissent: an Introduction to Luis Antonio de Villena* (1995). He is
currently writing on issues of masculinity and its representation in
Spanish cinema of the 1990s; he has co-authored *A New History of
Spanish Writing from 1930 to the 1990s,* forthcoming from Oxford
University Press.

Seth Clark Silberman is completing his dissertation on the representation
of male homosexuality in early twentieth-century African American,
Caribbean and African literatures at the University of Maryland,
College Park. He has taught at the European Humanities University in

Minsk, Belarus, and Univerität Tübingen, Germany. He is the co-editor of *Generation Q: Gays, Lesbians and Bisexuals Born around 1969's Stonewall Riots Tell their Stories of Growing Up in the Age of Information* (Alyson, 1996). His fiction is included in *Quickies: Short Fiction on Gay Male Desire* (Arsenal Pulp, 1998).

Alan Sinfield teaches on the MA programme 'Sexual Dissidence and Cultural Change' at the University of Sussex. His recent books include *Out on Stage: Lesbian and Gay Theatre in the Twentieth Century* (1999); *Gay and After* (1998); *The Wilde Century* (1994).

Lizzie Thynne is Senior Lecturer in Video at the London College of Music and Media and an award-winning film-maker. Since her original research on Renaissance literature, she has made documentaries for Channel 4's gay programming and shorts for gallery exhibition. She previously worked in cinema exhibition and education and has published work on lesbian representation in film. She is currently developing a film/book project on the surrealist photographer Claude Cahun.

Sarah Waters is the author of a PhD thesis and various articles on the idea of history in lesbian and gay writing, but is currently working as a full-time novelist. Her fiction so far has explored lesbian sexual identities of the Victorian period. *Tipping the Velvet*, her first novel, was published by Virago in 1998; it won a 1999 Betty Trask award, and was shortlisted for the John Llewellyn Rhys prize. *Affinity*, also published by Virago, appeared in 1999. She is currently working on her third novel.

1

Introduction

David Alderson and Linda Anderson

This is a remarkably productive time for thinking about questions of sexuality, a moment of significant shifts in attitudes, perceptions and definitions. In the academic world, the past fifteen years or so have seen the emergence of lesbian and gay studies, and subsequently queer studies, reflecting a broader self-confidence and visibility on the part of lesbian and gay communities, including higher public and media profiles. Such prominence is clearly a consequence of the gains made by those communities as well as a symptom of the broader liberalisation of societies in the 1990s, at least in western Europe and the United States. But one of the paradoxes of this greater prominence is that it has coincided with, or perhaps been partially responsible for, an intensification of debate around sexual identification, so that – again, both within and beyond the academic world – lesbian and gay identities have come under increasing scrutiny both for their coherence as ways of understanding sexuality and for their desirability as expressions of sexual dissidence. Simultaneously, liberalisation and the increasing lack of a perceived common objective in terms of cultural production and political activism have produced a diversification of voices in debates about the politics of sexuality ranging from the radical to the conservative. For the purposes of this collection it is important that we intially take stock of some of these developments.

It is a commonplace following Michel Foucault's work to note that lesbian and gay identities imply an essentialist conception of the subject,[1] and, following Eve Sedgwick, to acknowledge the 'minoritising'[2] logic attendant on such identities, which lead to demands for civil rights for a particular stigmatised group. Arguably this has been at the expense of a more radical, universalising impulse which aspires to undermine the polarities of hetero- and homo-sexual by emphasising their artificiality and even their role in policing sexual desire. Whether or not essentialism has in fact been characteristic of lesbian and gay identities and strategies is perhaps debatable, and those who assume that it has may be guilty of a kind of Foucauldian revisionism. In Britain the activist Peter Tatchell, for one, has argued that 'The more we succeed in asserting our human rights as homosexuals, the sooner the differences between heteros and queers lose their significance ... The end result of this erosion of sexual difference will be the demise of distinct homosexual and heterosexual orientations and identities.'[3] None the less, it may well be that Tatchell's is not a representative voice, and, in contrast to his position, of course, there are those who see the discovery of a gay gene as providing the (necessary?) biological justification for civil rights by disposing of the objection that sexual orientation is in some sense 'chosen' and might be altered.

In avowed contrast to the minoritising conception of same-sex desire, though, we have also witnessed in the 1990s the emergence of 'queer' positions in cultural and theoretical discourse as well as in activist circles, rejecting essentialism and focusing instead on the constructed nature of sexual identities, their contingency and instability. As a reappropriation of a term of abuse, 'queer' has been used to valorise those forms of sexuality which are not merely resistant to the 'norm' but which carry the potential to subvert the very grounds on which such normative judgements might be made in the first place by refusing or rendering incoherent homo/heterosexual and – often at the same time – masculine/feminine binarisms. As the title of this volume suggests, we intend it to be a contribution to and development of such work, albeit at times a critical one.

However, queer thinking, and the anti-essentialism which underpins it, has been far from universally welcomed. Indeed, it has been as unsettling, and possibly more so, for many who regard themselves as lesbian or gay as it has been for those 'straights' who are ostensibly the principal targets of its subversive challenge. Rictor Norton, for instance, has recently argued against social constructionism in relation to sexuality, simultaneously rendering 'queer' innocuous by treating it as a mere synonym for 'gay'. In a statement which runs precisely counter to the guiding principles of this collection, he claims that

> Not only have a very limited number of homosexual paradigms been observed throughout history and throughout different cultures, but they are very often found concurrently in a single culture. These models display more similarities to one another than do individual cultures, and it is remarkable that queer (sub)cultures have more in common with each other than with the larger cultures of which they are a part.[4]

Norton's insistence on subsuming different expressions of same-sex desire under an implicitly Anglo-American model contrasts with the close attention paid in these essays to the various determining factors of the ways in which same-sex desire is structured, experienced and represented at different times and in different places. Moreover, the writers collected here are conscious of writing at a time when, certainly in the West, the boundaries of what are considered legitimate and illegitimate are shifting and becoming less obviously coterminous with gay/straight oppositions, even though this is inevitably an uneven process. In this sense, the marginality and dissidence of same-sex desire is not taken for granted. Indeed, tacitly underpinning many of the chapters in this book are concerns with the degree to which same-sex desire represents a genuinely unsettling or subversive force, how it relates to other forms of dissidence or social challenge (feminism and 'racial' or class politics, for instance), the possibilities and the conditions for its assimilation to respectable bourgeois society, and even the desirability of this process of assimilation.

In this sense, these chapters reflect a further feature of queer thinking: in its tendency to invoke multiple forms of dissidence it encourages us to look beyond the dynamics of gay-versus-straight. According to Sedgwick, whilst 'gay' and 'lesbian' remain close to the 'definitional center' of the term, recent work has also spun queer thinking 'outward along dimensions that can't be subsumed under gender and sexuality at all: the ways that race, ethnicity, postcolonial nationality criss-cross with these and other identity-constituting, identity-fracturing discourses, for example'.[5] As Jeffrey Escoffier puts it, 'Queer politics offers a way of cutting across race and gender lines. It implies the rejection of a minoritarian logic of toleration or simple interest-representation. Instead, queer politics represents an expansive impulse of inclusion: specifically, it requires a resistance to regimes of the normal'.[6] It should not be surprising, then, that other recent work has reflected this 'expansiveness', suggesting perhaps a dissatisfaction with the mere articulation of difference as a form of distinctness or quasi-separatism; it may even be that this impulse stems from a desire to revive older imperatives of solidarity. When asked to edit a lesbian and gay issue of the journal *diacritics*, Judith Butler and Biddy Martin chose instead to focus on cross-identifications in order 'to expand our emphasis ... to avoid static conceptions of identity and political alignment ... by soliciting essays that analyze critical, even surprising, boundary crossings'.[7]

But assimilation too has its strong advocates, and has emerged as a dissonant counterpoint to queer thinking – possibly even as the dominant strain of lesbian and gay aspirations – in the 1990s. The right to serve in the military, for instance, has become a prominent demand of civil rights campaigns – raising questions about the relationships between same-sex desire, imperialism and masculinity – and this, along with gay marriages, is the cause which the avowedly conservative figure Andrew Sullivan makes central to his argument for lesbian and gay equality.[8] The strand of thinking represented by Sullivan, then, is clearly hostile to the 'queer' impulse to expand, rather than narrow, dissident sympathies and is directed at least as much at removing conservative anxieties about homosexuality as it is at encouraging lesbians and gay men to embrace 'normality'; it is about removing the perceived threat which homosexuality – conceived in essentialist terms – represents.

These essays, then, focus on the interrelated questions of desire, definition, history, cultural difference, assimilation and emancipation. They demonstrate an awareness of the necessary cross-identifications between sexuality and the broader cultural and political contexts in which identities are elaborated, and in some cases question the adequacy of the very term 'cross-identification', implying as it does a mere intersection of otherwise discrete formations, rather than a reciprocal, dialectical or even contradictory structuring of various forces and processes of identification. Notably, there is an emphasis throughout on the complicating questions of gender, national and 'racial' difference and the material construction of (male) gay subcultures by market forces, concerns which themselves cross the sectional divisions of the volume. The word 'territories' in the book's title is therefore intended to draw attention to the material (geographical and spatial) as well as metaphorical (for instance, cultural and temporal) boundaries which help to contain – in the sense of set limits to – perception, analysis and debate. Our aim is to foreground these limits, frequently in order to call them into question.

Part 1 of this book considers questions of history and our relationships to the past as they are mediated by various cultural phenomena. In particular, these essays are concerned with the legacies of the past and, more importantly perhaps, the ways in which our understanding of the past is determined by changing contemporary exigencies. Laura Doan and Sarah Waters discuss the ways in which lesbian historical fiction has tended to imagine the past in the restrictive terms of contemporary identity politics, a process which has been challenged in the work of Jeanette Winterson in particular. Winterson's writing, and the kinds of arguments put forward by critics such as Doan and Waters, clearly carry implications for the more traditional demand to increase lesbian visibility by recovering a history which has thus far been neglected or obscured. David Alderson looks at the sense of history in Alan Hollinghurst's fiction, paying particular attention to the novels' ambivalence towards past and present, an ambivalence determined by Hollinghurst's relations to a particular English literary-cultural tradition which, as Andrew Moor demonstrates, is shared by the otherwise self-consciously avant-garde Derek Jarman. In this respect, both Alderson and Moor draw our attention to culturally influential – though possibly socially residual – class inflections of same-sex desire in English society and analyse in detail the ways in which these two very different figures have responded to the development of a gay/queer subculture and politics.

But desire itself has a history. As Jonathan Dollimore has recently argued in his book *Death, Desire and Loss in Western Culture*,[9] there has been a long tradition within European culture of seeing desire and death as intrinsically linked. Significantly this relation has also been gendered, with femininity and death often aligned and woman being used to represent the living threat of death within sexuality, or desire's deathly consummation (a theme which Dollimore revisits in our final chapter). By contrast, Elizabeth Grosz, in her recent work, has sought ways of disentangling the gendered dialectic between death and desire, arguing that their cultural linking is neither universal nor inevitable. The tradition of thinking about desire as a relation to loss is bound up with sexual polarisation, that is, with seeing the sexes as complementary, filling up a lack in each other. Desire has therefore been heterosexualised, placing woman as the passive object of the man's active desiring. Grosz's argument is that it is impossible to think lesbian desire according to such a model and that we need to rethink desire not as a relation to negativity but as 'an intensity, innervation, positivity, or force'.[10] Queering desire may mean transforming what we have meant by desire into something else – 'movement, processes, transmutations' – using desire to 'rearrange, reorganize the body's forms and sensations, to make the subject and the body as such dissolve into something else, something other than what they are habitually'.[11] Desire, then, might be freed from its own past into the transformative energy of becoming. Taking up the theme of nostalgia introduced by Alderson and Moor, Linda Anderson's essay develops Grosz's insights by suggesting that nostalgia itself is a form of desire which creates a complex temporality for queer subjects for whom the past offers neither explanation nor origin. Anderson thus offers a more radical view of nostalgia as overflowing the texts she discusses, creating new affects and unsettling boundaries.

Part II, 'Relocating desire', takes us beyond the metropolitan centres of those Anglo-American societies which have been associated most closely with the elaboration of lesbian and gay sexual, social and political identities, to explore contemporary French, Spanish, Greek–Australian and northern British imaginings of same-sex desire in both film and fiction. Bill Marshall takes issue with Simon Watney's attack on Cyril Collard's *Les Nuits fauves*, brilliantly dissecting its typically French lack of engagement with identity politics, and this emphasis is complemented by Santiago Fouz Hernández and Chris Perriam's chapter on contemporary Spanish cinema, which suggests that Anglo-American paradigms of gay and even queer sexuality offer only problematic interpretative grids for understanding recent Spanish films.

If Marshall, Fouz Hernández and Perriam are alert to the different constructions of same-sex desire across national contexts, though, the other two chapters in Part II focus more closely on the internal divisions of particular spaces. As Gill Valentine has argued, space, as it is experienced in relation to sexuality, is never singular or homogeneous, since 'there are usually "others" present who are producing their own relational spaces', or who are reading 'heterosexual space against the grain – experiencing it differently'. [2] Bounded spaces are comprised of scattered or overlapping locations which possess the potential to generate tensions or conflicts at both the social and subjective levels. This is no less true of attempts to generate or define gay spaces, as Deborah Hunn implies in her account of the ways in which ethnic and class divisions complicate sexual identity in an Australian context, and more specifically the ways in which the urban geography of Melbourne maps on to experiences of both gender identification and same-sex desire as these are represented in Christos Tsiolkas's novel *Loaded* and its filmic adaptation by the lesbian director Ana Kokkinos. At the same time, Hunn demonstrates that the closet of the central character, Ari, is 'one of complex dimensions', and involves resistance to the assimilation of ethnic and sexually dissident groups into a liberalising Australian society as well as a form of alienation. A similar concern with divisions within certain boundaries – in this case, those of Britain – and with the class divisions which are often assumed to structure its internal north/south polarities is the focus of James Knowles's chapter on the novels of Paul Magrs.

It is a grounding assumption of most contemporary work on sexuality that sex, gender and desire do not map neatly on to each other but rather have been assumed, or made to do so in order to maintain the logic of compulsory heterosexuality. None the less, it may be, as Alan Sinfield suggests in his essay which opens Part III of this collection, that the post-Stonewall lesbian and gay emphasis on sexuality has itself so far tended to displace and obscure forms of gender dissidence. To make his point, he looks at non-Western cultures in which same-sex desire does not correlate with same-gender attraction. He thus develops the critical impulses of the previous section by refusing to assimilate the dissident strands of other cultures to the civil rights paradigms which have tended to dominate the Anglo-American scene, and in doing so he refuses to privilege Western norms as the enlightened ideal to which all cultures should aspire. None the less, Sinfield's agenda is self-consciously determined by developments within Western debates, and in particular by the questions increasingly raised by transgendered identities, a theme taken up, in a different context, by Seth Clark Silberman who also continues the volume's engagement with 'racial' matters in his discussion of the different strategies of RuPaul and Andre Charles (the figure behind Ru) in challenging sexual and gender identification.

The final two chapters of Part III, though, emphasise the difficulties of crossing boundaries. In this respect, they offer valuable correctives to certain tendencies within contemporary queer thinking which might be said to exhibit a peculiar optimism of the intellect in their detection of subversive and unstable currents in various cultural phenomena despite the fact that the dominant regime of sexuality remains relatively stable and, in certain parts of the world, is being reinforced by state initiatives which accord priority to marriage and the nuclear family. It is this regime itself which is interrogated in *Safe* by queer film pioneer Todd Haynes, discussed here by Glyn Davis. This is not a film which celebrates a possible, still less achieved, state of queerness; indeed its concern with sexuality is rather oblique. Rather, Davis argues, its subversive power lies in its presentation of illness as a metaphor for an alienated relation to the 'normality' of suburban domesticity which is interrogated in the film's preoccupation with the racially potent symbolism of whiteness. Here it is the constraining, claustrophobic territory of the home which is being critiqued. Lizzie Thynne similarly demonstrates an awareness of hegemonic forces in alerting us to the fact that the desire for change is often held in check by the power of a culture to reappropriate differences and re-inscribe them as the same. Thynne discusses the obdurately persistent discursive limits to the representations of women's same-sex desire on British television which have gone largely unchallenged by the

otherwise liberal institutional agendas on sexuality, even where these
have led to the greater prominence of relationships between women.

We end this volume, though, with reflections on the state of theoretical debates themselves and, simultaneously, by looking to the future with
Jonathan Dollimore's intricate examination of the complicities and
contradictions between and within what he terms the reformist, enlightenment view of sexuality, which envisages the social assimilation of
same-sex desire, and the more radical investment of sexuality with a
revolutionary potential. Dollimore's argument is valuable not merely for
its exploration of the history and implications of current debates but also
as a self-reflexive piece on the institutionalisation of lesbian and
gay/queer studies and the establishment of its own territory – a necessary
process in itself, perhaps, and one in which Dollimore himself has played
a significant part, but one which has, at the same time, produced its own
limits and orthodoxies.

Dollimore's chapter is, in its consideration of future possibilities,
inevitably at times speculative, and is perhaps therefore symptomatic of
a contemporary moment characterised by flux and uncertainty. Indeed,
it is this uncertainty that makes inevitable the diversity of this volume as
a whole. Though these chapters may be said loosely to occupy the
common ground which we have set out in this introduction, they do not
represent a consensus and should not be made to do so. Instead, they
provide examples of the potential of queer thinking to chart changing
configurations and alignments; ultimately to provide some kind of map
– if inevitably a provisional and bounded one – of present complexities
and future possibilities.

Notes

1   Michel Foucault, *History of Sexuality*, trans. Robert Hurley (Harmonds-
    worth, Penguin, 1981).
2   See Eve Kosofsky Sedgwick, *Epistemology of the Closet* (Hemel Hempstead,
    Harvester Wheatsheaf, 1991), p. 1.
3   Peter Tatchell, 'It's just a phase: why homosexuality is doomed' in Mark
    Simpson (ed.), *Anti-Gay* (London, Cassell, 1996), p. 53. It should be noted
    that Tatchell's piece is in striking contrast to much of the mere polemical
    disenchantment with gay identification which characterises this volume,
    and which the present volume hopes not to reproduce.
4   Rictor Norton, *The Myth of the Modern Homosexual: Queer History and the
    Search for Cultural Unity*, (London, Cassell, 1997), p. 24.
5   Eve Kosofsky Sedgwick, *Tendencies*, (London and New York, Routledge,

1994), p. 9.

6   Jeffrey Escoffier, 'Under the sign of the queer' *Found Object*, 1994, p. 135; quoted in Ruth Goldmann, 'Who is that *queer*queer?' in Brett Beemyn and Mickey Eliasan (eds), *Queer Studies: a Lesbian, Gay, Bisexual and Transgender Anthology* (New York and London, New York University Press, 1996), p. 170.

7   Judith Butler and Biddy Martin, introduction to *diacritics*, 24:2–3 (1994), 3.

8   Andrew Sullivan, *Virtually Normal: An Argument about Homosexuality* (London, Picador, 1995).

9   Jonathan Dollimore, *Death, Desire and Loss in Western Culture* (Harmondsworth, Allen Lane, 1998).

10 Elizabeth Grosz, 'Refiguring lesbian desire' in Laura Doan (ed.), *The Lesbian Postmodern* (New York, Columbia University Press, 1994), p. 74.

11 Elizabeth Grosz, 'Animal sex' in Elizabeth Grosz and Elspeth Probyn (eds), *Sexy Bodies: the Strange Carnalities of Feminism* (London and New York, Routledge, 1995), p. 295.

12 Gill Valentine, 'Lesbian productions of space' in Nancy Duncan (ed.), *Bodyspace* (London, Routledge, 1996), p. 150.

Part I

Another country: desire and the past

2

Making up lost time: contemporary lesbian writing and the invention of history

Laura Doan and Sarah Waters

For as long as 'homosexuality' has been available for meaningful deployment, commentators have traced its history, identifying traditions of same-sex love for purposes of diagnosis, censure, celebration, defence or apology. In a sense, retrospection is a condition of homosexual agency. If, as Foucault suggests, the homosexual was 'born' out of the conjunction of particular cultural factors, at a distinct historical moment, then s/he was born yearning for a genealogy with which to transcend that moment.[1] Many practitioners of sexology drew up roll-calls of famous homosexuals in which to situate their modern inverted subjects; and we know both from the testimonies in the case histories themselves (Richard von Krafft-Ebing, for example, refers to 'viragines' who take as their models 'certain female characters who in the past or the present have excelled by virtue of genius and brave and noble deeds')[2] and from the homophile literature that proliferated at the beginning of the twentieth century that retrospection has played a vital role in the culture of homosexual self-definition.

But while the interests of lesbians and gay men have often coincided in their quest for historical precedent, history itself has appeared to offer them an unequal balance of resources for the fulfilment of such a project. The male homosexual tradition, which interested commentators have pursued from Plato to Michelangelo, from Shakespeare to Wilde, has both subverted historical master narratives and substantially overlapped with them; the pederastic model cherished by nineteenth-century homosexual apologists, in which one generation passes its masculine privileges on to the next, is often indistinguishable from patriarchal accounts of cultural reproduction more generally.[3] The suppression or absence of lesbian activity from the historical record, on the other hand, has limited the constituency across which a lesbian genealogy might be

traced, and made it difficult for women to imagine themselves as participants in an unbroken tradition of same-sex love. While John Addington
Symonds (himself recently identified by Rictor Norton as 'the father of
queer history')[4] could look confidently and nostalgically to the
homophile communities of classical Greece, ancient Rome, Persia and
Renaissance Europe, early lesbian fantasists Renée Vivien and Natalie
Barney understood the search for lesbian originals to centre on a single,
highly-charged figure – Sappho of Lesbos.[5]

With the expansion of lesbian publishing in the past two decades, and
the emergence of distinctly lesbian popular fiction genres, historical
fiction has been rehabilitated for queer consumption alongside romance,
crime and science fiction; lesbians may now indulge the serious pleasure
of repossessing their own lost histories, through the speculative or reconstructive work of British and American writers such as Caeia March,
Ellen Galford, Penny Hayes and Sarah Aldridge. Yet on what terms does
history appeal to the lesbian writer and how is the past negotiated in
lesbian literary production? Should the popular novel be a site to
recuperate the names and lives of 'suitable' or famous lesbians of the past,
or is it better approached as a starting-point to invent a 'history' haunted
by the present and understood to take its authority from the imperatives
of contemporary lesbian identities? Should we read lesbian historical
novels as 'performative' rather than 'descriptive' texts – as indices to the
myths and fantasies through which lesbian culture is maintained and
reproduced?[6] We propose a two-fold approach to such questions by
surveying, in the opening section, a wide spectrum of popular realist
lesbian historical novels to explore how writers engage in diverse ways in
the project of 'making up lost time'; we then move on to an examination
of one particular writer – Jeanette Winterson – who is arguably the most
high-profile British lesbian novelist, and whose historiographic metafiction crosses over established notions of time and identity. We believe that
this juxtaposition of the genre of popular lesbian historical fiction against
Winterson's inventive use of postmodern literary strategies (for instance,
the ironic and self-conscious recognition of the fictionality of fact) will
reveal the lure of history in lesbian writing, but also its limits.

'Provoked to tender dreams by a hint': contemporary lesbian historical fictions

As we have suggested, the location of a lesbian genealogy is a project that
has impelled women's writing since the emergence of self-identified

lesbian groups; but it was given a particular, urgent, feminist agenda by the Sapphic fantasising of Vivien and Barney, at the turn of the twentieth century. Their contributions to classical debate helped to rescue Sappho from the misrepresentations of male-dominated scholarship; in their own lives and writing – via what Susan Gubar has termed a 'fantastic collaboration'[7] – they restored the woman-centred eros of Sappho's verse, and attempted to emulate and regenerate it for a modern lesbian culture. This involved the claiming of a matriarchal, pre- or ahistoric ancestry, audacious both in statement and in intent: in 'Thus would I speak' (1906), for example, Vivien's narrator tells a disapproving Christ, 'Let me return to the ancient splendour / And, when eternity finally comes, / Rejoin those women who never knew you at all.'[8] The *re* prefix is a prominent one in Vivien's Sapphic writing (as it was in her life: born plain Pauline Tarn, she renamed and rebirthed herself through the adoption of that suggestive Renée). Her poetry offers a re-enactment of the Sapphic original as both a rehearsal and a return; she understands the lesbian pilgrim to the isle of Lesbos to be a kind of revenant, and she constructs a lesbian historiography based on empathy, immediacy and mysticism: 'From the depths of my past I return to you, / Mytilene, across the disparate centuries.'[9] This reconstructive model, in which centuries dissolve under the weight of modern erotic imaginings, has proved profoundly influential or symptomatic for a lesbian culture still preoccupied with the recovery of Sapphic originals in the face of an attenuated historical record.

But if the impulse towards the tracing of an erotic genealogy remained strong in lesbian writing in the twentieth century, then the eras and icons across which such a history might be pursued have changed significantly, as discourses of sex and gender have shifted and evolved. While Sappho once dominated the lesbian historical imagination, she is conspicuous in modern lesbian fiction only by her absence. One of the few novel-length treatments of the Sapphic setting to emerge from the lesbian and gay presses is Ellen Frye's significantly titled *The Other Sappho* (1989), which offers us an ancient Greek culture in which erotic relations between women are routine and unremarkable, but ultimately unthreatening to patriarchal interests. Frye recasts Sappho herself as a bourgeois feminist, schooling her well-bred female students in the composition of wedding-songs and civic verses. In contrast, Frye's other Sappho is Lykaina, a peasant girl raised by wolves and trained in the music of the people: she establishes an alternative lesbian academy on the periphery of Sappho's island, a community of women dedicated to the worship of the Great

Mother and the celebration of ancient female heroines. The oral poetry produced here is radical, but ephemeral: it remains unconfined by literary records, but also unrecorded. 'This story is a history', Frye tells us in the novel's 'Prolegomena'. 'Not the history found in scholarly books, all carefully annotated, but the other kind, the kind that comes out of people's mouths from memories that have been passed on from generation to generation.'[10] Lykaina's history has been passed on to Frye herself, we are told, in just such a manner, for she has learned it through a chance encounter with an aged female storyteller in modern-day Lesbos. By this construction, to read the novel is to be implicitly cast as the legend's latest natural recipient, and charged with the responsibility of maintaining or transmitting it in one's turn.

Other lesbian historical novels position their readers in similar ways. Jeannine Allard's *Légende* (1984), which retells a nineteenth-century Breton story of women lovers who disguised themselves as husband and wife, is also prefaced by an 'Author's note': here Allard hopes that her novel will give her readers 'dreams and visions, and courage to make them true'.[11] Similarly, Isabel Miller appends an 'Afterword' to *Patience and Sarah* (first published as *A Place for Us*, 1969) which reveals the model for her novel to have been the 'romantic attachment' enjoyed by two early nineteenth-century women, Mary Ann Willson and her 'companion' Miss Brundidge. To Willson and Brundidge's story, Miller writes in her 'Afterword', 'we know our own response. We are provoked to tender dreams by a hint. Any stone from their hill is a crystal ball.'[12]

This is an appealing, romantic rhetoric: all three novels simultaneously satisfy the lesbian hunger for genealogy, and answer feminist anxieties that that genealogy has hitherto been elided or suppressed by patriarchal historiographical practice. Like Vivien and Barney, who sought to secure Sappho's pertinence for a modern lesbian audience via interventions in Sapphic debate that were at once scholarly and imaginative, the authors of recent lesbian historical fiction both invoke and abjure the authority of 'fact'. The recurrent stepping outside of the periodising frame through prologues and afterwords is not so much evidence of an appeal to historical record as it is testimony to the political charge of lesbian imagining: it recruits the reader into a community of shared lesbian interests understood to extend across history, and across the border separating history from fiction. It seems to affirm that – as Miller puts it – 'we' can, and must, intuit a meaningful history from the most insignificant of evidence: stones, hints, fragments; and it offers fantasy and wishful thinking as legitimate historiographical resources, necessary correctives or missing links to the impoverished lesbian archive. In this way, these novelists echo Monique Wittig's famous plea that we should '[m]ake an effort to remember, and failing that, invent'.[13]

In much recent lesbian fiction, indeed, this making up of lost time is a project into which characters are unwillingly or even traumatically drawn, at the urging of a suppressed history erupting into the present in the form of queer conjunctions, coincidences and hauntings. In Ellen Galford's *The Fires of Bride* (1986), contemporary artist Maria is troubled by messages from and glimpses of the matriarchal history of her island home, Cailleach; Denny, in Caeia March's *Fire! Fire!* (1991), gives voice to the seventeenth-century Roarie Brewster through a form of automatic writing; and Susan, in Paula Martinac's *Out of Time* (1990), becomes haunted by a group of lesbians from the 1920s when she finds an album of their photographs in a New York antique shop.[14] All three of these novels also figure as allegories of female creativity. Just as Vivien and Barney were enabled to write by their impassioned communings with Sapphic ancestors, so Maria, Denny and Susan overcome depression, aimlessness and artistic blocks through their encounters with the past, ultimately advertising the lives of their suppressed lesbian forebears in creative works of their own. This is lesbian historiography as exemplary feminist practice, a collaboration in which historical subjects are aware of their own significance for lesbian scholarship to the extent of organising the material remnants of their lives in anticipation of subsequent recuperation. And, again as in Vivien's verse, collaboration here is both artistic and erotic: the past and the present rub together, tribade-fashion, in intimacy and recognition, as Galford's and Martinac's protagonists are quite literally seduced by the restless lesbian phantoms that haunt them. "'It's for your education,'" purrs Harriet's ghost in *Out of Time*, 'her tongue exploring the curves of [Susan's] ear. "Tell yourself it's for history."'[15]

Such a scenario seems to enact the spectacular return of what Terry Castle has termed 'the "repressed idea"' of patriarchal culture, an 'apparitional' lesbianism she has found flitting across the master-texts of the western literary canon.[16] Like the lesbian spectre as Castle identifies it, the ghosts of Galford's, March's and Martinac's novels occupy abject but troubling positions on the borders of dominant structures of knowledge; like legends, they function as the natural repositories of subversive secrets, offering those secrets for recognition and retrieval by the empathetic reader of historical texts. 'I wonder', says a watchful ghost in Jane Eiseman's novel *Home Again, Home Again* (1990), as a modern lesbian couple discover the grave in which she and her lover are buried, 'Do you suppose they think they are the first ones to have found us?'[17] As Castle argues, the apparitional lesbian is paradoxically powerful: at once 'derealized' and resilient, flimsy and durable, robbed of her subversive sexual threat yet 'endlessly capable of "appearing"'.[18] This paradox, through which lesbian ghosts are simultaneously 'there' and 'not there', sustains the empowering historical vision of much recent lesbian fiction; but it must work ultimately, through tension and contradiction, to deflate that vision. The novels we have been examining here offer accounts of a lesbian past that are, in Eve Sedgwick's terms, at once 'universalizing' and 'minoritizing': they understand history to be bursting with lesbians ripe for modern recuperation (as in the utopian formula, We Are Everywhere), yet envisage lesbian history itself as a series of obscure romances, each one of them a struggle against patriarchal odds and available for retrieval through heroic but – as we have seen – unpredictable, abject or occult processes.[19] They identify a lesbian tradition that has been both routinely overlooked by the historical record and calculatedly expunged from it.

Ellen Galford's *Moll Cutpurse: Her True History* (1984) is typical here. Galford identifies spaces in the interstices of historical master-narratives for the maintenance of a secret tradition of female pleasures: such pleasures, she suggests, form 'An old story. It takes little wit to realise that women's joys are safest when kept secret.'[20] At the same time, however, the novel implies that lesbianism has been suppressed by men, 'who being jealous that a woman might get her pleasure without submitting to them, would strive to keep the very notion of such things from infecting the ears of their wives and daughters'.[21] The tension here relates to a sexual identity that is rich in meaning but nevertheless part of a gnostic tradition requiring recovery and elucidation. Moll herself must be educated by her apothecary lover Judith that her cross-dressing impulses are a symptom not of transgenderism, as she supposes (she initially approaches Judith for a potion to transform her into a man), but of lesbianism:

> 'Love,' she sighed, 'is also part of the problem. For when I love, and when I lust, it's a woman who's my object … They offer friendship, but I want something more. And when I have made this known to them they shun my company … Because I'm nothing to them without a stiff bull's pizzle and a pair of wobbling balls.'
> 'The more fools they,' I said, stroking her arm. 'I think perhaps you have been unlucky in your choice of women. For there are those of us who know that such machinery but gets in the way of a woman's true pleasure' …

> Her voice shook slightly. 'I've never met a woman who wanted me without them.'
>   'Now that proves it, Moll. You are a fool.' I kissed her over and over again, then drew her close and taught her otherwise.[22]

As in many lesbian historical novels, lesbian identity is offered here as taking its ultimate authority from the imperatives of the body; but it is a 'natural' identity in which the desiring subject must, paradoxically, be schooled.

Even more problematically, to appeal to the authority of the desiring body is to imagine that body as unlocated, undefined, unmarked by the cultural discourses by which bodies and desires are constructed and contained; it involves, in fact, a refusal of history, an embracing of the trans- or ahistorical. 'We are leaving behind a legend', says the sole surviving lesbian character at the end of Allard's *Légende*. '[B]ecause we have lived here, others will know that it has been done ... And the world will go on. Plus ça change, plus c'est la même chose.'[23] Similarly, when Denny in March's *Fire! Fire!* is offered a vision of a seventeenth-century lesbian partnership, she is challenged: 'Did you think you ... invented it, Denny, in your times?'[24] March's novels in particular – with their limited cast of recurring characters, their interweaving of individual and familial stories with larger national histories – collectively testify to a shared lesbian community extending over a range of different eras and cultures; a typical scene has a lesbian couple reading Adrienne Rich's *The Dream of a Common Language*: they might, they think, 'have been any women lovers, anywhere in the world, any time, in any living-room'.[25] Facilitating such a vision is March's more general presentation of lesbian intimacies as essentially pre- or alinguistic, uncorrupted by patriarchal discourse: 'Vonn's mouth is on Rachel's breast and Vonn's fingers are miming love stories to her clit, with a women body knowledge that reaches back to ancient times when women were birthed to be lovers for one another, women lovers brought forth from the primordial womb of the sea.'[26]

However, as Diana Fuss notes, 'The dream of either a common language or no language at all is just that – a dream, a fantasy that ultimately can do little to acknowledge and to legitimate the hitherto repressed differences between and within sexual identities.'[27] The past – which ought to proliferate with such differences – emerges from the lesbian historical genre as an erotic and political continuum through which alterity can be mystically overridden. Historical difference is located instead in the form of impediments to the expression of a basic lesbian teleology – impediments such as the necessity for one partner to adopt male disguise, or the lovers' ignorance of a distinctly lesbian vocabulary. 'Boy,' say the contemporary lesbian couple of *Home Again, Home Again*, as they confront the suggestive gravestone that is our lead into the novel's historical narrative, 'that would really have taken guts in those days.'[28] It is precisely this model of lesbian heroism – this sense that every lesbian couple in history must have been *Patience-and-Sarah*-style pioneers, raising new edifices upon the drab erotic landscape – that has impelled lesbian historical fiction into what appear to be its most appropriate forms; actually, of course, the genre's continual and dogged re-staging of lesbian ingenuousness leading to isolated romance is no more natural or authentic a vehicle for the recovery of pre-sexological same-sex configurations than any other. The recurrence of Miller's model, indeed, suggests that the genre and the communities it serves have an interest in *maintaining* a version of lesbian history that is underfunded, peripheral, unmarked by sexology; and it is perhaps not surprising that so many writers of lesbian historical fiction share that Fadermanesque model of 'romantic friends' which, as critics have noted, appears reassuringly to anticipate a modern lesbian feminist paradigm, but actually simply replicates it.[29] Ultimately, the motivating impulse behind much lesbian historical fiction is not historicism so much as nostalgia: the genre's ingenuous lesbian protagonists all undergo experiences similar to that of Eiseman's heroine Joan who, on first reading the poetry of Sappho, feels 'her confusion gradually lift[ing] … It was like coming home again. She felt like she had come home.'[30]

The narratives apparently 'recovered' by the genre, therefore, resemble nothing so much as the modern lesbian coming out stories analysed by Biddy Martin, and may be described in similar terms, as 'tautological': they detail 'a process of coming to know something that has always been true, a truth to which the author has returned'.[31] Such narratives imbue the past with lesbian meaning, even as they seem to extract meaning from it; and the urgent, clamorous artefacts with which the genre is cluttered – those photographs, stories, fragments and hints – operate as exemplary historical texts precisely to the extent that their coincidence with lesbian historiographical expectations is so complete. Consider again the grave with its stone carved with two female names, in *Home Again, Home Again*: 'Not a family plot, its cluster of stones identifying generations of spouses and children. And not an individual plot, mute testimony to a solitary life and death. But something outside the pattern, like a square of rose stitched into a quilt of reds and pinks.'[32] That elusive 'something' –

lesbianism – exists courageously here 'outside the pattern', as it does in other lesbian historical novels; but it can be isolated from its monochrome background only at the expense of other, vaguer identities and non-identities. The women subsumed into the 'family plot', the 'solitary life and death': there are no spirit-voices accompanying these; they testify to nothing, perhaps, except lost Sapphic potential, thwarted romance. And yet they may represent precisely those 'troublesome' historical subjects identified by Martha M. Umphrey – that is, the married, the celibate, the bisexual, the transgendered: men and women not quite identifiable as 'gay' but nevertheless offering a 'critique of compulsory heterosexuality' – whose place upon the queer family tree ought to be equally prominent alongside Symonds, Oscar Wilde and Sappho, but whose narratives the lesbian and gay past has so far signally failed to accommodate.[33]

The postmodern turn to 'history'

In her two 'historical' novels, *The Passion* (1987) and *Sexing the Cherry* (1989), author Jeanette Winterson features female protagonists – Villanelle and the Dog-Woman respectively – who, to borrow Umphrey's phrase again, are indeed 'not quite gay'.[34] This refusal simply to insert a mirror-image of a contemporary lesbian into an earlier historical period marks a break with the unwillingness of the genre of the lesbian historical novel to abandon limiting paradigms, and the beginning perhaps of a more inventive use of history. Unlike those popular novelists who locate lesbian stories in the spaces beyond, between or beneath dominant historical narratives, Winterson confronts the heart of the historical record; her construction of characters of both sexes who do not conform to any conventional or modern label of sexual identity familiar to the contemporary reader leaves her free to interpret the protagonists' desires or acts outside the conventions endorsed by the historical genre. In *The Passion*, for example, Villanelle, hopelessly in love with a married woman, is sold into sexual slavery by her own husband the cook who, before their marriage, had demanded she should continue to nurture his fantasies by cross-dressing as a boy. As a prostitute servicing Napoleon's troops in Russia, Villanelle meets Henri and, in this way, public war is supplanted by a more important, noble and heroic personal one as Henri shifts his (homoerotic) allegiance from his idol Napoleon to the boyish Villanelle. Villanelle, who holds power over the impressionable Henri – a man she loves like a brother – is a woman who desires another woman; yet she is free of labels such as lesbian or bisexual, unlike those lesbian pioneers celebrated in the historical genre whose identities nevertheless approximate a modern (feminist) model; she is a hero with the audacity and agency to enact her own liberation.

Similarly, while the lesbian bodies of popular historical fiction are scarred and impeded by heterosexist imposition – whether restricted by full skirts and corsetry, as butch Blanche is in Penny Hayes's *The Long Trail*, or confined to an awkward male disguise, like Biff in March's *The Hide and Seek Files* (1988) – the bodies of Villanelle and Dog-Woman represent a convergence of traits culturally associated with both the female and male, ultimately 'exceeding and ironizing' normative gender models.[35] Villanelle, for instance, possesses the 'clean heart' associated with femininity as well as the 'boatman's feet' found only on the body of the Venetian male gondolier: 'There never was a girl whose feet were webbed in the entire history of the boatmen', Villanelle declares.[36] While this most visible sign of Villanelle's congenital masculinity is tucked away discreetly in her boots and revealed only on the rarest of occasions, the young Venetian woman traverses the streets and canals of her city with complete physical freedom in her masculine clothing. Villanelle testifies matter-of-factly about the extraordinary nature of her cross-sexed body, just as Dog-Woman nonchalantly describes her own monumental size as comparable to, if not greater than, an elephant.

Dog-Woman too, in playing an active and interventionist role, is an archetypal 'sister doing it for herself': she 'mothers' a child, Jordan, without having experienced heterosexual sex or the act of childbirth when she discovers him as a foundling abandoned by the Thames: 'I would have liked to pour out a child from my body but you have to have a man for that and there's no man who's a match for me', she proudly exclaims.[37] Once again Winterson unsettles conventional expectations in assigning Dog-Woman the visual icon of a half-peeled banana (the emblem of the occasional cross-dresser Jordan is that of the pineapple), and, lest anyone presumes that the gender assignment of these icons is arbitrary, when a banana is first exhibited in the streets of London Dog-Woman observes that it 'resembled nothing more than the private parts of an Oriental. It was yellow and livid and long.'[38] Dog-Woman, in possession of the power of the phallus, literally devours a hapless exhibitionist's penis ('biting it off with a snap')[39] and deploys, in a manner both startling and hilarious, the most erotic parts of her female body as weapons of crass destruction. In one passage, for example, Dog-Woman threatens the man who proposes to charge for a glimpse of the exotic

banana from the Island of Bermuda: 'I told Johnson that if he didn't
throw back his cloth and let us see this wonder I'd cram his face so hard
into my breasts that he'd wish he'd never been suckled by a woman, so
truly would I smother him.'[40] Elsewhere, during copulation, Dog-Woman
so tightens the muscles of her vagina that she sucks in the genitalia of her
partner, 'balls and everything. He was stuck.'[41] In the formidably huge
Dog-Woman who cannot find pleasure in any heterosexual act
Winterson creates a super female hero outside of any one kind of
sexuality.

Such bodily characteristics signal not freakishness but a bold new
vision of female superiority. Dog-Woman and Villanelle resist or
transcend labels of identity, and as women of vision with extraordinary
and rare talents they are wholly competent and confident in their
dealings with men and with the world of men. Released from the confine-
ment of domestic space, both protagonists witness and participate in the
violence and chaos of large-scale public events, from the perils of revolu-
tion to the futility of empire-building. Still, what is the point of
Winterson rescuing women – even the fabulous and heroic – from
cultural invisibility and inserting them into the grand narratives of sexual
and political history if time itself separates along gender lines, as
suggested by Henri's preference for the past tense ('It was New Year's Day,
1805') against Villanelle's commitment to the present: 'It is New Year's
Day, 1805'?[42] Here, and elsewhere in the novel, Winterson defines history
as man's history, as seen in Villanelle's remark: 'There is only the present
and nothing to remember', a lesson that Henri works hard to learn.[43]
Villanelle's hybrid body allows her to claim a (male) history which should
not be hers, yet she repudiates her genetic claim to this past in favour of
a female preoccupation with the 'now':

> Our ancestors. Our belonging. The future is foretold from the past and the
> future is only possible because of the past. Without past and future, the
> present is partial. All time is eternally present and so all time is ours. There
> is no sense in forgetting and every sense in dreaming. Thus the present is
> made rich. Thus the present is made whole.[44]

In this sophisticated critique of history, Winterson first fixes the past and
future as narratives always informed by a consciousness of the present
and then locates in the present a temporal space with the most potential
for the transformation of material conditions. If, as this passage suggests,
all paths lead ineluctably to the present, the past is made available for
both recovery and problematisation, and retrospection seems to be

simultaneously indulged and refused. Ultimately, 'history' as such hardly matters.

Yet halfway through *Sexing the Cherry*, the year '1649' appears starkly at the top of a page introducing a new section.[45] Nothing, one might argue, concretises our sense of the 'historical' as much as an actual date, a precise moment in time; in this case, the year in which Charles I was executed as a 'Tyrant, Traitor, Murderer and Public Enemy'.[46] Beneath the date 1649 hovers a visual icon of the act of regicide which, in foreshadowing one deadly consequence of the English Civil War, alerts the reader that the literary episode that follows represents an event of immense historical significance. Towards the novel's end another page marking a new section informs the reader that the narrative has shifted to a point in time rather nearer the present; in recent editions of the novel this page bears only a vague 'some years later'; in the earliest editions, however, it is marked '1990'.[47] Such chronological specificity, indeed the very linearity implicit in constructing a narrative that subsequently alternates between '1649' and '1990', is curious in a novel that opens with an epigraph celebrating the erasure of temporal distinctions: 'The Hopi, an Indian tribe, have a language as sophisticated as ours, but no tenses for past, present and future. The division does not exist. What does this say about time?'[48] More relevant to our purposes, we might ask: what does this inconsistency about time in *Sexing the Cherry* (abnegation followed by inscription) say about the limits or possibilities of history for the contemporary lesbian writer of historiographic metafiction? In other words, how or why can history, for Winterson, be both utterly irrelevant <u>and</u> highly significant?

Part of the answer can be found in the final '1990' section of *Sexing the Cherry*, where Winterson offers a more open-ended view of the imbrication of 'past' and 'present' by introducing a contemporary narrator, an unnamed radical feminist ecologist, whose visual icon – the same banana as Dog-Woman's, although now severed in half – suggests an unnatural or unworldly relationship with her historical counterpart: in a dream or mad hallucination, the modern woman imagines herself as 'a giant … Men shoot at me, but I take the bullets out of my cleavage and I chew them up.'[49] Has the Dog-Woman, from the very start, been nothing more than an invention of the contemporary woman's fragmented postmodern imagination? The precise nature of Dog-Woman's relationship to the unnamed narrator – as ghost, fantasy or even an earlier incarnation – suggests multiple approaches to history itself. If we suppose Dog-Woman an insubstantial ghost or spiritual forebear haunting the modern-day woman, then time itself, ironically, becomes hyper-substantial; as is so often the case in the lesbian historical genre, a kind of continuum is imagined, through which the modern woman is united with a powerful, empowering ancestress. If instead Dog-Woman is the contemporary narrator's fantasy, history becomes the means to explore contemporary culture, offering further evidence that Winterson regards the past more as a useful site to rewrite, and thereby intervene in, history-making. Winterson's creative use of history, therefore, involves less the recovery of a genealogy or a lost tradition for modern sexual subjects than the raising of a kind of screen on which to project for readers' scrutiny the sensibilities and identities of modernity itself. Whether history makes possible an exploration of contemporary consciousness or whether it coexists with the present in a nebulous realm of atemporality, what appears as a mapping of the past in Winterson's work is in effect the postmodern appropriation of the trappings of history, as evidenced in her snatching of the authority of 'fact', precise dates or allusions to significant political events.

'There is only the present and nothing to remember'

Winterson's achievement, then, is an affirmation of female agency and autonomy grounded not in history but in a metafictional utopian space, a space bound neither by temporality nor by limiting paradigms. Paradoxically, this has made her writing problematic for some lesbian readers. Critic Rachel Wingfield, for example, admonishes Winterson for abandoning her lesbian readers by taking a 'reactive shift into an increasing focus on the theoretical concerns of the (male) literary world [which] has meant that the experiences of lesbians, and women experiencing oppression generally, are written out of her work'.[50] Patricia Juliana Smith too finds it troubling that Winterson's two historical novels, although 'aesthetically innovative', 'provide little in terms of a new narrative model for lesbian life in the late twentieth century'.[51] Such criticisms reveal the burdens of responsibility that are placed, by lesbian reading communities, upon lesbian writers; they gesture to a kind of expectation which Winterson's increasingly complex writing must fail to fulfil. In her historical novels – as in any handling of lesbian history which attempts to address the real historical issue of cultural and erotic difference – 'lesbianism' itself can only disappear. Like a ghost indeed, the lesbian past grows increasingly insubstantial the nearer one draws to it; ultimately, perhaps, there is no 'it' to be recovered.[52]

It is surely in response to this paradox – rather than in spite of it – that popular lesbian historical fiction has emerged and thrived; for it is in its capacity for indulging empowering and consolatory fantasies – its precise answering of the angers and anxieties provoked by lesbians' marginalised relationship with what Sedgwick calls 'the discursive fabric of the given' – that the genre triumphs where constructionist work is sometimes understood to baffle.[53] It is the nature of genre, however, both to restrict and to evolve – to contain cultural narratives, and to expand or mutate in response to cultural change. The publication of recent novels such as Jay Taverner's *Rebellion* (1997) – in which eighteenth-century lesbian lovers find a secret haven for their union practising herbal medicine in the mystical matriarchal tradition of 'old dames' – suggests that some writers are still in thrall to a peripheral, underfunded historical model, still looking to the past largely in order to rehearse a version of the lesbian feminist present.[54] Jackie Kay's *Trumpet* (1998), on the other hand, attempts to address exactly the kind of 'troublesome' historical subject identified by Umphrey, by telling the story of a cross-dressing female jazz musician whose 'marriage' to another woman is precisely not – as in *Légende* and *The Hide and Seek Files* – reducible to a lesbian paradigm.[55] It is only, perhaps, in such testings of the genre – even, in the jettisoning of generic structures altogether – that we find a sophisticated treatment of lesbian historiographical issues and contradictions, one that problematises the very categories with which sex and gender are constructed. In the end, the relevance of historical fiction for 'lesbian life in the late twentieth century' may lie most fully in its capacity for illuminating the queer identities and acts against which modern lesbian narratives have defined themselves and which they perhaps continue to occlude.

Notes

1   Michel Foucault, *The History of Sexuality, Volume One: An Introduction*, trans. Robert Hurley (New York, Random House, 1978).

2   Richard von Krafft-Ebing, *Psychopathia Sexualis* (London, Rebman, [1886] 1899), p. 392.

3   Timothy d'Arch Smith, *Love in Earnest: Some Notes on the Lives and Writings of English 'Uranian' Poets from 1889 to 1930* (London, Routledge & Kegan Paul, 1970).

4   Rictor Norton, *The Myth of the Modern Homosexual: Queer History and the Search for Cultural Unity* (London and Washington, Cassell, 1997), p. 162.

5   See, for example, Renée Vivien, *A Woman Appeared to Me*, trans. Jeannette

H. Foster (Tallahassee, Naiad Press, [1904] 1979), *The Woman of the Wolf and Other Stories*, trans. Karla Jay and Yvonne M. Klein (New York, Gay Presses of New York, [1904] 1983) and *Poésies Complètes* (Paris, 1986); and Tryphe [pseud. Natalie Barney], *Cinq petit dialogues Grecs* (Paris, La Plume, 1902) and Natalie Barney, *Actes et entr'actes* (Paris, Sansot, 1910).

6   We borrow here the phrasing of Scott Bravmann, *Queer Fictions of the Past: History, Culture, and Difference* (Cambridge, Cambridge University Press, 1997), p. 98.

7   Susan Gubar, 'Sapphistries' in Estelle B. Freedman, Barbara C. Gelpi, Susan L. Johnson and Kath M. Weston (eds), *The Lesbian Issue: Essays from SIGNS* (Chicago and London, University of Chicago Press, 1985), p. 95.

8   Vivien, 'Ainsi je parlerai …', *Poésies Complètes*, p. 255. Our translation.

9   Vivien, 'En débarquant à Mytilène' ('Landing at Mytilene') (1906), *Poésies Complètes*, p. 268. Our translation.

10 Ellen Frye, *The Other Sappho* (Ithaca, Firebrand Books, 1989), p. i.

11 Jeanine Allard, *Légende* (Boston, Alyson, 1984), p. 10.

12 Isabel Miller [pseud. Alma Routsong], *Patience and Sarah* (London, The Women's Press, [1969] 1979), p. 190.

13 Quoted in Patricia Duncker, *Sisters and Strangers: An Introduction to Contemporary Feminist Fiction* (Oxford, Blackwell, 1992), p. 123.

14 Ellen Galford, *The Fires of Bride* (London, The Women's Press, 1986); Caeia March, *Fire! Fire!* (London, The Women's Press, 1991); Paula Martinac, *Out of Time* (Seattle, Seal Press, 1990).

15 Martinac, *Out of Time*, p. 55.

16 Terry Castle, *The Apparitional Lesbian: Female Homosexuality and Modern Culture* (New York, Columbia University Press, 1993), pp. 61–2.

17 Jane Eiseman, *Home Again, Home Again* (Austin, Banned Books, 1990), p. 139.

18 Castle, *The Apparitional Lesbian*, p. 63.

19 See Eve Kosofsky Sedgwick, *Epistemology of the Closet* (Berkeley, University of California Press, 1990); Mark Blasius and Shane Phelan (eds), *We Are Everywhere: a Historical Sourcebook for Gay and Lesbian Politics* (New York and London, Routledge, 1997).

20 Ellen Galford, *Moll Cutpurse: Her True History* (Edinburgh, Stramullion, 1984), p. 59.

21 *Ibid.*, p. 194.

22 *Ibid.*, pp. 45–6.

23 Allard, *Légende*, p. 125.

24 March, *Fire! Fire!*, p. 17.

25 *Ibid.*, p. 170.

26 Caeia March, *Reflections* (London, The Women's Press, 1995), p. 73.

27 Diana Fuss, 'Inside/out', in Fuss (ed.), *Inside/Out: Lesbian Theories, Gay Theories* (New York and London, Routledge, 1991), p. 7.

28 Eiseman, *Home Again, Home Again*, p. 2.
29 See, for example, Chris White, '"Poets and lovers evermore": the poetry and journals of Michael Field' in Joseph Bristow (ed.), *Sexual Sameness: Textual Differences in Lesbian and Gay Writing* (London and New York, Routledge, 1992), pp. 26–43.
30 Eiseman, *Home Again, Home Again*, p. 111.
31 Biddy Martin, 'Lesbian identity and autobiographical difference[s]', in Henry Abelove, Michèle Aina Barale and David M. Halperin (eds), *The Lesbian and Gay Studies Reader* (New York and London, Routledge, 1993), pp. 274–93.
32 Eiseman, *Home Again, Home Again*, p. 1.
33 Martha M. Umphrey, 'The trouble with Harry Thaw', *Radical History Review*, 62 (Spring 1995) 21.
34 Jeanette Winterson, *The Passion* (New York, Vintage, [1987] 1989) and *Sexing the Cherry* (London, Vintage, [1989] 1990).
35 Penny Hayes, *The Long Trail* (Tallahasee, Naiad Press, 1986); Caeia March, *The Hide and Seek Files* (London, The Women's Press, 1988); and Lisa Moore, 'Teledildonics: virtual lesbians in the fiction of Jeanette Winterson' in Elizabeth Grosz and Elspeth Probyn (eds), *Sexy Bodies: the Strange Carnalities of Feminism* (London and New York, Routledge, 1995), p. 120.
36 Winterson, *The Passion*, pp. 50 and 51.
37 Winterson, *Sexing the Cherry*, p. 11.
38 *Ibid.*, p. 12.
39 *Ibid.*, p. 41.
40 *Ibid.*, p. 12.
41 *Ibid.*, p. 106.
42 Winterson, *The Passion*, pp. 45 and 76.
43 *Ibid.*, p. 43.
44 *Ibid.*, p. 62.
45 Winterson, *Sexing the Cherry*, p. 61.
46 *Ibid.*, p. 70.
47 See the 1989 edition of *Sexing the Cherry* with Bloomsbury Publishing, London, p. 125.
48 *Sexing the Cherry*, p. 8.
49 *Ibid.*, pp. 121–2.
50 Rachel Wingfield, 'Lesbian writers and the mainstream: Sara Maitland, Jeanette Winterson and Emma Donoghue,' in Elaine Hutton (ed.), *Beyond Sex and Romance: the Politics of Contemporary Lesbian Fiction* (London, The Women's Press, 1998), p. 67.
51 Patricia Juliana Smith, *Lesbian Panic: Homoeroticism in Modern British Women's Fiction* (New York, Columbia University Press, 1997), p. 185.
52 We are here paraphrasing Carole S. Vance, who asks of lesbian and gay history, 'Is there an "it" to study?' in 'Social construction theory: problems in

the history of sexuality' in Dennis Altman *et al.*, *Which Homosexuality?: Essays from the International Scientific Conference on Lesbian and Gay Studies* (London, GMP, 1989), p. 22.

53   Sedgwick, *Epistemology of the Closet*, p. 43.
54   Jay Taverner, *Rebellion* (London, Onlywomen, 1997).
55   Jackie Kay, *Trumpet* (London, Picador, 1998).

3

Desire as nostalgia:
the novels of Alan Hollinghurst

David Alderson

Back in 1982 a disdainful review of Stephen Coote's *Penguin Anthology of Homosexual Verse* appeared in the *TLS*: 'If this book has few surprises', wrote the reviewer, 'it is in part because the increasing *self*-segregation of gays has had an enfeebling effect on their art' (my emphasis). The author of this was Alan Hollinghurst, then Literary Editor of the *TLS*. Its critical emphasis might come as a surprise to those who have come to regard him as the foremost English gay novelist. None the less, the basis of his argument is revealing, and tells us something about Hollinghurst's ambivalence towards gay identity and its literary expression. The problem with the anthology was that it contained only explicitly gay verse, leaving aside a large amount of poetry which is 'predominantly indirect' in its presentations of same-sex love, having been written in contexts which were legally and socially circumscribed: 'the unspeakable love demands metaphor, and conscripts other ways of seeing to its purpose'.[1] In this sense, Hollinghurst suggests, poetry of the necessarily more discreet period prior to partial decriminalisation was obliged to be more mainstream and was therefore in some sense more universal in its appeal, less self-regarding and particularistic; it was consequently – according to this avowedly 'literary' judgement – less facile in its treatment of same-sex love.

It seems hard to square this with the seemingly unapologetic sexual explicitness and almost exclusively gay milieux of Hollinghurst's novels.[2] Indeed, most critics – relieved no doubt to have novels dealing with gay life which are so well-crafted, witty and genuinely erotic – have tended to assimilate Hollinghurst's work to a unilinear sense of history and a more or less affirmative perspective. Richard Dellamora, for instance, suggests that the denouement to *The Swimming Pool Library* presents Will

Beckwith with 'a quick course of study' in the state persecution of gay men.[3] On one level, this is unquestionably the case, but, as I will argue here, the novel is also more complicated than this, and establishes themes and motifs which recur throughout Hollinghurst's work. Indeed, Hollinghurst's strictures on the 'self-segregation' of gays in relation to Coote's anthology were repeated – if in rather more circumspect terms – on the publication of *The Swimming Pool Library* which, Hollinghurst claimed, represents in part at least a critique of 'a passing subcultural gay world of people who "to gratify their sexuality, are forced into stylised, ritualised environments" of clubs, pubs and cinemas'. Crucially, too, the novel had its origins in an Oxford MLitt. dissertation which Hollinghurst completed in 1980 and which dealt with precisely that paradoxically legally circumscribed but in some ways more holistic past which had preceded subcultural segregation: '"I was dealing with three gay novelists [L. P. Hartley, Forster and Firbank] and what they could write about at a time when they could not write about homosexuality, and their ways of deflecting their interests."'[4] Despite obvious differences, these figures are very much the literary and ideological antecedents of Hollinghurst's work, informing his perspective on history, sexual identification and subcultural life. Since, in this respect, I also regard *The Swimming Pool Library* as a formative work, and one to which the later novels are indebted, I want to begin by discussing it in some detail.

Innocence and desire

The Swimming Pool Library is self-evidently concerned with history. First published in 1988 but set in 1983, it focuses on the summer experiences of a gay future peer, Will Beckwith, who, partly because of his leisurely existence, is able to make the most of the freedoms which the gay scene offers. But the hedonism embodied in Will is complicated from the outset for the reader by an enforced awareness of an impending disaster, AIDS, which will irretrievably consign this moment to the past. Consequently Hollinghurst opens the novel by evoking a sense of loss. However, if this anticipation of a supervening state of things is intended to condition our response to what follows in the narrative, that narrative is further compli-cated by episodes from a period of gay history prior to the legal reforms of 1967 in which Will Beckwith's uninhibited sexual behaviour would have been impossible. That period of history is presented to us in an almost synoptic form[5] through the diaries of Lord Nantwich, an elderly gay aristocrat whose biography Beckwith agrees to write, and this may at first suggest that the moment of the novel is that of an Edenic moment hard won and tragically lost. But this too would be misleading, since Nantwich's diaries reveal a past which was not merely repressive, and Beckwith's own insistent sexual urges are driven by the desire for a fulfilment which is ultimately unobtainable, as he experiences something approaching the condition that Jonathan Dollimore has labelled 'the impossibility of desire':[6] he is, as we will see, driven by a sense of the passage of time to find satisfaction in the apparent timelessness of the objects of his desire, though in his case this experience is bound up with the novel's specific ideological perspective.

Nor is gay history the only history with which the novel is concerned. In a *Guardian* interview prompted by the novel's release, Hollinghurst made a connection between the state persecution of gay men and the emergence of popular racism: 'In 1954, the year I was born, there was the beginning of a gay pogrom and also the first fairly organized hostility and violence against coloured immigrants.'[7] This history of race relations – both in the colonial situation, and subsequent to black immigration to Britain – also becomes integral to the novel's reflections. Moreover, black and gay histories are not discretely articulated, but complexly interwoven throughout: we discover, for instance, that Nantwich was a colonial administrator in the Sudan who brought his manservant Taha, with whom he was in love, back to England. Taha, though, was eventually killed in a racist attack while Nantwich himself was serving time for gross indecency as a consequence of a gay pogrom instigated – as his diaries finally reveal – by the then Director of Public Prosecutions, now Lord Beckwith, from whom Will is to inherit his title. Beckwith, too, focuses much of his libidinal attentions on black men and at one point is beaten up by a group of racist skinheads who haunt the council estate on which his black lover lives.

This may sound as if the novel attempts to create some kind of facile equivalence between the histories of gay and black oppression, but, again, this is not the case, not least because Will's, and others' attitudes towards black sexual partners are obviously conditioned by Western preconceptions. When Beckwith first comes across Abdul, the chef at Nantwich's club, Abdul is described 'sharpening his knife on the steel and gazing at me as if I were a meal',[8] and this sexual potential figured as cannibalistic threat – a kind of savage promise – is fulfilled towards the end of the novel when Abdul fucks Beckwith over a chopping board, using corn oil as a lubricant. But Beckwith's eroticisation of black men is also more complex than this, returning us once again to questions of history, as in these early ironic reflections on his penchant for West Indian youths:

I used to think … Edwardian names were the denial of romance: Archibald, Ernest, Lionel, Hubert were laughably stolid; they bespoke personalities unflecked by sex or malice. Yet only this year I had been with boys called just those staid things; and they were not staid boys. Nor was Arthur. His name was perhaps the least likely ever to have been young: it evoked for me the sunless complexion, unaired suiting, steel-rimmed glasses of a ledger clerk in a vanished age. Or had done so, before I found my beautiful, cocky, sluttish Arthur – an Arthur it was impossible to imagine old.[9]

The white past is inverted by a black present in which those names which suggest Edwardian sexual fastidiousness are transformed into bywords for desirability and, importantly, availability. At the same time, the symbolic duality of these names mimics the kind of desire which dominates much of the novel – that is, a flight from respectable English-ness in search of exotic pleasures, even though in the cosmopolitan present sexual tourism is no longer a necessity (one of Beckwith's usual haunts, the Corinthian Club, has a 1930s façade which includes a banner whose motto is 'Men Of All Nations', hinting – again with a historical irony – at the sexual commonwealth inside). However, Beckwith's comments here reveal something else about the qualities which attract him and others in the novel, qualities which, at least potentially, abolish any sense of history: Arthur appears to him ageless, inhabiting some realm beyond the processes of time, managing effortlessly, naturally to combine innocence *and* sexuality, and thereby embodying a condition beyond the western postlapsarian economy of sexual guilt and physical mortality. In other words, Arthur is idealised in his primitivism, and this idealisation is an integral factor in all of Will's desires, directed as they are towards those he clearly regards as his social subordinates, black and working-class white characters alike, whose lack of 'cultured' sophistica-tion permits Will to invest them with precisely this eroticised innocence.

At the same time, though, this lack of sophistication ascribed by Will to his lovers results in his explicitly snobbish contempt for them. In other words, if they are conceived in terms of an innocence which does not preclude, and even enhances, their sexual appeal, this is also the basis of their perceived inferiority: idealisation and disdain are two sides of the same coin, since if one response to the perceived primitivism of the colonised or socially inferior male subject is to project on to him a lack of refinement, self-consciousness or inhibition, another – as Fanon has famously pointed out in relation to colonialism[10] – is to attribute to his pre-cultural condition a greater degree of animality figured in that same sexual potential. One of the controversial features of *The Swimming Pool*

Library, indeed, is precisely this sexual objectification of black men in particular, and not only on the part of Beckwith. However, this is done self-consciously by Hollinghurst and therefore carries the potential to disarm criticism, since the novel, it might be claimed, simply acknowledges, without at all endorsing, the fact that contemporary gay culture has participated in what Kobena Mercer has called (in a more specific context) the 'ontological reduction' of the black man to his phallus.[11] When Will visits a porn shop at one point he notes the range of dildos on offer, including, most prominently, 'mighty black jobs'.[12] Indeed, such commodities are part of a more pervasive fetishisation of 'primitive' or 'innocent' figures and their sexual potential to the extent that this process becomes virtually inseparable from the novel's account of desire.

The Swimming Pool Library, then, impresses on us an awareness of the class and racial dynamics of its central protagonist's desires, and in this and other ways opens up a critical distance between narrator and reader. But if the novel's ideological perspective is not straightforwardly articulated by the narrator, nor, I think, is the novel an attempt to lay bare the roots of present-day sexual projections in historically grounded power relations, since if the novel is, in part, a critique of the present, this is because it is not an unqualified condemnation of the colonial and sexually circumscribed past. There is no question that Hollinghurst indicts the legal proscription of male same-sex desire – this is one of the more obvious 'messages' of the novel – but that does not mean that the past is in every way denigrated: rather, the sexual liberties of the present are in many ways presented as a violation of older ideals.

For this reason, Nantwich is a crucial figure in the book, and not simply for the part he plays in Beckwith's own enlightenment and disenchantment. In the present, of course, Nantwich is distanced from the reader as a result of being mediated through the youthful eyes of Beckwith, for whom he is eccentrically elliptical and verging on senility; but in the memoirs he addresses the reader directly, and is lucid and self-reflexive – far more so than the self-deluding Beckwith. Nantwich also appears in many ways a humane figure, very much the liberal colonist, as in these observations on the 'openness and simplicity' of the Nuba:

> no one wears a stitch of clothing … I saw one pair of adolescent boys – very tall & elegant – sauntering along with their fingers intertwined, wearing scarves of red cotton tied round their upper arms. One old man, too, had a watch, & encouraged people to ask him the time, which had to be done in a very respectful manner. Then he wd. listen to its ticking, & give a knowing & superior smile.

It is this, which I hardly dare to call innocence, for fear it might not be, or
that I do not understand, which has moved me particularly.

The passage goes on: 'The beauty of the men is so openly displayed that
it seems a reproach to lust.'[13] Nantwich's complex response here – sexual
longing chastened by an idealisation of the Nuba's simplicity which, he
realises, may itself be a mistaken apprehension – is indicative of certain
characteristics which he later claims typified the colonial service of gay
men of his class: he comments to Will that gays were preferred for
positions in the empire on account of their proneness to "immense
idealism and dedication"'.[14] But we might also note that Nantwich here
strikes a typically Firbankian note, not least in the reference to the unselfconscious nakedness and intimacy of the adolescent boys.[15] This is not
merely another of those literary allusions with which the novel is replete,
but reminds us that Firbank is, in many ways, a presiding influence over
the novel, providing its epigraph as well as making appearances in
Nantwich's diaries and, towards the end of the book, on film, close to
death.[16]

Given this focus on black sexuality in Nantwich's diaries, it is revealing
to turn to Hollinghurst's own reflections on Firbank. In his MLitt. dissertation, Hollinghurst is brief and rather uncritical in his references to what
he describes as Firbank's 'negroism'.[17] This, he remarks, is the product of
an imaginative investment in the exotic necessitated by the repressive
features of Firbank's home culture. He goes on to note that Firbank's
'negro' characters play 'central roles in the fiction. Their naturalness is
their innocence, but part of their significance to Firbank is that they allow
him more fully to sexualize his concept of innocence, to diminish his
indirectness, and to describe the more overtly libidinous quality of his
imagination.'[18] If this is the primary significance of the black characters
in Firbank's fiction, Nantwich's earlier diaries reveal similar attitudes: the
apparent innocence of his Africans is undiminished by their erotic attrac-
tions for the white viewer, since they appear largely oblivious of the
Western stigmas attached to sexuality in general, and same-sex intimacies
in particular. In this context, then, it may be legitimate to interpret the old
man with the watch in the above passage as a symbol, not merely of cross-
cultural incomprehension but more specifically of a consciousness
untainted by the perception of time passing. Nantwich therefore
perceives the Nuba as figures outside western perceptions of time in a way
which mirrors Beckwith's attitudes to West Indian men. But crucially
Nantwich does not demonstrate the disdain which is integral to

Beckwith's desires – or, at least, not at this point – and is even self-consciously hesitant about this idealisation.

Nantwich's colonial idealism is pervasive, but it is embodied principally in his relationship with his manservant in Africa, Taha, whose beauty precipitates Nantwich's devoted service to him. The relationship never becomes fully sexual, though, since paternalist feelings always hold in check Nantwich's lust, as in the incident in which Taha is bitten on the calf by a scorpion: Nantwich records that 'fussily, unnecessarily, I shoved back the gathered folds of [Taha's] djellaba, baring his thighs, glancing at them as well – though with a curiosity almost annulled by the ethical transfiguration I was enabled for a few minutes to undergo'.[19] Later, though drunk, Nantwich claims to have realised that Taha '*was* my responsibility made flesh: he was all the offspring I will never have, all my futurity'.[20] It is this genuinely idealistic – if (because?) eroticised – paternalism which Nantwich ultimately betrays in the novel, since one of its devastating revelations is that Abdul, the figure who features in the present-day pornographic enterprises of Nantwich and his friend Ronald Staines, is Taha's son and once visited Nantwich while he was in prison. Again, one possible reading of this revelation may be that the relationship between Nantwich and Abdul represents an unmasking of the exploitation which was always at least latent in the colonial situation, but this seems to me an unsustainable interpretation, a wilful attempt to enlist the novel for an anti- or post-colonial agenda which it does not actually endorse. Rather, Nantwich's relationship with Taha is presented with few reservations as reciprocal and disinterested, if clearly unequal – part of that integration, if not sublimation, of gay desire into broader social structures and relations which Hollinghurst has found appealing – whereas Nantwich's present-day financially and sexually motivated paternalism in relation to Abdul is presented to us as a degeneration of former principles, even an exploitative parody of them.

This returns me to the elegiac qualities of the novel, since, though the imagined appeal of racially alterior and lower-class figures lies in their imagined prelapsarian qualities, the principal ideological template of the novel is the familiar one of a fall from innocence to experience: desire in the novel is a restless and inevitably doomed need to repossess a former moment of innocence prior to the self-consciousness implied in the formation of sexual identity and the consequent absorption into the 'segregated' world of the present: physical and moral degeneration is integral to Nantwich's development, just as disillusionment is to the development of Beckwith, whose social eminence and privilege is revealed to be indebted to an Establishment homophobe, and whose attributions of naivety to his lovers are themselves finally unmasked as illusions; moreover, the hedonistic present of Will's existence is, as we have seen, the prelude to a less carefree, AIDS-afflicted future. The fall from a state of innocence, then, acts as a counterpoint to the familiar history of progressive legal reform, and the colonial context figures as part of an overarching transformation from a genuinely idealistic, if necessarily reticent, past into a present in which that idealism has become the source of an explicit fetishisation. It is true that this history does not take the form of a pure opposition – at one point in the Sudan, for instance, Nantwich records being discreetly offered pornography – but the overall sense is that of a deterioration which has accompanied the growth of an urban and largely commercial scene – indeed, this deterioration is implicit in the incident in the Sudan, since Nantwich waves the merchant away – reflecting Hollinghurst's apparent disenchantment with modernity.

The reason that this mood of disenchantment has become so integral to Hollinghurst's aesthetic is surely that gay identity has taken on peculiarly modern forms at odds with that English tradition which is such an important influence on this novel: an identity which had been constructed in terms of its sexual object (homosexuality) found its 'liberation', in the post-decriminalisation period, largely through the discrete place available through the market and the commodity forms through which that market promises the satisfaction of desire. According to David T. Evans, 'When illegal, gay male sexuality was objectified but not commercialised. With legalisation gay male sexuality was inevitably affected by material discourses commensurate with men as potent earners … Commodification of the sexual socially constructs because it requires active, objectifying commodifiable eroticism.' Moreover, 'for all the dissemination of rights news and political information, such journals [as *Gay News*] have predominantly been devoted to charting the growth of homosexuality as a commodity and how to obtain it'.[21] This commodification of gay sexuality – the *form* which sexual explicitness has predominantly taken in the contemporary situation – is presented in Hollinghurst as a violation of those socially integrated, yet eroticised relations of earlier times which centred on the innocence of their object. In *The Swimming Pool Library*, this is most clearly indicated by the degeneration of Nantwich's ideals, but the appeal of innocence is not exclusively bound up with the colonial context (or even with other formerly paternalistic relations): it exists more generally in the historical or individual past, prior to the emergence of an explicitly gay scene or the acquisition of an individual sexual identity and entry into the corresponding subculture, hence the generalised condition of nostalgia in the novel and the way that this structures desire. Beckwith himself, for instance, associates an originary state of sexual innocence with the public-school swimming pool of which he was 'librarian' (i.e. prefect) in his youth:

> I still dream, once a month or so, of that changing-room, its slatted floor and benches ... Sometimes I think that shadowy, doorless little shelter – which is all it was really, an empty, empty place – is where at heart I want to be ... There was never, or rarely, any kissing – no cloying, adult impurity in the lubricious innocence of what we did.

Immediately, his present-day lover, Phil, breaks in on these reflections:

> 'Are you into kids?' Phil asked.
> 'I'm into you, darling.'[22]

The clearly symbolic location of the swimming pool – this 'empty, empty place' – invested with a perhaps revisionary charm, represents the uncomplicated moment which Will seems insistently to be attempting to recapture not only through his usual haunt at the 'Corry', but also through his habitual infantilisation of his lovers, signalled immediately here in the rapid transition from the idealisations of memory to Will's present-day conversation with Phil, and the 'cloying, adult' line which implies that Phil is still a kid. Nantwich feels similarly about public school that 'there will never again be a time of such freedom. It was the epitome of pleasure.'[23] Again, this kind of freedom enjoyed by both Will and Nantwich at their respective public schools contrasts with those freedoms – moral, legal, commercial – which make Will's adult sexual adventures possible.

In this sense, then, the explicitness of Hollinghurst's first novel is precisely *not* what the moralists might call 'gratuitous', since that very explicitness participates in but at the same time critically highlights the pornographic – that is, the reductively sexual, standardised and fetishistic – quality of contemporary desires. Hence, the ambivalence of many readers' responses to the novel, finding it deeply erotic yet simultaneously, if vaguely, troubling. Possibly the prime instance of this is again to be found in the infantilisation of Phil in that very carefully orchestrated passage in which – having already dressed Phil in a revealingly tight-fitting pair of Beckwith's own trousers and a 'boyish, blue Aertex shirt' prior to a visit to Nantwich's and Staines's porn studio where Phil is photographed – Beckwith, on getting him home and 'restoring his porno image' forces him childishly to piss himself before fucking him in the pool that this creates.[24]

Beckwith's own relative state of innocence – that is, his initially hedonistic, carefree existence – is itself undermined, as we have seen, as the revelations the novel has in store for him contribute to his greater self-knowledge. Significantly, given the novel's themes, this disenchantment is perhaps best demonstrated in his rejection of his former delight in power play in the comic sex scene with a wealthy Argentinian pick-up, Gabriel, who is visiting England in order to buy pornography unavailable in his country – though produced there (imperialism has been reduced to this) – as well as various sex toys and bondage gear which he is keen to try out on Beckwith. As their sexual encounter progresses, Gabriel reveals his black leather briefs and cock ring, mimics the rhetoric and accents of American porn, triumphantly dons a black mask and threatens to bugger Will with 'a gigantic pink dildo'. The final straw is Gabriel's offer to whip Beckwith '"for what your country did to mine during the war"' – 'I could see the whole thing deteriorating into a scene from some poker-faced left-wing European film', comments Beckwith. However, at the point at which Beckwith abandons the encounter and dresses to leave, Gabriel takes off his leather mask 'and his clear olive complexion was primed with pink – as it might have been if we had simply made love'.[25] Will is now able to perceive the appeal of an innocence which he would have liked to possess without violation.

None the less, Beckwith refuses to remain disillusioned. Immediately following this incident, he resumes his search for Phil – 'the only true, pure, simple thing I could see in my life at the moment'[26] – only to have his disenchantment completed with the discovery of Phil in bed with the boxing trainer Bill Hawkins, another of the beneficiaries of Nantwich's patronage. But even this does not defeat the compulsive condition to which Beckwith is condemned by his alienated condition, as the final line of the book has him chasing after another cute young thing in blue swimming trunks.

Wasting hope

In many ways, *The Folding Star* is a continuation and development of the themes and ideological perspective already established in the previous novel, except that the nostalgic qualities of that novel – those expressions of the desire to repossess some former moment of pure, unselfconscious sexual being – are, if anything, intensified and bound up even more explicitly with the awareness of mortality enforced by AIDS. This is especially the case in the elegiac central section of the novel which deals with the death of Edward Manners's first lover, androgynously – but with a heavy-handed symbolism – named Dawn. Though Dawn has AIDS, he dies not from this but in a car crash, and his funeral forces the return to his home town of Rough Common of the thirty-three-year-old Manners from the Flemish city in which he is pursuing his seventeen-year-old pupil, Luc. But the elegiac qualities of this section are doubled. Manners reflects on his relationship with Dawn, the first fully sexual relationship of his life (in contrast to his earlier closeness to the aesthete Lawrence Graves, who clearly resembles Clive in Forster's *Maurice*). This was, he considers, 'the motor of my grandest feelings and most darting thoughts, the ground bass to those first intense improvisations ... And what had there been since then? Nothing quite the same. Everything in some way melancholy, frantic or foredoomed.'[27] As the musical metaphor here indicates, though, these memories of Dawn are indissociably mingled with memories of the fatal illness of his father, a professional singer, so that even at this stage the experiences of desire and loss are interwoven. But this early relationship is also invested – at least retrospectively – with another sense of loss, prefigured in the very landscape which is the backdrop to Edward's and Dawn's relationship. Their first sexual contact is in the open on the Common, but has to be abandoned for the privacy of the nearby woods. Edward is at first apprehensive of this change of scene in ways which signal his intuitive resistance to sexual identification: '"that's where the queers go"', he thinks, 'imagining some nice distinction between what they did there and whatever we were going to do.'[28] The distinction, though, persists. The first night that Edward and Dawn spend together in a tent on the Common is a disaster, partly because of the intrusion of an older man – one of the many who cruise the area at nights – who attempts to 'comfort' the vulnerable, because grieving, Edward. They are interrupted by Dawn, who forces the man away, shouting '"Fucking queers ... He can fucking look after himself"' before rugby-tackling him. Meanwhile, Edward notices that 'Beyond them both, on the crest of the hill, figures were moving among the trees',[29] an obviously sinister portent of Edward's own future; and at the end of this section, back in the present, he is picked up on the Common.

Once again, there are connections between Hollinghurst's writing here and that earlier twentieth-century English tradition of gay writing which is arguably more of an influence on this novel than either of the most frequently invoked prototypes, *Death in Venice* and *Lolita*. According to Hollinghurst, E. M. Forster's novels

> imaginatively transform his own past into fictional material which is actually imbued with the intervening sense of loss. And this connection between the transfigured, eroticized landscapes of the past and the memory of the adolescent phase of homosexuality is a pattern found too in Forrest Reid and (more complicatedly) in A. E. Housman; in all three writers we can see the disruption of this kind of innocence (which is yet deeply erotic) by harsher adult forces untransmuted by fantasy.[30]

In this tradition, then, rural England acts in much the same way as the Orient does in Firbank's fiction as the site of a naturalistic eroticism at odds with both the puritanism and degeneracy offered by the city (for Forster, of course, the alternative to bourgeois conformity, effete bohemianism and racial degeneracy seemed to lie in an alternative version of England, that of the greenwood to which he consigns his ideal lovers at the end of *Maurice*, and in this sense Scudder is the representative of an indigenous English primitivism in that novel). At the same time, this eroticised site of opposition to modernity was already threatened for Forster *et al.* and therefore imbued with a sense of loss: the general mythicisation of rural England in the Edwardian period,[31] and Forster's particular version of it, recognised that it was already something in danger of disappearing, because in need of restoration. Moreover, Forster's 1960 terminal note to *Maurice* reaffirmed his hostility to urban modernity, even while it acknowledged that the contemporary city afforded some relief from those forces of respectability to which his fiction is so hostile:

> There is no forest or fell to escape to today, no cave in which to curl up, no deserted valley for those who wish neither to reform nor corrupt society but to be left alone. People do still escape, one can see them any night at it in the films. But they are gangsters not outlaws, they can dodge civilization because they are part of it.[31]

The tone of this – its sense of an irrecoverable past and a present whose freedoms are compromised – very closely anticipates Hollinghurst's response to the development of a self-conscious, urban gay scene (and in these terms Beckwith, for instance, is clearly a gangster not an outlaw).

The central section of *The Folding Star*, though, is not abstractable from the rest of the novel, and casts its shadow over the events which both precede and succeed it. Manners's pursuit of Luc, of course, is itself an attempt to repossess that moment prior to, if portending, his assumption of a sexual identity. Indeed, Luc embodies this condition and Hollinghurst has stated that he intended Luc as precisely such a liminal figure:

> I wanted Luc to be someone who is as big as Edward and physically and sexually mature but who still has all this unformed and vulnerable quality of youth ... the not knowing, it being impossible to decide whether he is interested in boys or girls. Luc probably does not know himself that he's at a stage where sexual feelings and instincts are still in a state of suspension or solution.[32]

Even Manners's brief, if spectacular, sexual possession of Luc is only the prelude to an intensification of loss, as Luc becomes the object of a search (rather than a pursuit), culminating in Manners's final encounter with him: fixed in a photographic image which will defy the processes of time, amongst the missing persons whose faces are displayed at the port at Ostend, Luc becomes the very embodiment of that clearly illusory unageing youthfulness which generates Manners's desires.

There are further parallels with the first novel, since, though Manners imagines his desires as uniquely pure, the book suggests this is mere self-delusion. Not only does he have a rival for Luc's affections in the figure of Ronald Strong, whom Manners comes irrationally to despise, but his rifling of Luc's washing basket for trophies is only a more direct version of Manners's friend Matt's trade in boys' stolen underwear which Manners finds so sordid. Moreover, Hollinghurst attempts to universalise Manners's obsessive condition by extending it to include heterosexual desire in the form of the sordid discoveries Manners is allowed to make about the life of the Belgian Symbolist painter Edgard Orst. Orst's early love for his model Jane Byron gives way to what is finally revealed to have been a pornographic obsession with a prostitute who resembled her. The photographs of this replacement are explicit and are accompanied by a lock of her hair which 'one knew ... had not been taken from her head'.[33] Again, we encounter the formal device of the past being carefully pieced together in a way which sheds light on the narrator, and this also reinforces that sense of desire as an attempted, but degenerate, recovery of the past. Moreover, in the description of Manners's sexual climax with Luc, Luc's appeal is fused with Manners's fascination with Orst's work in a way which positions Manners as the artist and leaves this consummation unfulfilling: 'I made a grieving moan at the bitterness of it, craving the blessing of his gaze, though his eyes were oddly veiled, fluttering and colourless like some Orst temptress's.'[34] More poignantly, in reflecting on the mysterious disappearance of Jane Byron – whose body was never found after she had gone missing while swimming – Manners unconsciously anticipates the disappearance of Luc in a way which also prefigures his own final condition: 'I was impressed by this, as I always was by the idea of a total disappearance, the vertigo of it, and the way it none the less left room for wasting hope.'[35]

Post-nostalgia?

If *The Swimming Pool Library* manifests alienation from the contemporary gay scene as much as and at the same time as it does excitement at the scene's possibilities, there is another feature of the novel which suggests a distance from gay identity as many of us experienced it in the 1980s. At this time, lesbian and gay rights, as we then – quaintly, it now seems – called them, were advocated most prominently by the left and were consequently seized on, along with a host of other causes – among them feminism, nuclear disarmament, anti-racism, Irish self-determination – and stigmatised by the Thatcherite right as self-evidently loony. The legislative expression of this stigma came with Section 28 of the Local Government Bill, around which there was considerable mobilisation on the part of lesbian and gay communities (though this failed to halt the Bill's passage). It is a signal feature of *The Swimming Pool Library* that such political consciousness is entirely elided, even though Hollinghurst was in part motivated in the writing of this novel by a desire to defy the censoriousness of the times.[36] For sure, there is a hint in the novel of Hollinghurst's disdain for the illiberal and bellicose Thatcherite vision of England. When Beckwith meets the Argentinian, Gabriel, he feels torn between apologising to him for the Falklands/Malvinas war and castigating him for his patronage of British porn shops: 'Surely if any British self-esteem could have been thought to have survived the recent war it must be something to do with our ... cultural values?'[37] The ellipsis clearly indicates Beckwith's sudden sense of the hollowness of his assumed superiority, and Thatcherism is implicitly assimilated to the more general vulgarity of the present (once again, Beckwith is too astute to be considered a mere anti-hero).

But there is surely a sense in which politics *are* vulgar for Hollinghurst, just as Stephen Coote's criteria for selecting homosexual verse are not properly *literary* judgements. Speaking of the political climate at the time of this first novel, Hollinghurst suggested that '"there is a general sense of a creeping totalitarianism. It's as if homosexuality were some kind of political creed. It's an absurd idea.'"[38] In one sense, this is correct, since the subversive potential of same-sex desire is clearly context-bound. But the fact remains that in the 1980s, lesbian and gay rights were politicised and assimilated to British left-right oppositions which were themselves subsumed – certainly for the right – by Cold War ideology. It seems to me that Hollinghurst's critical relation to gay identity was at least as much determined by an ideological dislike of such strident, unEnglish assertiveness – as evident in Coote's anthology – as it was by the commodification of desire, though he also implicitly integrates these two (often conflictual) elements of gay identity under the rubric of self-segregation.

In this respect, it is significant that the narratorial consciousness of *The Swimming Pool Library* is hardly the representative voice of the 1980s gay man. (Of course, it might be argued that Hollinghurst is not obliged to be representative, but the novel clearly does attempt a synoptic vision and his choice of narrator is surely revealing.) More specifically, Beckwith's assertion of sexual freedom is assimilated to an older tradition of the rake[39] rather than the radical, the libertine rather than the libertarian, thus further contributing to the novel's representation of the present as merely decadent rather than emancipated. Hence, too, the dominant tone of Beckwith's voice: its connoisseurial appreciation of everything from cocks to *haute cuisine*, arses to architecture. But then this tone pervades the other novels too, a characteristic feature of Hollinghurst's style: Manners is only superficially different from Beckwith – though older, not quite so well-born and less heavily ironised, Manners is still both cultured and rootless – and the third-person narration of *The Spell* really only provides access to the concerns of a group of upper-middle-class gay men who tend to embody facets of Beckwith's and Manners's personae.

Times have changed, though, and Cold War antagonisms have receded. In these rather more liberal days, politicians are only too keen to appeal to minorities: while Middle England concerns are most influential in the formation of party policies across a range of social and economic matters, there are simultaneously – if often contradictorily – attempts to cultivate the support of different 'communities' beyond this, and for a party leader *not* to have a letter of support read out at Pride these days would constitute a significant press office *faux pas*. Indeed, pride itself has lost much of its earnest tone, having in 1999 become a privatised mardi gras, and if it retains any political edge at all it is as (licensed) carnivalesque rather than agitprop, reflecting the way in which being gay now feels more like being part of a broader relaxed cosmopolitanism than being part of some conspiracy – or at least it does for those of us who live in cities and have some money – and I don't intend this merely as an intrusion of my own leftist brand of nostalgia: this is what progress is bound to feel like for 'minority groups' in a bourgeois democracy whose ideological legitimacy goes largely unchallenged.

This seems to me the appropriate context in which to read Hollinghurst's latest novel, which has a relaxed 1990s, 'post-issue' feel about it, signalled not least by its rather less ambitious scope in comparison to those of its predecessors. Both the mood of disenchantment and the attendant foredoomed desire to transcend the commercialisation and self-segregation of the present by appeal to a supposedly more integrated past are diminished as the gay scene is simply a given, no longer so disturbingly haunted by the impossible desire for an innocence which can be obtained only through violation. Urban and rural contexts are still juxtaposed – the events of the novel move between London and the country hamlet of Litton Gambril – but the urban appropriation of the rural is more comic, barely at all inflected by nostalgia, as in this cameo of an Italian rent boy in London:

> There was something superficially outward-bound about Carlo, in his homosexual boots and socks; the padded straps of his knapsack set off the curves of his chest and shoulders like a harness, and his black shorts, though baggy in cut, still caught and stretched around his thighs and buttocks as he moved. He was the urban parody of a hiker that you saw in any gay bar. He was by no means as tall as expected, but he was swelteringly good-looking; he had the mask-like orangey tan that comes from using the wrong 'no sun' lotion.[40]

There is a mildly fetishistic quality to this in the reference to Carlo's harness, but the parody, down to the fake healthy skin colour, is hardly sinister. Indeed, the tendency here is, if anything, to sexualise an otherwise rather staid original, the hiker, and this is part of a more general refusal of familiar city and country oppositions which works to undermine the idealisations which dominate the earlier novels. After all, Litton Gambril is characterised more by Middle England intolerance than earthy primitivism, and even that marginal Scudderite figure, Terry Badgett – whom Robin 'didn't really think of … as being homosexual'[41] – is a rent boy rather than a representative of spontaneity. The cosmopolitan world of London, on the other hand, turns out to be a source of a transcendence of sorts through the rejuvenating influence of drugs.

There are other significant variations on established themes, principally in relation to the opposition between youth and age. The youthful
Danny, for instance, finds himself in a relationship with the thirty-six-
year-old Alex who, Danny explains, is '"so innocent, and strange'',[42]
requiring Danny's tutelage in taking e and having a good time. Danny is
in control, and – to use the phrase of the book – is a taker rather than a
giver in his sometimes manipulative power over the doting Alex. Once
this fling is over, though, Alex is able to find satisfaction with a partner
slightly older than himself who is able to reconcile, or at least alternate,
off-yer-face clubbing with an interest in church architecture. The novel's
ending is a scene of reconciliation amongst thirty- and forty-something
peers significantly different in tone from either Beckwith's reassertion of
restless compulsion in the pursuit of youth or Manners's condemnation
to a future of wasting hope. Finally, this is also a post-AIDS novel, at least
in the sense that AIDS is invoked not as a future which colours our
perspective on the past, or as part of an elegiac contemplation on desire
itself, but as part of a superseded past in the form of Robin's memories of
his former lover: the present is no longer so heavily clouded by this
particular affliction.

The Spell, then, provides a sense of closure in relation to the earlier
novels (though it is also difficult to imagine Hollinghurst doing anything
strikingly new): nostalgia is not displaced entirely from its world –
indeed, there is an assumption that the condition is almost constitutional
(as when Alex scans Robin's cottage 'with an Englishman's nostalgia as
well as a tall person's sense of immense discomfort')[43] – but the critical, if
ultimately conservative, edge which this relationship to the past provided
in the earlier novels has clearly receded. It is, then, a novel which achieves
some kind of reconciliation between the Firbankian and Forsterian ideals
of same-sex love so influential on Hollinghurst's work and a modern,
scene-oriented identity apparently at odds with those ideals. This,
though, is largely because the modern context has itself changed as the
downturn in political activism during the 1990s has, paradoxically, been
accompanied by an intensification of the capitalist investment in gay
spaces and the commodification of gay lifestyles in ways which have, far
from increasing their segregation, contributed to a pluralistic queer
chic.[44] Not that Hollinghurst's latest work is conspicuously queer – in the
sense of celebrating desire's perversity and lack of fixity – but it is the
product of a moment in which being gay no longer feels so marginal or
oppositional. It is this which has made possible Hollinghurst's aesthetic
rapprochement between past and present, country and city, innocence

and experience; in short, between a residual, English leisure-class sensibility and a spell-binding, drug-oriented scene.

Notes

1 'The unspeakable spoken', *TLS* (22 April 1983), 397.
2 On the relationship between explicitness and literariness in *The Swimming
   Pool Library*, with some rather different conclusions from mine, see Alan
   Sinfield, 'Culture, consensus and difference' in Alistair Davis and Alan
   Sinfield (eds) *The Culture of the Postwar* (London, Routledge, forthcoming).
3 Richard Dellamora, *Apocalyptic Overtures: Sexual Politics and the Sense of an
   Ending* (New Brunswick, Rutgers University Press, 1994), p. 186.
4 Nicholas de Jongh, 'The deep end', *The Guardian* (27 February 1988), 25.
5 Joseph Bristow notes just some of the novel's explicit and allusive references
   to gay history in *Effeminate England: Homoerotic Writing After 1885* (New
   York, Columbia University Press, 1995), p. 175.
6 This is Jonathan Dollimore's term for the way in which 'mutability animates
   desire even as it thwarts it. Put slightly differently, the very nature of desire
   is what prevents its fulfilment' (*Death, Desire and Loss in Western Culture*
   (Harmondsworth, Allen Lane, 1998), p. xvii).
7 De Jongh, 'The deep end'.
8 Alan Hollinghurst, *The Swimming Pool Library* (London, Chatto & Windus,
   1988), p. 42.
9 *Ibid.*, p. 2.
10 See Frantz Fanon, *Black Skin White Masks* (London, Pluto, 1986), especially
   p. 165. For reflections on Fanon's comments in relation to homosexuality,
   see Jonathan Dollimore, *Sexual Dissidence: Augustine to Wilde, Freud to
   Foucault* (Oxford, Clarendon Press, 1991), pp. 344–7.
11 Kobena Mercer, 'Reading racial fetishism: the photographs of Robert
   Mapplethorpe' in *Welcome to the Jungle: New Positions in Black Cultural
   Studies* (London, Routledge, 1994), p. 174. For further discussion on
   Mapplethorpe, see David Marriott, 'Bordering on: the black penis', *Textual
   Practice*, 10:1 (1996), 9–28.
12 Hollinghurst, *Library*, p. 48.
13 *Ibid.*, p. 108.
14 *Ibid.*, p. 241.
15 Cf. this passage from *Prancing Nigger* in which Mrs Ahmadou Mouth looks
   on as 'two [naked] young men passed by with fingers intermingled … As the
   mother of oncoming girls, the number of ineligible young men or
   confirmed bachelors around the neighbourhood was a constant source of
   irritation to her' (*The Complete Firbank* (London, Duckworth, 1961), p.
   594).
16 Hollinghurst invents the film, but the incident is typical of Firbank's

behaviour towards the end of his life according to Miriam J. Benkowitz in *Ronald Firbank: a Biography* (London, Weidenfeld and Nicolson, 1970), pp. 292–3.

17   Significantly, Hollinghurst makes no reference in his dissertation to Edward Said's groundbreaking *Orientalism*, first published in 1978.

18   Alan Hollinghurst, *The Creative Uses of Homosexuality in the Novels of E. M. Forster, Ronald Firbank and L. P. Hartley*, MLitt. thesis, University of Oxford, 1980, p. 138.

19   Hollinghurst, *Library*, p. 208.

20   *Ibid.*, p. 210.

21   David T. Evans, *Sexual Citizenship: The Material Construction of Sexualities* (London, Routledge, 1993), p. 101. For further reflections on the relationsip between queer communities and consumerism, see in particular Alan Sinfield, *Gay and After* (London, Serpent's Tail, 1998), pp. 160–89.

22   Hollinghurst, *Library*, p. 141.

23   *Ibid.*, p. 113.

24   *Ibid.*, pp. 154–63.

25   *Ibid.*, p. 275.

26   *Ibid.*, p. 270.

27   Hollinghurst, *The Folding Star* (London, Chatto & Windus, 1994), p. 200.

28   *Ibid.*, p. 219.

29   *Ibid.*, p. 251.

30   Hollinghurst, *Creative Uses of Homosexuality*, p. 19.

31   See, for instance, Alun Howkins, 'The discovery of rural England' in Robert Colls and Philip Dodd (eds), *Englishness: Politics and Culture 1880–1920* (London, Croom Helm, 1986), pp. 62–88. Cf. Andrew Moor's comments on Derek Jarman's relationship to the English countryside in chapter 4 of this volume.

31   E. M. Forster, 'Terminal note', *Maurice* (Harmondsworth, Penguin, 1987), p. 221.

32   David Galligan, 'Beneath the surface of *The Swimming Pool Library*: an interview with Alan Hollinghurst', *James White Review*, 14:3 (1997), 6.

33   Hollinghurst, *Folding Star*, p. 304.

34   *Ibid.*, p. 337.

35   *Ibid.*, p. 302.

36   See De Jongh, 'The deep end'.

37   Hollinghurst, *Library*, p. 273.

38   De Jongh, 'The deep end'.

39   Cf. Ross Chambers's discussion of Beckwith as a *flâneur* in 'Messing around: gayness and loiterature in Alan Hollinghurst's *The Swimming Pool Library*' in Judith Still and Michael Worton (eds), *Textuality and Sexuality: Reading Theories and Practices* (Manchester, Manchester University Press, 1993), pp. 207–17.

40   Hollinghurst, *The Spell* (London, Chatto & Windus, 1998), p. 197.
41   *Ibid.*, p. 187.
42   *Ibid.*, p. 103.
43   *Ibid.*, p. 15.
44   On a theoretical level, Donald Morton has argued that queer theory is symptomatic of an erosion of the enlightened, libertarian project of lesbian and gay emancipation and is a consequence of the more general contemporary valorisation of exchange value (desire) over use value (need) which has given rise to 'ludic postmodernism': 'Birth of the cyberqueer', *PMLA*, 110:3 (1995), 369–81.

4

Spirit and matter:
romantic mythologies
in the films of Derek Jarman

Andrew Moor

Only the niceties and constraints of an English upbringing stop me from
reaching for a gun.

Derek Jarman, *Modern Nature*[1]

To say that Derek Jarman's last completed film, *Blue* (1993), secures its
author's avant-garde reputation is hardly to court controversy.[2] A film
without images, it is a rare instance of creative puritanism: a cinema of
denial. Consisting of an uninterrupted aquamarine screen, accompanied
by a rhapsodic soundtrack revolving around Jarman's experience of
AIDS, it achieves for queer cinema what Laura Mulvey had advocated for
feminist film practice in the mid-1970s, namely an ascetic denial of visual
pleasure.[3] Mulvey's polemic, drawing support from psychoanalysis, had
damned classical cinema for being an inherently phallocentric form.
Pleasure should be rejected because, according to her model, it is born
out of processes of identification which are channelled towards servicing
the masculine gazing subject, and thus towards maintaining patriarchal
power relations. There is no happy place within that regime for the objectified female on screen, and neither is there any reassuring theoretical
space for female spectatorship. Marking its non-signifying aesthetic,
Blue's single conceptual image, in so far as it can be called an image,
likewise abdicates any authority for fixed subject positioning along the
voyeuristic or fetishistic lines which Mulvey so roundly castigates.
Paradoxically it helps to keep the issue of AIDS visible, yet pointedly does
not let us look at its symptoms. This unwillingness to direct a lens on to
those with the syndrome, and to subject their bodies and the disease's
inscriptions to a prurient, medicalised surveillance, illustrates *Blue*'s
formal aversion to assertions of authority. Any documentary-style 'literal'

approach to AIDS might well seek truth in science, but can easily encroach upon the personal integrity of the sufferer, the effect being sentimental, demonising or disenfranchising. Viewed negatively, images of infected gay men risk connoting homosexuality with contagion itself, invidiously playing into the hands of homophobic rhetoric. 'If the doors of Perception were cleansed', *Blue*'s soundtrack vainly hopes, 'then everything would be seen as it is.' *Blue* searches for an uncontaminated way of transmitting its narrative, responding to the complaint that, as Lee Edelman has remarked, 'there is no available discourse on Aids that is not itself diseased'.[4] In this crisis of signification, *Blue*'s radical denial seems only to confirm the thrust of Edelman's observation.

The debates spawned by Mulvey's argument, including her own subsequent interventions, question the heterosexist assumptions behind her notion of a male gaze, and have finessed the solid demarcations of gendered and sexual identity upon which it is based. The importance of context, of audience response, and of issues of perfomativity and masquerade have since been emphasised, and the 1990s phenomenon of new queer cinema relishes in unstable or subversive oscillations of identification and desire.[5] Any images perceived in *Blue*'s blank canvas may be prompted by the soundtrack but are put there by the consciously engaged, 'projecting' viewer. Jarman has often criticised the manipulative character of traditional feature films, preferring open texts and democratically encouraging an interpretative response from his 'active audience'.[6] In offering scope for such a theoretically infinite set of identifications to the emancipated, imaginative spectator (and denying any to the unimaginative), *Blue*'s queer credentials begin to accrue. Paradoxically, however, the way the soundtrack works to suggest visual images in the viewer's 'inner eye' also suggests that a deeply romantic philosophy of art is actually in play. Such appeals to imaginative vision have a personal resonance for Jarman, of course: *Blue*'s rejection of photographic representation comments primarily upon the loss of sight which he suffered as a result of his own illness.[7] This inscription of the autobiographical is characteristic of his work.

Mulvey's analysis of classical cinema had, of course, been part of the 1970s feminist project to interrogate the conventional production of images of women. Likewise, *Blue*'s blank screen is an urgent, politicised response to other unsatisfactory representations of the AIDS crisis. In each case, avant-gardism has to engage with, and is thus shaped by, its binary opposite: namely, the tradition it seeks to reject. Perhaps this is inevitable. Alan Sinfield has remarked that dissident discourse 'can always, ipso facto, be discovered reinscribing that which it proposes to critique ... All stories comprise within themselves the ghosts of the alternative stories they are trying to exclude.'[8] Yet 'the traditional' is rather more than a spectre to Jarman. Even *Blue* is not quite the clean break which it first seems to be. In fact, it can be seen as the culmination of an established line in his career, marking his preoccupation with vision, with the imaginative spectator and with a brand of romanticised spiritualism. This is not to deny that Jarman's work is often radicalised, most obviously by Thatcherism and then by AIDS. *Blue*'s soundtrack, for instance, refers to Britain's National Health Service, to the 'state of the nation' and to other contemporary crises such as the Bosnian conflict. Yet the polemic needs to be placed in context. The British Establishment may be attacked, but exactly what Jarman defends is open to question.

Jarman's career is marked by, and is the marker of, transformations in subcultural identity politics from the 1970s to the 1990s. His first full-length feature, *Sebastiane* (1976), abandons the English landscape altogether for the sunnier Mediterranean climes of the Roman Empire, although the very banishment of a contemporary English *mise-en-scène* works as an implicit critique of it. Graven images of naked male bodies are generously paraded, and the film encompasses homosexual desires both loving and violent, reciprocated and rejected. For offering such images alone, *Sebastiane*'s very existence can be seen as a seminal cinematic event in the British history of gay liberation and solidarity, based squarely within the parameters of identity politics. Adrian's and Anthony's relationship in the film, for instance, is clearly to be read as a 'positive representation'. However, the exclusively male group they belong to is, emphatically, no model 'gay community'. Sebastian is the object of an aggressive, implicitly sodomising male gaze from his commander, Severus, a look unambiguously structured through point-of-view shots into the text; and Sebastian is finally executed for resisting these sexual advances. By the film's focusing on the hostile attention to Sebastian's body, the innocent enjoyment of Adrian's and Anthony's lovemaking (gratifyingly suspended for us in slow motion) is inevitably compromised. Jarman's accepted complicity here establishes what is an ongoing discomfort throughout his work with any clearly marked position of authority. Yet there is an unresolved tension, for elsewhere Jarman celebrates the commanding superiority of marginalised artist-figures whose own mystical authority is left unquestioned.

While there may be no simple continuum from the homoerotic pleasures of *Sebastiane* to *Blue*'s free-floating immateriality, what does

remain constant is Jarman's repeated reformulation of what is a fundamentally idealistic aesthetic. There is a sado-masochistic subtext to
Sebastian's death scene, with an implication of religious ecstasy which has
an obviously sexual redolence. This said, the indifference shown for the
martyrdom which might otherwise form the film's dramatic crux is
readable as Jarman's first major cinematic indictment of the Judeo-
Christian division between spirit and matter. This becomes a constant
line of attack. In *Chroma* he writes of the 'chasm opened up between the
terrestrial and celestial world',[9] a division which is seen as both unnatural
and catastrophic. Sebastian's unendorsed self-sacrifice is motivated by his
pious separation of divine and earthly pleasures; while conversely Adrian
and Anthony's loving relationship seems to fuse these polarities ideally.
Similarly, Jarman's *The Garden* (1990) allegorises homophobia by
replaying the story of the Passion with two male lovers occupying the
place of Christ. It conceives non-hierarchical, same-sex love as a gentle
mutual response to the queer-bashing violence of the Establishment. The
frequently idealised passivity of Jarman's gay lovers is not, then, a desex-
ualisation, but rather it marks the extent to which such images are a
retreat from a hostile world. The (ab)use of the sacred text in *The Garden*
also collapses categories of sex and transcendence between which
dominant western cultural traditions have long drawn a wedge. Whether
or not it is placed within a specifically religious context, the melding of
matter and spirit forms the basis of Jarman's romantic quest.

Jarman's confrontationalism is a consciously adopted posture. In his
copious writings and numerous interviews, he is repeatedly found undercutting the prevailing demonisation of queer subculture. He is often
impishly provocative, inverting norms and targeting his rhetoric on what
he sees as a brutal, philistine, middle-class power base, the dominance of
which reached exaggerated, grotesque proportions in the economic neo-
liberalism and bourgeois authoritarianism of 1980s and 1990s Britain.
The invective of 'Heterosoc' (his term for the powerful conflation of
family, suburbia, the bourgeoisie and all the repressive machinery which
shores it up) is often turned back on itself. Ironically, it is Jarman's
favoured tactic never to lose the semblance of what his public schooling
made him: a charming, polite and very eloquent English gentleman.[10]
Moreover, Jarman's genteel anglophilia may be calculated to undermine
the homophobia and muscular nationalism of the Conservative government, but what he is ultimately engaged in is nothing less than a battle for
the custodianship of English culture itself. It is a national tradition which
appeals to him, and it is often queerly inflected in his work. Entering the

public sphere both as a speaker about AIDS and as an artist and film-maker, this is the persona which Jarman strove to present.

Even Jarman's involvement in the confrontational politics of OutRage in the last decade of his life expressed anti-Establishment feelings born out of an affiliation to time-honoured romantic values, from which Thatcherism is seen as an aberrant deviation. To emphasise this is to situate Jarman in a sometimes submerged and often critically disparaged anti-realist tradition within British cinema history. Jarman's work forges correspondences between authority and seeing, between magic and art, and between some of his protected ideals: 'Home', nostalgia and English-ness. This particular nexus of motifs suggests, in particular, a close affili-ation to the British film-makers he most frequently claimed to admire, the partnership of Michael Powell and Emeric Pressburger.[11] Like Jarman's, their relationship to the Establishment was deeply quizzical. The effect of Pressburger's flight to Britain from Nazi Europe, and Powell's highly cosmopolitan romanticism, meld together in texts which problematise nationhood, craving roots while fearing assimilation. The idealistic images of magical, 'homely' and sometimes eroticised spaces in Powell and Pressburger's work enjoy a radical transformation in Jarman's, becoming sequestered havens, often for happily subversive same-sex love. The shared experience of displacement (whether geographical or cultural), and the associated fascination with frontiers, survives none-the-less. They each draw on an English Romantic heritage and on the Renaissance, and each has a highly conventional vision of art as emanating from the autonomous, transcendental genius, a character who is often inscribed into their films. Furthermore, this character imports a quasi-magical tone denoting a rejection of both realism and reality itself. The criticism can be made that this is an evasive romantic fantasy of the most fatal kind.

How credible, then, is this stance? It is not, of course, a novel one. The critique of Britain which Jarman, and Powell and Pressburger make derives from the Romantic movement's hostility to the Industrial Revolu-tion (notably in Blake, whom Jarman frequently quotes, and Wordsworth), a line of protest which survives through Ruskin, Morris and Wilde and into the twentieth century.[12] Yet this reaction against technological modernisation, urbanisation and the rampant entrepre-neurial advances of unregulated capitalism was not confined to the dissenting margins, but was (and still is) embedded within High Tory culture too. By the end of the nineteenth century, England's economic base no longer rested upon the country estate, yet a sense of national consciousness based upon the myth that it still did was perpetuated within the culture. Old feudal allegiances survived. In Martin Weiner's neatly observed diagnosis, 'the Tory party shifted its base from the land to property in all its forms, making room for the new middle classes ... [yet] many of the attitudes of Toryism lived on within the reconstituted party, alongside industrial and capitalistic values. The party continued to invoke the rustic spirit of the nation. Conservatism was enamoured of rural England, as much an England of the mind as of reality.'[13] A major version of the nation's sense of identity is thus invested in an emotional reservoir dislocated from the fact of modernity. This well-rehearsed argument offers up a valuable insight into the perseverance of romanticism in British cinema.

Kevin Macdonald has noted that Powell and Pressburger express what is basically an 'old-fashioned Anglican Tory'[14] vision. Despite his fight with Thatcherism (whose neo-liberalism was also at loggerheads with the traditions of Conservatism), and his ongoing sympathy with left-wing politics, including a brief flirtation with the Workers Revolutionary Party,[15] Jarman also admits that the work he has produced 'has always been Tory art'.[16] It is clear why Powell and Pressburger's work appeals to him. Their idealisation of the nation gelled with the official rhetoric of the so-called 'people's war', mythologising the audience's commitment to the preservation of the Home Front, and in works such as *A Canterbury Tale* (1944) and *I Know Where I'm Going* (1945) Pressburger's self-confessed 'crusade against materialism'[17] is clear. In *A Canterbury Tale*, disenchanted modern pilgrims are immersed in the Kentish countryside, and following the 'old road' to Canterbury they discover a cathedral which symbolises transcendental aspiration, the value of the past and the utopian possibility of the future (victory, peace, and possibly the high ideals of the Welfare State). In tension with these communal ideals, their work shows a fascination with lone outsiders. Deriving from a more individualistic brand of romanticism, and speaking an alternative language of visionary idealism, they often represent an irrational, authoritarian force. Thus we have, for example, the Svengali-like Lermontov in *The Red Shoes* (1948), an impresario presiding like a high priest over the film's quasi-religious attitude to art (their *Black Narcissus* (1947) likewise charts a drastically melodramatic schism between transcendental spirituality and sexual desire among a group of nuns exiled to a sublime Himalayan outpost). Such figures are alter egos for Powell, whose occasional appearances in his own films further inscribe his self-consciously artistic status, although this act becomes self-condemnation in *Peeping Tom* (1960) where he appears, in Mark's inherited home-movies, as the tyrannical, voyeuristic father-figure (the young Mark in this home-movie footage being played by Powell's own son). This sequence anticipates Jarman's use of his own family home-movies in his work, and closely rehearses his ambivalence towards his own father. Jarman senior was an Air Commodore in the Royal Air Force, and Derek has publicly admitted that their relationship was uneasy, the father's example being blamed for the son's recorded 'aversion to all authority'.[18]

Of all the magus-like 'seers' in Powell and Pressburger's output, Thomas Colpeper in *A Canterbury Tale* most expresses the romantic longing and the feudal values at the 'heart of England'. Another disturbing, disturbed, patriarchal figure, Colpeper is the local magistrate whose lectures on local landscape and history make him a spirit guide to the disoriented latter-day pilgrims. The name Colpeper (meaning 'herbalist') harks back to Nicholas Culpepper (1616–54), a writer on herbalism, medicine and astrology, whose work is referred to in Jarman's own journals.[19] Indeed, Jarman's diaries are littered with references to other Renaissance scholars, to gardening and in particular to alchemy, displaying his interest in premodern and dissident forms of knowledge. In his films, characters such as Prospero in *The Tempest* and John Dee in *Jubilee* (another historical figure, of course) represent the magically subversive possibilities of such learning, and the autobiographical current running through all of his work suggests a somewhat aristocratic identification with such fabled 'magicians'.

Regretting Kent's suburbanised commodification, Jarman complains that 'it is impossible to recapture, walking through Canterbury today, the emotions that fill that last reel of … *A Canterbury Tale*. The city of pilgrims has become an empty "theme park". The land of England was once the home of dryads and nymphs, every now and again you can feel the last of them lurking round a corner.'[20] Jarman overlooks the fact that Pressburger's script for *A Canterbury Tale* anticipates a postwar tourist boom in which, democratically, city dwellers might enjoy holidays in the English countryside. While Jarman might see this tourism as a consumerist debasement of a once romantic ideal, he is nevertheless open to the charge of elitism. Hence the following passage from *Modern Nature*: 'Sissinghurst, that elegant sodom in the garden of England, is "heritized" in the institutional hands of the National Trust. Its magic has fled in the vacant eyes of tourists … The shades of the Sackville-Wests pursuing naked guardsmen through the herbaceous borders return long after the last curious coachload has departed, the tea shoppe closed, and the general public has returned home to pore over the salacious Sundays.'[21] There is a humorous jibe at commercialised country-house culture here; and the patrician voice is inflected with a tone of arch irony, but any critique of exploitative property owners seems to pale next to a barely hidden aversion to the 'general public'. Significantly, perhaps, Jarman blames the blankness of the visitors' gaze for the ruin of Sissinghurst's 'magic', an attack which echoes his hope that his films might be greeted by a more imaginative audience. His lament for the loss of a faerie realm (with echoes of Tolkien's elves endlessly forsaking a Middle-England Middle-Earth) is fanciful, of course. But in its defence, Jarman's capriciousness is invariably an attack upon heterosexism and capital. These twin evils are, to him, vigorously conflated in the brutal dogma of Thatcherism, the moral hypocrisy of which is suggested in his image of the masses, in their domestic privacy, salivating vicariously at the latest sex scandals written up in the Sunday papers. Furthermore, the fantasised debauchery of the naked Sissinghust guardsmen clearly implies that, for Jarman, homosexuality itself is possessed of an aura of elitism.

'Heritage', of course, was a ripe term in British cinema of the 1980s. Films such as *Chariots of Fire* (dir. Hugh Hudson, 1981) and the work of Merchant Ivory constitute a genre of costume dramas with period settings, purporting to recreate the past faithfully. Occupying a prestigious position within the industry, they are predominantly readable as conservative works, signalling, according to Andrew Higson 'the desire for perfection, for the past as unimpaired paradigm, for a packaging of the past that is designed to please, not disturb'.[22] 'Packaging' is a choice word. This commodified culture satisfies the demands of a restrictive notion of 'national cinema' which works to promote and to secure national identity along middle-class lines, not least by drawing narratives from marketable 'classics' of the English literary canon such as the works of E. M. Forster. It is notable that, however much Forster himself was part of a Romantic anti-bourgeois English tradition, these cinematic adaptations seem to conform instead to the material pleasures of 1980s Britain. If Jarman belongs to a paradigm of 'national cinema', then it is a more pluralistic one, predicated upon a toleration of difference and a celebration of diversity, rather than on the rigid parameters and policed borders of a more tightly delineated 'official' model. Of course, even the more reactionary films of the heritage genre may comprise subversive elements, and may offer dissident pleasures, whatever their overall project seems to be. Thus issues of gender, class, race or sexuality may all find space to be tested progressively. Rupert Graves's roles in Merchant Ivory's *A Room with a View* (1985) and *Maurice* (1987) are notable cases in point.

Jarman does not participate in this ultimately hegemonic enterprise. He dismisses the manufacturers of such spectacles as 'Brideshead recidivists',[23] calling instead for an imaginative treatment of the historical which breaks away from the polished actorly artifice of so-called 'classical' quality cinema. His own period films often only gesture towards re-creating the past. Rather, they modernise it, making it rough and immediate, disjointing it with anachronisms, resisting the fetishistic aesthetic of mainstream 'heritage' cinema, which he perceived as being bound up too intimately with the current Establishment. Of course, much smaller budgets tend to enforce upon Jarman an aesthetic of makeshift artisanship. Confining his films to the specialised pocket of the art-house circuit, the production constraints he works with inevitably and directly decommercialise his films, and apparently shield them from the vicissitudes of the Thatcherite free marketplace. Indeed, their relatively non-commercial status within the industry and their minimal involvement with large-scale corporate enterprise reinforce the anti-materialistic sentiments which the texts so frequently defend. Jarman's use of video, the freedoms granted to him by Super-8, and his splicing in of his and his family's old home-movies, confirm the line of noble English amateurism in his work, and grant him an enviable scope for that most sought-after goal of the Romantics: uncompromised self-expression. As he admits himself, 'I am the most fortunate film-maker of my generation, I've only ever done what I wanted. Now I just film my life, I'm a happy megalomaniac … Making films our way makes all the others seem fabricated.'[24] This egotism goes hand in hand with his detachment from the mainstream.

What Jarman argues is that the past he tenaciously identifies with has been suppressed or warped by those forces now occupying the middle ground. The true culture of this past both antedates and should be divorced from those who now call themselves the Establishment. He draws upon a queer artistic canon, from Caravaggio to Shakespeare's sonnets, Britten's *War Requiem* and *Edward II*, to make the specific point that this culture has been criminally appropriated, normalised and neutered in the name of bourgeois suburban respectability and of capital, and more generally he declares that his own *oeuvre* actually harmonises with the central customs of English art. His work literally keeps this culture alight: images of torch-fires illuminating his films may occasionally signify destruction or cremation (and even there, the loss is generally of a value which is to be mourned), but more commonly they take on elemental connotations which are more to do with perseverance or rebirth, with the magical and the messianic. In the concluding image of *The Last of England* (1987), downtrodden refugees from an urban blighted dockland sail off, guided by just such a light. In *The Garden*, guardian angels carrying similar torches wade around a sleeping Jarman as the incoming tide washes around his bed, the film becoming a hypno-gogic sequence conjured from the inspired, dreaming artist.

Jarman and his subculture may have been demonised and driven underground by Heterosoc, but, by taking with him 'the best' of an artistic heritage, he attempts to bring the centre back to himself and the more ancient tradition he says he represents. There is a double motiva-tion here. By Jarman's reclaiming custody of this 'best', the state's spurious proprietorship of it is shown to be a dishonest appeal to misconceived 'old-fashioned values', and its cultural paucity will be left all the more exposed. Furthermore, this ancient tradition should and can be, for Jarman, a more positively liberating cultural space, where natural freedoms, both spiritual and sexual, may be enjoyed. To sing the praise of this other space, he celebrates the closeted or nocturnal homosexual subculture as one of magical potential. A dominant national discourse which criminally purports to tell the truth is wholeheartedly rejected; and the values of orthodoxy and unorthodoxy are inverted. 'I never believed in reality', Jarman maintains, 'because if reality was the way it was served up, who wanted it?'[25]

But just beyond the jurisdiction of Heterosoc, Jarman cruises noctur-nally among the nymphs of Hampstead Heath, venturing, as he says, 'over the invisible border [where] your heart beats faster and the world seems a better place'.[26] This is the forest of Arden, or the woods outside Athens: a memorable scenario in the journals contrasts the 'real fairies' of the Heath, gay men at ease in a moonlit natural setting, with an incongruous and artificial group of designer-clad film-makers struggling nearby to shoot their version of *A Midsummer Night's Dream*.[27] Jarman's favoured other space is a pastoral carnivalesque alternative to commercialised urban Britain (not least the gay club scene). Furthermore, the sense of kinship paradoxically found on the Heath, and mirrored in Jarman's film-making collaborations with a close circle of friends, suggests a nostalgic endorsement of values of 'community' (whose existence Margaret Thatcher denied) rather than with the atomisation of modern capitalist society. Nostalgia was always present in Jarman's paintings.

Despite arriving at Slade Art College in the early 1960s just at the moment of the London pop-art explosion, Jarman was, even then, out of step with the celebration of popular culture by artists such as David Hockney. While the tide of fashion faced squarely towards Warhol's America, Jarman was painting Dorset landscapes with the soft surrealism of Paul Nash, Henry Moore and the English neo-Romantic school.

Where, then, is this aesthetic in his films, when works such as *The Last of England* depict city blight so thoroughly? As with the footage mentioned earlier of Jarman sleeping in *The Garden*, the opening shots of *The Last of England* show him writing in his study and clearly mark him as its author, yet given the lack of any classical narrative form to the film, they also mark his consciousness as one possible locus of meaning. His old nib pen and his monastic appearance cut him loose from the late twentieth century, and suggest a mythic aura of timeless artistic genius. Jarman's very act of protest against oppression, squalor and injustice implies, of course, an alternative, a principle of hope which predictably is rooted in the past (for the only transcendence the present seems to offer is that gained through heroin or solvent abuse). A voice-over commentary, spoken by Nigel Terry, sounds elegiac: 'Poppies and corn-cockles have long been forgotten here, like the boys who died in Flanders ... The oaks died this year. On every green hill, mourners stand and weep for the last of England.' The rusticity of Georgian poetry ghosts through this passage, however much it has degenerated, and, symbolically, the curative knowledge of herbalists (for whom the corn-cockle had been an ancient and useful weed) is now lost to us, conflated with a failure to remember the war dead, in a general mourning of any sense of history in contemporary Britain.

Among the riotous dystopia of the image track, muted moments of calm can nevertheless be glimpsed. Brief shots of bees, flowers, and of Tilda Swinton among a host of daffodils are matched to reflective music scored for strings, and all hint at the possibility of regeneration. As if emulating a classical deity, one of Jarman's dispossessed wanderers, a tattooed, leather-jacketed youth (an actor ironically nicknamed 'Spring') plays pan-pipes. Intercut with metropolitan businessfolk advancing in hordes towards the camera, Spring's playing implicitly lures these agents of capital out of their rat race, although any natural celebration connoted by the pipes is incongruous in Jarman's wasteland. More plaintively, a gentle harp melody, gesturing to the older sonorities of folk music, accompanies shots of homeless refugees gathering on a disused dock, with the lyrics of 'The Skye boat song' sung by Marianne Faithfull suggesting a narrative of exiled hope. Edited into Jarman's new footage, however, are snatches of his father's and his grandfather's home-movies, and in these are located some of the film's strongest appeals to nostalgia. These brightly coloured, sun-drenched sequences mainly show Jarman in the 1940s as a toddler, with his sister and mother, playing in their childhood garden. The image of the smiling mother, in particular, seems to radiate love, and the accompanying classical guitar soundtrack sets up a range of idyllically Mediterranean connotations. But just as this significantly amateur footage idealistically equates 'Home' and nostalgia, the clear cutting within *The Last of England* to and from this very different film stock marks its separation from the present, and the relationship between the childhood scenes and the 1980s material remains ambivalent. Continuous soundtrack stitches the images together, and the presence of the adult Jarman in the film imposes an autobiographical linearity; yet the collision of different film (and video) formats leaves the work fragmented. The sequence may be read as a flashback from the current, or may signify a fated transition from the 1940s. If the relationship is merely one of historical association, then the earlier sunshine of England's 'Blitz culture' mythic optimism clearly seems to be in dialogue with the hopeless nihilism of the more utterly blitzed 1980s. Jarman's keen and questioning sense of the historical is, in any event, visible. Particularly, his rose-tinted haven for healthy 1940s children encapsulates the high idealism of the Welfare State: the starkly contrasting urban underclass of Thatcherite Britain becomes a direct consequence of the dismantling of those ideals.

The Jarman family biography is implicated in this sense of questioning. This other Eden, Derek's childhood playground, is RAF Abingdon: a compromised idyll. The barbed wire surrounding it, and the drone of planes and of an air-raid mixed on to the soundtrack, all remind us of oppressive power structures, and of the absent, filming father (he is caught on camera once, in the Alps with his wife). The inclusion of aerial footage, clearly shot in the 1940s by Jarman senior from his aeroplane, symbolically gives the offscreen patriarch a troubling airborne omniscience, while his military lifestyle is, by implication, bound up with the entire film's oppositional stance to abuses of authority.[28] While Jarman's incorporation of himself into his work is readable as a self-promotional admission of his own directorial agency, its effect is, rather, to personalise the film, and strip it of its own authoritative objectivity. With the textual status diminished, an active spectatorial response is required. The audio-visual collage which constitutes the work requires, in any case, an imaginative and synthesising response (although admittedly, there are times when Jarman's images of violence, and use of sound recordings such as 'Rule Britannia' and a Hitler speech, lack either subtlety or ambiguity – the meaning is all too crushingly clear).

This said, on occasions the text mischievously records the director's presence. Such disruptive moments significantly queer what is not otherwise flagged as a 'homosexual film'. Shots of the magus-like Jarman in his study are cut to Spring, bare-chested and in ripped jeans, nihilistically attacking Caravaggio's painting *Profane Love*, an obvious intertext harking back to Jarman's biopic of the painter. Yet this is no simple or deplored defamation of 'high art', for, given Jarman's recognition of anti-Establishment iconoclasm in Caravaggio himself, Spring's attack is deeply ironic. Yet it is also ambiguously erotic. Cutting from shots of himself to footage of Spring, Jarman clinically splices himself to his imagined piece of 'rough trade'; but a later shot, in which Spring effectively rapes Caravaggio's famous portrait of the naked boy, makes explicit the sexual meaning: a hand-held camera purposefully revolves around Spring so that Jarman's shadow falls on to the youth's rutting body. Abusing and destroying the classical integrity of his cinema image, Jarman underscores his fantasised participation in Spring's masturbatory sex act, and prompts the spectator to do likewise, as an orgiastic chain of homosexual encounters is enacted between bodies, shades and images.

The other sex scene in the film is differently disruptive: rather than displaying its effect, it does the opposite, keeping its secret from all but a knowing coterie. A drunken 'yuppy' (a public schoolboy 'type') strips naked and climbs on to a bed draped in a Union Jack, upon which a khaki-clad, balaclava-masked terrorist (or soldier) is sleeping. An overhead camera emphasises the flag, and the connotations which are prompted by the couple's clumsy sexual wrestling suggest the homoerotics of soldiery and the public school system, and a subversive (homo)sexualisation of Great Britain's Establishment. None of these meanings is entirely undone, but they are mockingly upset, by the hidden truth that the soldier is a woman – a fact disguised in the text and therefore privileged only to that community involved in the film (and later to readers of Jarman's accompanying journal of its making).[29] The perception of apparently cogent and stable gender positions is thus tricked, and aspects of performance, masquerade and costume are brought into play, albeit invisibly. The signs have misdirected us. The stereotypes of the foppish rake and the sexually available squaddie are the regular fare of gay pornography, but here these seemingly uncomplicated fantasy images are deployed deceptively, and the expectations of Jarman's customary gay audience are apparently satisfied, yet are ultimately tricked. Perversely, the sequence is queered by the hidden disparity between the soldier's outward appearance and her biological sex. By so wrong-footing us, it serves as a warning against easy categorisations of biology, gender, sexuality and performance. The invisibility of the strategem provides another layer of significance though. It comments upon Jarman's belief that homosexuality is structured around a secretive exclusivity.

His reading of gay subculture stresses the importance of codes, imaginative connections and unearthing meanings: a cabbalistic activity which rests upon an alternative, esoteric language, known to an inner circle of preferred initiates. It is worth stressing that for Jarman, this subculture amounts metaphorically to a form of magic, which, as he says, is 'banned and dangerous, difficult and mysterious'.[30] Not only is the sense of segregation acknowledged but it is, by implication, celebrated. The very existence of this marginalised, enigmatic culture might alone trouble the confidence of society's dominant values; but it is imbued by Jarman with a superior faculty of perception, not bound by the supposedly material certainties of rationalism. Hence his 'queer magus' figures are subversive tribal visionaries, inhabiting, like Prospero, a cultural space fantastically divorced from ordinary reality, and explicitly connoted with premodernity. Jarman's version of The Tempest (1979) incorporates ciphers from Egyptian hieroglyphics and from Renaissance scholars, with Prospero's wand being modelled on John Dee's insignia, symbolising, as the director confirms, the alchemical unity of spirit and matter.[31] John Dee had, of course, been fictionalised in Jubilee (1978), where he transports himself and the first Queen Elizabeth to the punk anomie of 1970s Britain, a territory so alien that they ultimately flee to the fringes, seeking out the 'great elixir' of the seashore, where in Dee's words 'one can dream of lands far distant, and the earth's treasure'.

A mathematician and scientist in the late Tudor period, Dee had by repute been associated with alchemy and the summoning of angels. In old age he fell out of favour with the court of King James, dying neglected and in poverty, an anti-Establishment figure.[32] It is characteristic of Jarman that he should identify with him. Jarman's own conjuring, of course, is in the province of the arts, and a sorcerer's language informs his aesthetic pronouncements: thus he declares film to be 'the wedding of light and matter – an alchemical conjunction'.[33] It is a highly romantic concept which echoes, incidentally, Michael Powell's more consciously egotistical assertion that in his films 'miracles occur on screen'.[34] Such metaphysical aspirations finally achieve their apotheosis in *Blue*.

I opened with the suggestion that *Blue* is chiefly significant for marking absence, that it is a metacinematic meditation on the dilemmas of depicting what cannot satisfactorily be represented. It sidesteps the political ramifications of objectifying sufferers of AIDS, and shifts instead to pure abstraction, avoiding what its soundtrack refers to as 'the pandemonium of image'. But cannot that negation be read, alternatively, as a sublimation? While, as Richard Porton has suggested, 'it is impossible for the viewer to fetishize Jarman's film as pure transcendent form',[35] the religious yearning for the immaterial in the work is nevertheless to the fore, creatively in tension with its more self-reflexive aspects. The blueness may represent a semiotic void, but it is still a signifier, and its cultural connotations of spirituality or infinity propel the film towards the sublime. Images of the sea – an elemental infinitude and, to Britain's island race, a space beyond the nation's repressive rule – form a recurring motif in Jarman's work, from *Sebastiane*'s Mediterranean, to the blue-filtered shots of Bamburgh's beach and dunes in *The Tempest*, through the waterfront footage in *The Garden*, *The Angelic Conversation* and *The Last of England* (and not forgetting Jarman's own beach home, Prospect Cottage at Dungeness). *Blue*'s aquamarine screen alludes to these earlier symbols of possibility.[36] In line with his characteristic language of romantic-pastoral, the closing lyrical moments of the film speak of a magical-marginal zone for Jarman's chosen few: in waters 'washing the isle of the dead … We lie there, … lost boys … in a deep embrace, salt lips touching in submarine gardens, … deep love drifting on the tide forever.'

Blue's stated antecedents lie in the monochrome abstraction of the painter Yves Klein (1928–62), the film being based on a sample of ultramarine blue from one of his canvases. Anticipating Jarman's eventual shift into a cinematic non-pictorialism, Klein's messianic, deeply mystical view of the sacred function of art was expressed in a series of works, notably his solid blue screens.[37] These screens, marking Klein's deep religiosity and his longing for a 'primal state', position themselves squarely within a zone of the ideal, unsullied by matter. Jarman's comment in *Blue* that the 'image is a prison of the soul' thus captures the essence of Klein's work. What Jarman does is write that spirituality into the narrative of AIDS.

On the verge of death, Jarman abandons *terra firma* altogether. The concrete physical reality of gay experience (and more generally of mortality) is raised to some elevated condition. This sublimation, read in the context of Jarman's earlier work, is one of alchemical transmutation. As a conclusion to his career, it recollects his alter ego, Prospero, declaring the end of his own revels and the vaporisation of what has been an insubstantial pageant. Certainly, after the carnivalesque excess of *Edward II* (1991) and *Wittgenstein* (1993) there is a post-ludic quality to the last work, and, while the familiar voices of John Quintin, Nigel Terry, Tilda Swinton and Jarman himself are to be heard, the bodies of the actors are now rejected, melted into thin air.

This ethereal response to his illness is not, however, Jarman's sole artistic comment on it. Painting until near the end of his life, Jarman's late canvases, such as those exhibited in his *Queer* exhibition of 1992, are the visceral converse to *Blue*.[38] In these aggressive paintings (such as *EIIR, Love, Sex, Death* and *Queer*) Jarman takes multiple photocopies of homophobic tabloid front pages and almost covers them in paint – mainly reds, browns and yellows. He then scores graffiti-like obscenities into the paint, directly invoking blood, sex and the plague. These works are emotional declarations, literally and passionately incorporating the nation's public discourse of AIDS into themselves, and the overriding sensation of series is its redness. Connoting carnality and rage, and provocatively suggesting the body's fluids and the disease of the flesh, this red is a stark antithesis to the cool of *Blue*.[39]

Blue and red, spirit and matter, segregated into different media: the gap between these regimes is seemingly unbreachable in Jarman's final output. But his work is all acutely intertextual, each piece knitting into a wider pattern, often shaped along auteurist, or blatantly autobiographical, lines. Mediating between this late work is Jarman himself, the self-styled Romantic artist. One of the last images we have of Jarman is an oil portrait. Painted by Mike Clark in 1993, it hangs in the National Portrait Gallery. Its title, *Seer*, suggests how far that figure of the 'gifted magus' had been absorbed into the Jarman persona. Clark's portrait shows a close-up image of Jarman staring out at the spectator. Encrypted in mirrored text over him is an untranslated prophecy, implicitly Jarman's: 'Enjoy the luscious landscape of my wound … But Hurry! … Time meets us, and we are destroyed.' Another secret code: Jarman addresses his private coterie, to whom his *carpe diem* pleasures are exclusively afforded. The invitation here comments upon the astonishing late burst of creativity sparked by Jarman's very public decline into ill health, yet with the plural pronouns 'us' and 'we' he is allied to a community which is being wiped out by the disease. Again, the mystical insight allotted to the Jarman persona, and by implication to his threatened community, invests queer culture with a special quality, even if what it perceives so clearly is no more than political indifference and moral hypocrisy. Like the magic spaces charted in his films, Jarman's diseased body is now a rich territory, a fertile 'landscape' to be enjoyed. That this 'wound' itself becomes a positive source of inspiration indicates how far Jarman's own experience of AIDS is pervaded by a romantic discourse. On the point of death in this interconnected triptych of images, *Blue*, the *Queer* paintings and Clark's *Seer* portrait, there is a collapse between autobiography, biography, art and politics, written through with a keen sense of the need to reconcile the material with the spiritual. However anti-Establishment the sentiments, however avant-garde the work, the mediator between these regimes is Jarman himself, and the central position afforded to his role places his work within a highly traditional artistic discourse.

Notes

1   Derek Jarman, *Modern Nature* (London, Century, 1991), p. 127.
2   I am excluding Jarman's *Glitterbug* (1994), the edited collage of old film and video footage released after his death.
3   See Laura Mulvey, 'Visual pleasure and the narrative cinema', *Screen*, 19:3 (1975), 6–18. The essay is reprinted in Laura Mulvey, *Visual and Other Pleasures* (Basingstoke, Macmillan, 1989).
4   Lee Edelman, 'Politics, literary theory, and AIDS' in Ronald R. Butters, John M. Clum and Michael Moon (eds), *Displacing Homophobia: Gay Male Perspectives in Literature and Culture* (London, Duke University Press, 1989), p. 304.
5   'New queer cinema' covers such films as *Poison* (Todd Haynes, 1991), *My Own Private Idaho* (Gus Van Sant, 1991), *Young Soul Rebels* (Isaac Julien, 1991), *The Living End* (Greg Araki, 1992), *Swoon* (Tom Kalin, 1992) as well as Jarman's later work. Such films collide queer narratives with postmodern strategies such as parody, pastiche and intertextuality, while importantly constructing multiple 'non-straight' subject positions.
6   Derek Jarman, *The Last of England* (London, Constable, 1987), p. 194.
7   Jarman first tested HIV-positive in December 1986, and died of AIDS in February 1994.
8   Alan Sinfield, *Faultlines: Cultural Materialism and the Politics of Dissident Reading* (Oxford, Clarendon Press, 1992), p. 47.
9   Derek Jarman, *Chroma* (London, Vintage, 1995), p. 45.
10 See Jarman, *The Last of England*, p. 118.
11 See Jarman, *Dancing Ledge* (London, Quartet Books, 1984), p. 216. See also Simon Field and Michael O'Pray, 'Imagining October, Dr. Dee and other matters: an interview with Derek Jarman', *Afterimage* 1985 (12) 45.

12   See Lawrence Driscoll, ' "The rose revived": Derek Jarman and the British tradition' in Chris Lippard (ed.), *By Angels Driven: the Films of Derek Jarman* (Trowbridge, Flick Books, 1996).

13   Martin J. Weiner, *English Culture and the Decline of the English Spirit, 1850–1980* (Cambridge, Cambridge University Press, 1981), p. 98.

14   Kevin Macdonald, *Emeric Pressburger: The Life and Death of a Screenwriter* (London, Faber & Faber, 1994), p. 233.

15   See Jarman, *The Last of England*, p. 213.

16   Quoted by Mick Brown, *Daily Telegraph*, 16 August 1993 (see the British Film Institute library microfile on 'Derek Jarman').

17   Macdonald, *Emeric Pressburger*, p. 233.

18   Jarman, *The Last of England*, p. 179.

19   Jarman, *Modern Nature*, p. 37.

20   Jarman, *The Last of England*, p. 138.

21   Jarman, *Modern Nature*, p. 15.

22   Andrew Higson, *Waving the Flag* (Oxford, Clarendon, 1995), p. 122.

23   Jarman, *Dancing Ledge*, p. 14.

24   Jarman, *Modern Nature*, p. 131.

25   Derek Jarman, television interview, *Know What I Mean* (YoYo Films, made for Channel 4, 1988), broadcast as part of Channel 4's posthumous tribute *A Night with Derek*, 16 September 1994.

26   Jarman, *Modern Nature*, p. 84.

27   *Ibid.*, p. 103.

28   Jarman, *The Last of England*, p. 179.

29   *Ibid.*, p. 196.

30   Field and O'Pray 'Imagining October', p. 59.

31   Jarman, *Dancing Ledge*, p. 188.

32   See Frances A. Yates, *Occult Philosophy in the Elizabethan Age* (London, Ark Paperbacks, 1983).

33   Jarman, *Dancing Ledge*, p. 188.

34   Michael Powell, *A Life in Movies* (London, Mandarin Paperbacks, 1992), p. 612.

35   R. Porton, 'Language games and aesthetic attitudes: style and ideology in Jarman's late films' in Lippard (ed.), *By Angels Driven*, p. 149.

36   Paul Julian Smith sees in *Blue* a link to the French autobiographies of AIDS, Cyril Collard's film (and novel) *Savage Nights*, and Hervé Guibert's novel *Compassion Protocol*, both of which treat the sea as an image of transcendence, although, in contrast to Jarman, these works repeatedly display their AIDS sufferers' bodies as unblemished and immaculate (an act, as Smith suggests, of narcissistic disavowal). See Paul Julian Smith, '*Blue* and the outer limits', *Sight and Sound*, 3:20 (1993), 18–19.

37   See Pierre Restany, *Yves Klein* (New York, Harry N. Abrams Inc., 1982).

38   These works were exhibited at Manchester City Art Gallery, 16 May–28 June

1992. See the published exhibition catalogue: Jarman, *Queer* (Manchester, Manchester City Art Galleries/Richard Salmon Ltd, 1992).

39 Powell and Pressburger's *Black Narcissus* also draws on this traditional division. In its symbolic colour code, a transcendent blue in the nun's costumes, matched in the Himalayan skies of the film's painted sets, is pitched against Powell's famous use of red, haemorrhaging an otherwise repressed sexual energy on to his screen.

5

Autobiographical travesties:
the nostalgic self in queer writing

Linda Anderson

A hypothesis worth making explicit: that there are important senses in which 'queer' can signify only when attached to the first person. One possible corollary: that what it takes – all it takes – to make the description 'queer' a true one is the impulsion to use it in the first person.

Eve Sedgwick, *Tendencies*[1]

Let us now imagine reintroducing into the politico-sexual field ... *a touch of sentimentality*: would that not be the ultimate transgression? the transgression of transgression itself? For, after all, that would be love: which would return: *but in another place.*

Roland Barthes by Roland Barthes[2]

According to Eve Sedgwick sexual difference has an almost infinite variety of forms. However, the self-evident truth for Sedgwick that 'people are different from each other' in sexual, as well as in other, more or less fraught and contested ways, is difficult to theorise even though we may well 'know' less systematically through literature or gossip about the small, unregistered gradations of difference which abound and which require the 'making and unmaking and remaking and redissolution of hundreds of old categorical imaginings': the project of 'nonce taxonomy' as Sedgwick calls it.[3] Knowing does not necessarily mean that we know in a definitive or conceptual way, in ways we always recognise as knowledge. 'Queer' finds itself at this unstable or blurred boundary between knowing and not knowing. In the early 1990s this vituperative term was re-appropriated by theorists as a 'defiant adjective'[4] which could cross the normative categories of gender, sexuality and theory, opposing any claim to certainty (knowledge which does not also acknowledge its own ignorance) and the idea of 'normality' it supports. If same-sex object choice must remain near its 'definitional centre' for queer to mean anything, as Sedgwick argues, it is also against 'identities', including gay and lesbian ones, which are prescriptive or monolithic, which do not allow for the complex crossings and interruptions of other 'identity-constituting, identity-fracturing discourses', including the ones we may not yet know.[5]

Yet however radical queer theory is, it may be difficult for it ever to be radical enough. Talking about deconstruction – from which both queer theory and her own writing has taken its momentum – Sedgwick has complained that it has both 'fetishised' the idea of difference and 'vaporized' its possible embodiments.[6] The problem becomes how to stop difference disappearing into thin air when it is *only* an idea, a general term for what is quite specifically different about our lives. Like decon-struction, queer can imply differences which somehow become so abstracted – so decarnated and theoretical – that the term difference, rather than re-animating meaning, becomes another way of inhibiting its unpredictable diversification. Biddy Martin has referred critically to a tendency within queer theory to reduce individual histories to the effects of power; whilst she acknowledges that queer theory enables us better to understand the social and discursive constructedness of gender – and in particular how sex, gender and sexuality are not necessarily aligned – she also believes that we have lost a language in which to address the internal and subjective dimension of our lives and relationships. While gender is 'more than a fixed ground', according to Martin, more than the unchangeable core of the person which heterosexuality assumes, it is also 'less than that which structures everything, the deconstruction of which would take apart personhood itself'.[7] This is why Sedgwick's use of the first person, cited in the epigraph to this chapter, seems particularly important. It is first of all a way of dislodging queer from its possible definitional role and putting it to work as a word – an adjective – which actively changes meaning. As *performed* meaning, Sedgwick argues, queer is always different from itself. 'Anyone's use of "queer" about themselves means differently from their use of it about someone else'.[8] Sedgwick's personalising of queer also returns us to the question of interiority raised above, and what it can mean within a deconstructive critical practice. If interiority is, as Judith Butler has argued, 'an effect and function of a decidedly public and social discourse', and as such a 'fabrication' or 'an illusion',[9] this conclusion – both overarching and negative in function – can account neither for affectivity nor for more localised, individual and perhaps positive forms of knowing. For Sedgwick such 'strong' and 'fixated' or 'paranoid' knowledge, as Butler argues for in *Gender Trouble*, is always bound by, in Paul Ricoeur's phrase, a 'hermeneutics of suspicion', a relation to texts which sees them as inherently falsifying and in need of demystification by the critic/reader. This narrative of 'tracing-and-exposure', which has become almost compulsory for 'radical' critics, can end up being both tautological and predictable, finding what is already assumed to be so in order not to be caught out. 'It's strange' Sedgwick wryly comments, 'that a hermeneutic of suspicion would appear so trusting about the effects of exposure.'[10] Her own use of the first person in her essays is, as she suggests, more about experiment and surprise: it is about validating divergence and movement away from the inevitable truth of theory, even when it's posing at its most radical: like the word queer, the value of the first person lies in its continuing re-inflection of meaning: 'Anything that offers to make this genre [criticism] more acute and experimental, less numb to itself, is a welcome prospect.'[11]

This is an essay about the queer use of the first person; it is also an essay about returning to the self from another place, coming back to it as if from a distance and refiguring its possibilities. Roland Barthes, in his fragmented, ludic autobiography, *Roland Barthes by Roland Barthes*, surprises us by inviting the word 'love' back into a writing which seems to have discredited all its usual humanistic connotations through displacement and deconstruction: Barthes asks whether this 'touch of sentimentality' does not become the ultimate transgression, another kind of meaning – a subjective one – insisting on its difference from the subject-less discourses of the 'politico-sexual field'.[12] 'Love' could be said to act as a reminder of the past in the context of a different future; to insist on an imaginary wholeness despite the subversions and deprivations of desire; it tells us that textuality is not all there is by bringing into play a different dream of coherence. Sedgwick similarly imagines a 'reparative critical practice', modelled on Melanie Klein's notion of reparation or making whole – which Klein also called love – which can turn us away from paranoia, the 'hermeneutics of suspicion', even if only temporarily, towards an imagined plenitude. Such wholeness, Sedgwick stresses, should not be thought about in terms of a pre-existing whole: it's 'something like a whole', an assemblage of part-objects into a form of wholeness with which one can then identify and derive nourishment. Replacing the whole it can never be, the object thus conceived provides a way of thinking about wholeness for the instable and fragmented self. It creates a phantasmic space for the release and recognition of real affect.[13]

I want to go on and link this return of 'sentiment' to the use or uses of nostalgia in queer writing. It is an important part of Sedgwick's point, of course, that there's something locked and rigid about the temporality of 'suspicious' criticism that leaves no room for different times but inter-prets the future only in terms of a repetition of the past: 'paranoia requires that bad news be always already known'.[14] Nostalgia on the other hand invokes the uncanny effects of time: if nostalgia is characteristically turned towards a past conceived as fuller and more authentic than the present, it also confronts the impossibility of making the past and the present cohere into a single narrative line. Nostalgia denies the present for the sake of an impossible past; it yearns for an irrecoverable point of origin before the subject's inscription in time; however, in its desire for unity, it has the effect of generating distance and discontinuity, a disjunc-tive temporality where time is always different from itself. As Susan Stewart notes, nostalgia produces a narrative which must always lack 'fixity and closure' since it is turned towards 'a future-past, a past which has only an ideological reality'. Nostalgia is 'enamored of distance' since to close the gap between present and past, between sign and signified, would be to 'cancel out the desire which is nostalgia's reason for existence'.[15]

In her discussion of childhood in her essay 'Suspended beginnings' Elspeth Probyn has emphasised the mobility which has characterised nostalgia's history. From describing the 'normal' state of homesickness, nostalgia was later pathologised and associated with the regressive desire of the melancholic. It ceased to be a condition which could be remedied through direct physical action – returning the soldier to his home – but was interiorised, becoming instead the disease of the intellectual. From a wish to return to a place, nostalgia comes to denote the return to a partic-ular time, the past understood as a personal past, recaptured through memory.[16] Freud believed that the longing to return to a homeland could always be read psychoanalytically as a desire to return to the body of the mother. The dreamed-of, familiar place which produces symptoms of homesickness, is the womb.[17] However such an understanding only further serves to split nostalgia off from its object, for the mother, according to Lacan, never existed as she is imagined to be, but is already divided ('castrated'). There is no home to return to; the mother as 'homeland, source and grounding' is lost for ever. The subject is therefore always and inevitably abroad, in a foreign country.[18] Jane Gallop has gone on to offer an even more radical – or estranged – reading of nostalgia based on Lacanian notions of desire, which makes the 'object of desire' not just irretrievable but indefinable. If the history of the term suggests the progressive attenuation of 'what' it is we want to return to – a place, a time, an earlier state – in this definition it has also lost its direction. Nostalgia finally suggests a 'a transgression of return: a desire ungrounded in a past, desire for an object that has never been known'. Without an object, even in fantasy, 'what Lacan calls desire … yields up a nostalgia beyond *nostos*, beyond the desire to return'.[19]

From our point of view it is, of course, significant that nostalgia should be linked to the (psychoanalytic) narrative of sexual difference and that it should release itself from its fixation on origins in the same way as that narrative disproves its own point of departure. If Freud initially assumed a 'natural heterosexuality', the rest of his work, according to Juliet Mitchell, 'argued against this possibility'; bisexuality came to stand, for Freud, 'for the very uncertainty of sexual division itself'.[20] The same oedipal narrative, therefore, which had assigned the subject to his or her different sexual position also revealed it to be a fiction. The story could after all take another turn. Nostalgia accompanies the subject whose choices and identifications are no longer fixed and predetermined; unmoored from the narrative of cause and effect, nostalgia finds itself similarly free to wander in perverse ways.

Elspeth Probyn has seen nostalgia as a way of 'queering the past in the present', a mode peculiarly suited to the retelling of queer childhoods, which dispute both the 'truth' of sexuality and the 'straight' line which leads from the past to the present. Far from making childhood the point of origin for queer identity, the tracing of a commonality in which we can refind our difference – a structure familiar from 'coming out' stories – Probyn wants to deny the stability of both origins and identity: 'We need to re-make childhood into evidence of the necessary absence of any primary ground in queer politics.'[21] Memory in her account creates disturbance and dissonance, the fraying of identity as it encounters its own difference. The past does not lead to the present, finding its completion in the unified subject. Rather memory insists on a dissociation of self. Jeanette Winterson's *Oranges Are Not the Only Fruit* is used by Probyn as an example of a novel which queers the idea of a return. What we discover in that novel is that the strangest thing about Jeanette's return to her mother at the end is that her mother does not seem to have noticed she has left. 'My mother was treating me like she always had; had she noticed my absence? …There's a chance I'm not here at all, that all the choices I did and didn't make, for a moment brush up against each other.'[22] Going back, Jeanette is doubly estranged from both the past and the present; memory upsets who she is as the past draws her in, refusing to recognise her difference. Rather than re-connecting her to what is familiar and primary, the past disarranges who she has become. There is no straight line joining her past and present but rather a confused and confusing sense of many different possible trajectories consisting of 'all the choices that I did and didn't make'.

In what follows I want to explore two examples of queer writing in the first person which belong to different genres or categories – theory and fiction – but which both employ nostalgia as affect and as narrative mode. The first example is by the theorist who has already been much quoted in this essay, Eve Sedgwick. Her essay 'White glasses', the final one in her book *Tendencies*, is written as a personal tribute and an obituary for her friend Michael Lynch, who at the time of the essay's inception seemed close to death from AIDS. However the essay goes on to question the stability of the positionings that an obituary seems to establish in relation to death. In the case of this writing, Michael Lynch, against the odds, turns out to be not its dead but its living addressee, whilst Sedgwick, diagnosed as having cancer, finds her own relation to death changed. Later Sedgwick comments more generally on the 'rhetorical power' of obituaries, and the way they disrupt 'the conventional relations of person and address':

> From a tombstone, from the tiny print in the New York Times, from the panels on panels on panels of the Names Project quilt, whose voice speaks impossibly to whom? From where is this rhetorical power borrowed, and how and to whom is it to be repaid? We miss you. Remember me. She hated to say goodbye. Participating in these speech acts, we hardly know whether to be interpellated as survivors, bereft; as witnesses or even judges; or as the very dead.[23]

The obituary is 'inclusive' as well as 'relentlessly disorientating',[24] both opening up and mixing up positions for the addresser and addressee. The power of this rhetorical form is that it speaks for, or to, the silence of the dead and can therefore borrow many voices. It involves us: we are never safely beyond its appeal.

'White glasses' is both retrospective and nostalgic: it looks back to the time of Sedgwick's first meeting with Lynch and celebrates the significance of their relationship. Yet the nostalgia becomes difficult to 'place' since the anticipated loss – Lynch's death – has not yet happened, while another loss – Sedgwick's own from her life-threatening illness – has forced itself pre-emptively into the text. It is as if the distances of nostalgic vision – trained inevitably and disproportionately on the past – are suddenly intercepted by a new and more immediate perspective, creating a kind of double vision, where loss, still the pervasive background, has also taken on a different and sharper focus in the foreground. This doubling of vision is a figure which Sedgwick invokes in order to suggest her sense of becoming a different 'I', an 'I' who not only reflects upon obituaries but who is caught within their reflection: 'Now shock and mourning gaze in both directions through the obituary frame'.[25] The gaze, at first a gaze at the Other, is now turned round as well towards the self.

This perspectival doubling is also enacted in the form of this essay, with Sedgwick moving between short sections which juxtapose her relationship with Lynch and its queer energies with a more generalising commentary on loss and mourning. The symbol of her connection with Lynch is significantly enough a visual one, the 'white glasses' which Lynch is wearing at their first meeting and which Sedgwick subsequently desires as a chic sartorial signifier of gayness, a fashion statement which never, in fact, catches on. However the glasses also allow Sedgwick another chance to 'gaze in both directions': to feel 'like Michael', identified with him through the wearing of the same prosthetic device, seeing 'with Michael's eyes'[26] and to experience the gaze of others, viewing her differently and not as she desires to be seen. The white glasses, so telling on a man, fade into insignificance on a woman, shift from the 'flaming signifier' they had been for Michael to a banal pastel, the dull ordinariness of a white woman wearing white.[27]

What is at stake here, of course, is how far 'I' can identify across the naturalising discourses of gender and sexuality, how far 'I' can claim an identity which is at odds with how 'I' am perceived. For Sedgwick this leads to a 'defiant' positioning of herself as a gay man, but, it should be added, a gay man whose strongest shared interest with Lynch is in lesbian writers. For Sedgwick no positioning is stable or single, but is rather multiply traversed by others. 'If what is at work here is an identification that falls across gender, it falls no less across sexualities, across "perversions".'[28] Moreover it is through her experience as a 'fat woman', a woman who feels at odds with her body, and who has been intensively 'trained' in 'binocular vision', in trying to span the disjunction between how she is seen and how she sees herself, that Sedgwick believes she found the capacity for 'defiant' identification. There are many ways in which the body may not accord with our imaginings of it or ourselves. For Sedgwick the experience of breast cancer and a body changed by surgery, chemotherapy and hormone therapy puts into question the body's integrity or naturalness as the ground of identity. 'Every aspect of the self comes up for grabs under the pressure of modern medicine.'[29] Sedgwick refuses to identify as a woman or lesbian, or to be defined through her experience of breast cancer, when such an identification is posed against others, when woman is not only 'the thing defined by breasts' but also 'that-thing-that-is-not man'.[30] Rather solidarity exists for Sedgwick *because* the body does not fix us, because, even when thought of in strictly gender-normative terms, the body is already a fantasised body, and, as Judith Butler argues, not 'the ground or cause' of desire but 'its *occasion* and its *object*'.[31] In this way there may be less difference than there appears between the prosthetic device through which Sedgwick claims an alliance with Lynch and the imaginative investment in body parts required for gendered identification or for the structuring of desire. Our bodies are not simply a biological given – a set of empirical facts – but a construct – an image – created through our imaginary relation to them. The penis *becomes* the phallus – and white glasses become the desirable shared signifier of the gay man.

Sedgwick turns to Judith Butler's notion of the mask for its suggestive linking of loss with gender instability. According to Butler, who is in turn discussing Lacan, the mask becomes a way of incorporating the Other who is lost, when that loss is as a result of a refusal or denial of love. The mask is both the masking of the refusal, a double denial and a mask of the Other since it involves the wearing of a melancholy identification with them. According to Butler every refusal could be said to fail since 'the refuser becomes part of the very identity of the refused, indeed becomes the psychic refuse of the refused'. Picking up on Lacan's discussion of female homosexuality as 'disappointed heterosexuality' (love refused), Butler goes on to question whether heterosexuality might not also be seen as the result of disappointed homosexuality. What she calls the 'melancholia of gender' may involve unacknowledged mourning for a prohibited object relation and identification with the object which is lost. Heterosexuality therefore preserves the same-sex object relation (in a melancholic form) by substituting a process of identification with the object.[32] Sedgwick quotes Michael Moon's further elaboration of Butler's argument: he suggests that grief may be felt more generally for a whole range of 'inappropriate desires':

> Melancholy, homo or hetero, is not just about disavowal and lack of grieving for 'the other' desire, there are 'many other' desires – the entire range of 'perversions' – which many people feel compelled to deny and omit

grieving for the loss of … We want to conduct our mourning and grieving in the image of, and as an indispensable part of, this task of collectively and solitarily exploring 'perverse' or stigmatized desire.[33]

This section of Sedgwick's essay makes its point through the use of overlapping voices, through extended quotation from Butler and from Michael Moon which Sedgwick 'incorporates' into her own argument. In some ways, therefore, it mimics its own theme, drawing on the possibility of multiple identifications and the preservation of the Other's voice within the text of the self. However Michael Moon's final point still requires interrogation. Whilst the abjection or repudiation of homosexual desire may make it difficult for society properly to mourn victims of AIDS, for instance, it may still seem difficult to connect mourning the loss of friends, colleagues and lovers – real historical losses – with the more generalised notion of loss which Butler (and Moon) see as constitutive of the gendered subject. However it is also not an evasion of the problem to say that Sedgwick, in this essay, is less interested in constructing a theoretical argument than she is – in terms of her own subjectivity – in crossing between what are 'normally' held to be contradictory positions, the either/or which structures both heterosexuality and the symbolic. How can desire and identification be conflated in the same object and how can the 'opacity' of loss – and its negation of meaning – produce new ways of seeing and relating? Sedgwick's answer may be: only through a queer – and nostalgic – use of the first person.

Jackie Kay's novel *Trumpet*, published in 1998, offers an interesting comparison with Sedgwick's essay. Based on the life of Billie Tipton, the American jazz pianist and saxophonist, who was revealed on his death to be a woman, Kay's novel transposes her character, Joss Moody, to Scotland and makes him black rather than white. These changes, resonant in terms of Kay's own life, suggest autobiographical traces, a complex layering within the novel of self and other, even as the novel impersonates autobiographical discourse through a sustained – though multiply inflected – use of the first person. Significantly the novel is set after Joss's death and Millie, Joss's 'widow', whose nostalgic recollections of their life together forms the most powerful and important interior monologue in the novel, has fled 'over the border' to Torr, the family holiday home in Scotland, in order to escape the intrusive attentions of the press. We are therefore immediately confronted, at the beginning of the novel, with her sense of dislocation, with a subject who does not recognise her own external representation. 'Each time I look at the photographs in the papers, I look unreal. I look unlike the memory of myself.'[34] Millie is similarly cut off from a sense of her past, from childhood as origin of her identity in the present. 'Once I was a fearless girl … It feels so long ago, it is as if it was somebody else who lived that part of my life. Not me. The girl I was has been swept out to sea.'[35] A 'not me' is already instantiated in the self; her past self is 'at sea', providing no secure ground for a present understanding of who she has become. There is no straight line between past and present, no coherent narrative of the self.

Kay therefore locates Joss Moody's transgendered identity within a narrative of selfhood which disputes both external perception and childhood beginnings as secure grounding for the self. Millie's sense of self is disordered by time, memory and loss, by a nostalgic straying of subjectivity across temporal boundaries. Joss's loss is much stranger to Millie than his identification of himself as male, his practised performance of masculinity. 'I can't see him as anything other than him, my Joss, my husband.'[36] Joss becomes male through his identification of himself as male and Millie challenges us to tell the difference. For her, he was simply her husband. 'I didn't feel that I was living a lie. I felt like I was living a life. Hindsight is a lie.'[37]

Death exposes Joss to the gaze of others, consigns him to the body he has resignified as male through dress and performance. Hindsight reads the body as the repository of the stable truth of gender, the primordial materal basis of identity rather than a lived body, a set of variable meanings, including phantasmic ones, through which the subject relates to others and the world. Signing a death certificate means the registration of the body according to a rigid set of binaries – life/death, male/female – and is at odds with the doctor's subjective encounter with Joss's body. 'Everyone called it "the body", but for Dr Krishnamurty, so soon after the death itself, it was not just a body to her. It was a man, a person. Even a soul.'[38] It is part of Kay's strategy in the novel to disengage even the dead body from inertness, facticity, to suggest a penumbra and set of differences which exceed the body seen merely as corpse. For the undertaker death too is 'a slow business', never simply one 'event'. Death is also specific, particular to the person: 'There are as many different deaths as there are different people.'[39] The undertaker also finds the dead 'demanding', not pliable like an object simply to be disposed of. Kay challenges the objectification of death; even in death the body is not transparent, an object of knowledge, but opaque, involved in its own dying.

It is through Colman, Millie's and Joss's adopted son, who discovers the 'secret' of his father's sex only after his death, that Kay deconstructs the social meanings of masculinity. If Joss's lifetime endeavour has been to live a 'fiction' of normality, this has also involved a complex belief in the ability of the subject to live in terms of his own imaginings, in excess of what is given or socially determined. Joss is an artist and performer off stage as well as on. 'All jazz men are fantasies of themselves; reinventing the Counts and Dukes and Armstrongs, imitating them', Colman comments.[40] Colman's masculinity, crudely and violently expressed, is based on the rigid exclusion of its Others, on the abjection of femininity and on a sense of sexual difference established simply through his 'having' the phallus. 'My father didn't have a prick', Colman bitterly comments.[41] The problem with this version of masculinity is that it must constantly defend against not having, against the pervasive fear of castration. Colman's viewing of his father's nakedness in the mortuary is also a terrifying and hallucinatory invasion of him by his own primitive fears. 'I take a quick look. But that look is still in my head now. It has stayed in my head – the image of father in a woman's body.'[42] The absence of the paternal phallus creates a profound crisis for Colman, putting his own masculine identity at risk, challenging the notion of what 'having one' means.

Kay, like Sedgwick, suggests that the phallus need not simply be the penis. In many ways Joss's trumpet, the triumphant vehicle of his art, is a fetishistic object for Colman; both desired and prohibited, it functions within Joss's oedipal fantasies as a phallic signifier: 'I goes in my father's bedroom. I am six years old. I opens their wardrobe. My daddy keeps his trumpet in here. I opens the big silver box, and there it is, all shiny inside. I touched it. I did touch it. Then I strokes it like I've seen my father do and it purrs.'[43] In a sense Colman has never resolved his oedipal rivalry with his father since he never manages to possess his trumpet, his talent; rather he goes on experiencing his own inadequacy and failure, seeing himself as less of a 'man' than his father. What Joss offers Colman is the chance to make up his own life, to move outside the repetitions of a narrative which sees the father as the origin of meaning, and constructs history through biological succession. 'He said you make up your own bloodline, Colman. Make it up and trace it back. Design your own family tree – what's the matter with you? Haven't you got an imagination?'[44] There are alternative ways of imagining than the one handed on to us by the patriarchal family which claims for itself both hegemony and a kind of literalness. The meaning of fatherhood is in excess of the biological given: it is also an imaginary relation to someone who occupies the place of father. This is important not just because Colman's father is 'in fact' a woman but because, as adopted son, he is already displaced from his 'origins', from a biological family. Moreover as a black man living in Scotland, he is already in exile from his place of origin; the 'crossing' in the past is known only as a story, with no secure foundation. The final letter which Joss leaves Colman does not contain the secret of his life as a man, but the story of *his* father, the story Colman always wanted to know, but a story which, as it turns out, could be that of 'any black man who came from Africa to Scotland'. What is handed on is not the 'name of the Father' which might secure identity within the structures of patriarchy. Joss's father's name in any case is not his original name but a name he is given when he arrives in Scotland. What binds father to son is not the stability of a name or identity Joss suggests, but a repeated history of change, of transformation, of becoming. Joss's father 'came off a boat', was a part of particular history of immigration, but fatherhood as a biological given is also as random as that phrase suggests. The father's story therefore is a story of repeated destabilisation, of a lack of determination by the past, of the absence of origins. As Joss says of his father, 'odd his memory would trail back time and time again to recapture mist, fog, lack of substance'.[45]

In replacing historical fact with nostalgic subjective memory, Kay is also able to open up a space where the narratives of gender, race and the family can recirculate, can acquire new and different meanings. The nostalgic wandering of the subject across time is also a way of releasing the subject from a narrative of origins and the grounding of the subject in the past. This 'queer' narrative reads queerness across a range of inter-linked discourses of gender, race and the family by reading back into them their contingency, their instability and their availability therefore for new meanings. The novel is marked particularly by the mournful voice of Millie for whom loving fidelity to Joss has also meant faithfully sustaining the 'fiction' of his identity. The final risk that Kay has taken may be to have written this novel as a love story and by doing so to have brought us back to think about the place of love – its surprising meaning – within a narrative where so much is destabilised and reconfigured.

Notes

1   Eve Kosofsky Sedgwick, *Tendencies* (London and New York, Routledge, 1994), p. 9.

2   Roland Barthes, *Roland Barthes by Roland Barthes* (London, Papermac, 1975), pp. 65–6.

3   Eve Kosofsky Sedgwick, *Epistemology of the Closet* (Hemel Hempstead, Harvester Wheatsheaf, 1991), p. 23.

4   Eric Savoy, 'You can't go homo again: queer theory and the foreclosure of gay studies', *English Studies in Canada*, 20 (1994), quoted in Elspeth Probyn, *Outside Belongings* (New York and London, Routledge, 1996), p. 138.

5   Sedgwick, *Tendencies*, p. 9.

6   Sedgwick, *Epistemology*, p. 23.

7   Biddy Martin, 'Sexualities without genders and other queer utopias' in Mandy Merck, Naomi Segal and Elizabeth Wright (eds), *Coming Out of Feminism?* (Oxford, Blackwell, 1998), pp. 13–14; p. 33.

8   Sedgwick, *Tendencies*, p. 9.

9   Judith Butler, *Gender Trouble: Feminism and the Subversion of Identity* (London and New York, Routledge, 1990), p. 136

10   Eve Kosofsky Sedgwick, 'Paranoid reading and reparative reading: or you're so paranoid you probably think this introduction is about you' in *Novel Gazing: Queer Reading in Fiction* (Durham and London, Duke University Press, 1997), p. 12.

11   Sedgwick, *Tendencies*, p. 11.

12   Barthes, *Roland Barthes*, pp. 65–6.

13   Sedgwick, 'Paranoid Reading', p. 8.

14   *Ibid.*, p. 12.

15   Susan Stewart, *On Longings: Narratives of the Miniature, the Gigantic, the Souvenir, the Collection* (Durham and London, Duke University Press, 1993), p. 23.

16   Elspeth Probyn, *Outside Belongings* (London and New York, Routledge, 1996), pp. 114 –5.

17   Sigmund Freud, *The Uncanny*, Pelican Freud Library, vol. 14 (Harmondsworth, Penguin, 1985), p. 368.

18   Jane Gallop, *Reading Lacan* (Ithaca and London, Cornell University Press, 1985), p. 148.

19   *Ibid.*, p. 151.

20   Juliet Mitchell, 'Introduction 1' in Juliet Mitchell and Jacqueline Rose (eds), *Feminine Sexuality* (London, Macmillan, 1982), p. 12.

21   Probyn, *Outside Belongings*, p. 112.

22   Jeannette Winterson, *Oranges Are Not the Only Fruit* (London, Pandora, 1985), p. 169.

23   Sedgwick, *Tendencies*, p. 264.

24   *Ibid.*, p. 268.

25   *Ibid.*, p. 256.

26   *Ibid.*, p. 257,

27   *Ibid.*, p. 255.

28   *Ibid.*, p. 256.
29   *Ibid.*, p. 263.
30   *Ibid.*
31   Butler, *Gender Trouble*, p. 71.
32   *Ibid.*, pp. 49–50.
33   Sedgwick, *Tendencies*, p. 258.
34   Jackie Kay, *Trumpet* (Pantheon Books, New York, 1998), p. 1.
35   *Ibid.*, p. 8.
36   *Ibid.*, p. 35.
37   *Ibid.*, p. 95.
38   *Ibid.*, p. 43.
39   *Ibid.*, p. 103.
40   *Ibid.*, p. 190.
41   *Ibid.*, p. 66.
42   *Ibid.*, p. 63.
43   *Ibid.*, p. 49.
44   *Ibid.*, p. 58.
45   *Ibid.*, p. 273.

Part II

Relocating desire

6

The national–popular and comparative gay identities: Cyril Collard's *Les Nuits fauves*

Bill Marshall

Cyril Collard's *Les Nuits fauves* (*Savage Nights*, 1992) raises interesting questions regarding the comparative reception of films across national cultures. Its commercial and critical impact in France is well known: a national box-office hit of its year, its plethora of *césars* (the French Oscars) a few days after Collard's death from an AIDS-related illness. Its mixed reception by Anglo-Saxon audiences and critics was largely bound up with questions of identity politics. Typical was Simon Watney's article in *Sight and Sound*, which cast opprobrium on the film's narcissism, selfishness, misogyny and lack of political awareness of the issues affecting gay men and people with AIDS.[1] In *Les Nuits fauves*, Collard plays the bisexual camera operator Jean, whose affair with eighteen-year-old Laura (Romane Bohringer) is disrupted by his relationship with a young unemployed macho rugby player, Samy (Carlos Lopez), and moreover by his failure before they have sex to disclose to Laura his HIV-positive status. Laura embarks on a persecutory obsession with Jean, Samy moves in with him, but drifts into the milieu of racist gangs and the political far right.

The film has obvious shortcomings. None the less, evaluations such as Watney's are unsatisfactory for two interrelating reasons. One is that the film, the text, is seen as a totalised event, all its elements decoded as part of one single reading, that of falling short of some 'true' depiction of AIDS. Another is either the neglect of the French context, or the imposition of Anglo-Saxon political and cultural codes as some kind of master reference point: in France, unlike in Britain or the USA, 'the very idea of a *collective* social or cultural response to Aids on the part of homosexuals is unthinkable'. We need to ask why the film was so popular in France, and to interrogate its 'Frenchness' in terms of its approach to sexual identities, its straddling of auteur and popular cinematic codes, its address to 'youth', and the relationship it constructs *vis-à-vis* American mass culture. This 'Frenchness' is not totalisable as such, but is a question of competing discourses around definitions of national culture, and even around competing strata of French cultural history, between authenticity and inauthenticity, modernism and postmodernism, across the caesura of May 1968. In this way it is the film's plurality of discourses and therefore incoherences that are of interest, and these rhyme with its fundamentally realist codes and project, since, according to Bakhtin, the realist novel is to be seen as a text of heteroglossia, of heterogeneous social discourses and positions.[2]

Simon Watney is correct, however, to home in on the specificities of the French construction of political identities; that is the tradition of republican citizenship since 1789, in which the key relationship is between the individual and the state, with (apart from the idea of the 'nation' with which the state is coterminous) merely a weak civil society mediating between the two, if at all. If we consider the emergence of a collective gay identity in the USA, the Stonewall riots of June 1969 are very much part of an American culture and history that combine traditions of relatively weak national parties, and of ethnic voting blocks and interest groups, with those of liberal individualism and self-invention. The model of the black civil rights movement of the 1960s was not only a radicalising experience in itself for many later gay activists, but was one consistent with the demand for full citizenship rights to be extended to another self-identified subgroup in the American mosaic. The experience of the Second World War and the immediate postwar era shows similarities between France and the USA: the Kinsey Report, the groundbreaking first homosexual organisations in the 1950s, the coexistence in that decade of an officially conservative moral climate with the development of consumerism and the undermining of tradition. However, whereas in the USA the War, with its uprooting and combination of homosexual individuals, played a formative role in the construction of the postwar gay identity, leading directly to the settlement of self-consciously gay people in cities such as New York and San Francisco and in turn to a widespread bar subculture, in France the War uprooted but by and large did not combine them, for the context was that of Nazi occupation or collaboration, with vicious laws that specifically targeted homosexuals among others, many of whom were of course deported to death camps. The postwar climate was not at all conducive to an out gay culture.

All this is to say, firstly, that by the 1980s and 1990s gay men in France had made gains in terms of legislation (for example an equal age of consent after 1982 as a result of the Socialists' hegemonic adoption of certain cultural changes of the 1970s), and a developed commercial scene in Paris on the international model, but the community and cultural institutions taken for granted in Britain and the USA were relatively absent. This absence in *Les Nuits fauves*, set in 1986 even before ACT-UP Paris had come into existence, is thus no surprise. The second point, however, is that this model of French republican citizenship seemed to have run into a crisis in the age of AIDS. The late development of a gay infrastructure meant, for example, that safer sex campaigns were more difficult to disseminate, and the targeting of those most at risk was problematic. (This – and the now large Moslem minority – represent new and dramatic challenges to the system.) A result is the huge disparity between the French and British statistics. By the end of 1998, there had been since the start of the epidemic 49,421 declared AIDS cases and 30,190 deaths in France compared to respective figures of 16,018 and 11,280 in the UK (although the toll for Italy and Spain is comparable to that for France, which raises other issues).

However, it does not necessarily follow that the adoption of an Anglo-Saxon model of identity politics would save or would have saved France from this catastrophe. For instance, HIV infection rates among young men in the USA are stubbornly high, and identity politics imperialism has been demonstrated to be inappropriate in speaking to men in other cultures who practise sex with other men, but in a completely different interpretative grid. In any case, for example, three times as many people are killed in road accidents in France as in Britain, and it is clear that wider issues of different cultures of risk need to be addressed. This chapter on *Les Nuits fauves* can be read as a small part of a wider project which would seek to investigate the relationship between national cultural and political traditions and those recently emerged and emerging transnational categories of 'gay', or 'person with HIV/AIDS'. The argument here is that the specific Frenchness of sexual identity in *Les Nuits fauves* is very much a part of the film's discourse and project. Fredric Jameson has written of what he calls 'Third-World texts' that they are inevitably about nation-building or are narratives of the nation, in that 'the story of the private individual destiny is always an allegory of the embattled situation of the Third-World culture and society, whereas in the developed world the institutionalized split between private and public prevents this allegorization in the name of a placeless individuality'.[3] But it could be argued that, in the context of the American dominance of the world audio-visual industry, cinematic texts in Europe also have the tendency at least to include an allegorised discourse of the nation in them. Thus *Les Visiteurs* (Jean-Marie Poiré, 1993), for example, sought to rival the production values of Spielberg, but, or rather at the same time, mobilised an extraordinary national narrative around past and present, origins, history and republicanism. The story of the individuals in *Les Visiteurs*, as in *Les Nuits fauves*, is 'about France' and what it means to be French.

Les Nuits fauves's very French address and popularity with French audiences mean therefore that it partakes of that 'national-popular', that French-Jacobin success in constructing a civil society, a modern secularism, in terms of the national culture so envied by Gramsci, who saw Italians in the 1920s and 1930s reading and consuming foreign literature in preference to a 'high' culture perpetrated in Italian but isolated in rarefied social circles.[4] In *Les Nuits fauves*, Jean's sexual identity cannot be fixed as gay or even bisexual. He does not reject the label 'pédé', but for example in a conversation with his lover Laura formulates his situation in terms of acts ('tu sais j'aime aussi les garçons'/'you know I also love boys') rather than identity. In one of French cinema's most fascinating portrayals of the capital, Paris is mapped out in terms of desire and of the history of desire: not the 'international' commercial gay bars of the Marais, but Montmartre and Pigalle, the world of public cruising grounds at night, a legacy of the nineteenth-century urban. Within this is embedded a history of Parisian popular culture and subculture. Anglo-Saxon critics bemoaned the 'stereotypical' gay character, the transvestite who sings 'Mon homme' to Jean. What is interesting however is his presence in what is a socially and sexually mixed café, not predicated on sexual or any identity other than (largely male) French and Parisian, and the way in which his song is a dialogue with both the men in general and the emotionally irresponsible Jean in particular. It obviously quotes the prewar *chanteuses réalistes* such as Fréhel and Piaf,[5] their melodramatic performance (and *Les Nuits fauves* relies on this mode as well as on its realism for its effects), and construction of a community, indeed of an emotionally feminised popular community through that performance. And yet, at the same time, the film's music and also *mise-en-scène* of Paris mobilise other discourses that reach beyond the city and nation, destabilising its comforting traditions, undermining its depth and 'authenticity'. The 'national-popular' as embedded culture is now in dialogue with the contemporary and the unfixed: so in another scene the Eiffel Tower and other cityscapes are filmed to the music of the Pogues (a first), and the Spanish music of Samy's family raises new questions of ethnicity.

The particular construction of sexual identity in the film can thus not be disentangled from that of the nation. But if *Les Nuits fauves* is not 'gay', is it 'queer'? Jean's uncooptability as positive role model, his refusal of a monolithic signifying of his sexuality, including that of the homo/hetero binary, would seem to justify that adjective as it appropriates the abject (literally, that which is 'thrown out' or expelled) to deconstructive purpose. And yet a comparison with the films of Tom Kalin or Gregg Araki, the 'new queer cinema' with which it is roughly contemporaneous, would be absurd: not only because of the French cultural context and the very specifically American determinants of 'queer', or the moralising implications of the film's narrative closure, but also because of the film's investment in identification.

Les Nuits fauves's popularity with audiences and critics in France was matched by the positive response from AIDS organisations such as AIDES, who found that its appeal could be harnessed to their educational campaigns, and indeed, the film made a considerable contribution to AIDS awareness in France, particularly among the young. One of the keys to the film's popularity, and thus participation in the ongoing construction of the 'national-popular', is its strategy of realism rather than avant-gardism, identification rather than distance, and an auteurism which breaks out of the art-house owing to the auteur as star and as spectacular body. As Paul Julian Smith has argued in relation to Derek Jarman's *Blue*,[6] the avant-gardist strategy of not displaying the body at all gets Jarman out of the double-bind of presenting the HIV body either as diseased (and exposed therefore to an othering, mortuary gaze) or as intact (and therefore assimilable, acceptable only as the same). Since the strategy of *Blue* is not available or desirable to Collard, the way forward lies therefore with the HIV body as beautiful (crucial of course for that other popular requisite, narrative and narrativisation, for if Jean were visibly ill his non-revelation about his status to Laura would not be an issue). *Les Nuits fauves* thus mobilises certain discourses emerging in the 1970s and after around the politics of the gaze. The political risk, in feminist avant-garde circles, of putting a woman's body on the screen is echoed by that of the HIV body as voyeuristic or fetishistic spectacle. However, Collard's acceptance of that risk is counteracted in criticism of the film by the invocation of its narcissism, to which we must now turn.

The obvious parallel, that of the male director displaying himself in aestheticized form, is that of Warren Beatty in *Reds* (1981). However, there are crucial differences. Beatty/Reed's simultaneous orgasm with the storming of the Winter Palace, and the relentlessly goal-oriented narrative, present a totalising view of director, actor, masculinity, sexuality and history which is barely subverted by the varying discourses of his witnesses. While it would be inappropriate to deny the narcissism of *Les Nuits fauves*, this evaluation needs to be qualified by the self-consciousness about narcissism displayed in the dialogue (Jean to Laura: 'Tu n'es pas narcissiste, toi?'/'Aren't *you* a narcissist?'), *mise-en-scène* and narrative, and by the complexities of the term itself.

In 'Visual pleasure and narrative cinema',[7] Laura Mulvey argues of course that spectatorship partakes of a narcissism (the screen as mirror) that is mediated by a patriarchal culture's concern to construct via the protagonist a regime of male power associated with the active heterosexual erotic look and an overall satisfying sense of mastery if not omnipotence. Since the 1970s, not only has much interesting work been done on the male body as object of the erotic gaze,[8] but also the image culture of the West has seen a mainstreaming of the homoerotic previously confined to gay subcultures. In general, the representation of the male body beautiful takes place within ambiguous frameworks that disavow the 'power' of phallic presence but frame that disavowal within autoerotic or narcissistic discourses, or, more recently in pop culture, within iconographies that stress the boy or adolescent rather than the mature, socially empowered or responsible male (witness the twenty-nine-year-old Damon Albarn of the Britpop group Blur, or even Leonardo di Caprio). In *Les Nuits fauves*, Collard's youthful, hairless body and puppy eyes connote a male figure socially adrift and unfixed rather than patriarchal, a consuming and hedonistic male but one deprived of *la place*, of a mapping analogous to the certainties of the traditional bourgeois family glimpsed at his parents' dinner. Moreover, these ambiguities need to be articulated with those of narcissism itself. As Steve Neale points out,[9] the eroticisation of the male body permitted via narcissism in the male action movie is predicated on the refusal of, or resistance to, social integration in the form of marriage and the law, including that resistance to language whose splitting of the subject negates the narcissistic fantasy of an ideal ego.

In common parlance, Clint Eastwood or Sylvester Stallone in various roles are examples of male narcissism, strong silent types and/or men whose identity is based on physical (self-) mastery. So narcissism is 'narcissism' in its negative connotations if it arrests the process of psychic development and social signification, leading to masculinity as trap. On the other hand, narcissistic drives are an inevitable and essential part of any social and psychic process. The plenitude of the mirror stage is a misrecognition, it cannot be attained. The self desired as object is in a sense other and not the self. In Freud, narcissism is a stage which both looks back to the polymorphous perverse and forward to identity-based object desire as in the oedipal narrative, and he became interested in it for its potential to explain transformations in the libido. It is the first identification, without which identity, for good or bad, would not exist at all.[10] Indeed, it can be argued that narcissism is necessary for the culture to operate, in that the 'good' represented in hegemonic moral or other evaluating categories can be read as narcissistic, investments in external ideal standards, the ideal ego, that are then internalised. The changing, unfixed characteristics of those investments suggest that narcissism actually represents a way of reducing, not affirming, rigidity of self. This is of relevance to the rhetoric in the literal sense of *Les Nuits fauves*, since its effectiveness in both working within the grain of French culture and contributing in some small way to the process of cultural change suggests above all the dynamic relationship for its audiences between internalisations of external objects and libidinal models of aspiration and identity. Whereas Mulvey in 'Visual pleasure and narrative cinema' saw mainstream Hollywood cinema as a fateful relay of ultimately patriarchal looks, *Les Nuits fauves* can be seen as a relay of narcissisms, between director and star, between characters in the diegesis, between audiences and the screen, 'a structure and a stimulus for a fruitful dialogical relationship between the codings of an author's narcissistic text and a reader's narcissistic interest'.[11] Through narcissistic processes, then, a text may establish a community through effects of recognition and social reciprocity, in which the artist attracts the reader's recognition, and the reader recognises himself or herself in the signification produced.

Thus in *Les Nuits fauves* the shots of Jean looking in mirrors inspecting his body, and the early shots of both Laura and Samy both seen through his viewfinder (she enacting an emotional scene, he physical danger), rather than being crass expressions of the director's self-regard, foreground narcissism in its filmic, desiring and social modes. Jean's 'Tu n'es pas narcissiste, toi?' is not just a rejoinder to Laura's accusation, but implies that everyone is, although not all narcissisms are the same or have the same results. This perhaps partly explains the (rather tenuous) nature of Jean's final conversion to a more creative or dialogic integration of the self/other relationship which is none the less narcissistic: 'Je suis vivant; le monde n'est pas seulement une chose posée là, extérieure à moi-même:

j'y participe … je suis dans la vie'/'I am alive; the world isn't just a thing placed there, external to myself: I participate in it … I am in life.' In addition, the film consciously refers to and plays with the original Narcissus myth from Ovid. Narcissus too was indifferent to the feelings of his male and female admirers; his falling in love with his own reflection is the fulfilment of Tiresias' prophecy that he would live to an old age only 'if he never knew himself'. *Les Nuits fauves* turns this round, so that Jean's impending death is the means by which he comes to know himself. Echo, condemned to repeat the sounds of others, is paralleled by Laura, who is introduced to us in a scene in which she responds to the lines fed her by the ad director Kader and then by Jean filming her. Echo's fate of metamorphosing into a disembodied voice becomes Laura's endless messages on Jean's answering machine. Narcissus falls victim to the unreliability of surface perception: the film holds in tension that proposition – the regime of *le look* – and one that maintains cinema's ontological truth.

The pleasurable processes of identification and recognition in *Les Nuits fauves* rely on realist strategies. These perpetuate the illusion and illusionism of spontaneity *pris sur le vif*. What gives Collard's film its particular energy is the way in which it combines both the ontological real *à la* Bazin, the style of Maurice Pialat (for whom Collard worked as assistant director), with an emphasis on cinematic language (notably the long takes marked by editing cuts) and wider cultural codings. In *Les Nuits fauves*, the cultural identities foregrounded are those of the nation, but also of youth. If we are looking for identity, *Les Nuits fauves* is so much more a French youth movie than a 'gay movie'. Youth is both a metonym for the wider culture's social and political anxieties, and is itself traversed by those anxieties: unemployment (since the early 1980s youth unemployment has been at 25 per cent in France); the cutting edge of racial politics, with the high proportion of first- and second-generation North Africans; and the 'unfixing' of identity and identities which has affected French culture in its postwar modernisation. Moreover, romance, but also the emancipation from it, have been decisively affected by the threat of AIDS.

The question of youth subcultures in *Les Nuits fauves* focuses principally on music and with it competing discourses of what we might call the national-modern and international or hybrid postmodern, as we have seen. Collard even sings in English the closing song. 'Youth' becomes a sounding board for the ambiguities of contemporary French culture, just as its countercultural stances coexist uneasily with the anxiety of being unable to participate in the French consumer republic. Instead of a process of active subcultural production we see both Laura and Samy trapped on one side of the fixed/unfixed, caught/uncaught binary: Laura in the traditional gender masochism of romance; Samy, despite or because of his flirtation with homosexuality and hybrid status as the son of immigrants, drifting towards a hyperbolic reassertion of national plenitude through violence and the political far right. As we shall see, it is left to Jean dialectically to overcome these antagonisms and to assert both plurality and significance. The 'political' content of *Les Nuits fauves* should however not be underestimated: the absence of gay identity and community is balanced and explained by an emphasis on hybridity and pluralism within an ongoing national project in which individualism is to the fore as a model of citizenship and as the basis of consumer culture. Collard's earlier short film projects had included rock videos, a documentary on subway artists (*Taggers*), and shorts featuring *beur* protagonists: *Alger la blanche* (1981) and *Grand huit* (1983). In recent French cinema, *Les Nuits fauves* can be seen as dialoguing with two elements of 1980s production: the postmodern cinema of the image *à la* Beineix, Besson and Carax, and *le cinéma beur*. On the margins of the latter as a white director but interested in getting beyond the traps of fashion, tokenism and positive images, Collard also engages with the decentred and fragmented culture of the former while refusing its cult of artifice and its reluctance to get beyond the signifier. *Les Nuits fauves* can be seen as combining elements of two other moments marked by the importance of young audiences, namely Luc Besson's *Le Grand Bleu/ The Big Blue* (1988) and the currently prominent *cinéma de banlieue*: a social realism and portrait of cultural fragmentation combined with a basically masculinist and individualist 'solution' intensified by the proximity of death.

Les Nuits fauves also links with accounts of French modernisation and its so-called postmodern turn. Jean's sports car and what he does with it, like his walkman, is emblematic of this. The scene of the meal at his parents' house is followed by him speeding his car and colliding with another. The drag car race of *Rebel Without a Cause* (Nicholas Ray, 1955) exemplified the importance of peer rather than parental relations and judgement, validating masculine notions of freedom, independence and power with a more general validation of the confusion and alienation of 1950s youth. Some of these elements are present in this sequence of *Les Nuits fauves*, but there are subtle differences. Jean's car is much more an object of consumerism and signifier of material success, much more like the 'real' James Dean. The motives for his speed and crash are ambiguous: a cult of living close to the edge, a rebellion against the oppressive family ambiance exemplified by the almost ecclesiastical *mise-en-scène* of the meal, but also a reaction to the conflict between the partial 'truth' spoken by his mother that he must learn to love and his assertion to her that egoism is also important and might have given her a better life. What is important here is the intertextuality of 'James Dean' in both *Les Nuits fauves* and the secondary texts around Collard himself, and the way that intertextuality plays across different moments in postwar French history. As Kristin Ross has convincingly argued in her study of the culture of French modernisation 1950–65, the figure of James Dean – 'the mutinous but self-reliant teenager, at home neither in civilization nor adulthood'[12] – was particularly relevant for rapidly modernising countries such as France or Japan, whose traditional societies were being destroyed and for whose film audiences 'youth' could come to embody the anxieties of transition, of the symbolic abandonment of 'the home' without as yet a clear road map for how to reinvent 'the home' within the new order. One only has to recall Truffaut's article on James Dean,[13] or the references in his *Les Quatre Cents Coups* (1959).

Ross's work is suggestive for an analysis of *Les Nuits fauves* because of the categories via which she argues French culture was reworked, and the way in which they interact with the pluralism of this film. For Ross, these include: cars and their connotations not only of consumerism but also displacement, depthlessness, even irresponsibility, and the consequences for perception; the *disponibilité* (availability, openness) of the new man not rooted in tradition; the ideology of the couple, and couple-in-the-city, and the way in which it came to replace family bonds as the main affective link; race and the centrality of decolonisation in France's transition from dominant and exploiting to dominated and exploited culture, including the othering of Algeria as France's monstrous double, the logic of racial exclusion in the construction of a national and modern middle class, and the last use made of the colonies in the immigrant labour employed in reconstruction; the motifs of cleanliness and health implied in the reinvention of the home through domestic consumerism with its love of narcissistic self-satisfaction and its attempt to arrest the ravages of time by rendering things as if new.

May 1968 can therefore be seen to be an acceleration of this process which permitted French capitalism to intensify Fordism but then adapt to post-Fordism through the supposed suppression of class conflict and construction of an endless present, the end of history.

While the cars, the narcissism and perfect body of Jean would seem superficially to support a reading of *Les Nuits fauves* that confirms this dominant order, it is important to stress the always provisional and polyvalent nature of its discourses: if French modernisation is complete, for example, why is James Dean important forty years on? Moreover, the film actually suggests that some of the attempted closures of modernisation are no longer successfully operating. Romance and the couple are not a solution. Above all, the logic of racial exclusion leads to the *Front national* and a complete inability to reconcile the present with past colonialism or future multiculturalism. It is here worth mentioning the fact that Laura's mother is a repatriated *pied noir*, and that one of Collard's criticisms of *la mode beur* in 1985 was its suppression of 'un passé auquel nous sommes horriblement mêlés'/'a past which we are horribly mixed up in'.[14]

Les Nuits fauves's imaginary 'solution' to all this lies in its final sequences. Jean's illness is rendered visible when he slashes his hand and threatens to infect his racist adversary. The movement of the film stops – twice – at the sea: on the beach with Laura years later, and when Jean gazes out from the Lisbon lighthouse, at the edge of Europe. However, the ending is simultaneously insufficient to soak up the contradictions and polyvalences of what has preceded it, and itself partakes of them. Jean's stance can be read from a pick 'n' mix of French cultural traditions: Catholic redemption, Existentialism without the *engagement*, American individualism and self-invention, a postmodern, Nietzschean and why not Deleuzean identity-less proliferation of desire. The key to the film's popular success is perhaps there: rather like Madonna or Michael Jackson, it federates a spectrum of identities and discourses, including that of modern and postmodern, in a manner befitting the ongoing project of national elaboration.

Notes

1   Simon Watney, 'The French connection', *Sight & Sound*, 3:6 (1993), 24–5.
2   Mikhail Bakhtin, 'Discourse in the novel' in *The Dialogic Imagination*, ed. M. Holquist, trans. C. Emerson and M. Holquist (Austin, University of Texas Press, 1981).
3   Fredric Jameson, 'Third-world literature in the era of multinational capitalism', *Social Text*, 15 (fall 1986), 69.
4   Antonio Gramsci, *Selections from Cultural Writings*, ed. David Forgacs and Geoffrey Nowell-Smith, trans. W. Boelhover (London, Lawrence and Wishart, 1985).

5   See G. Vincendeau, 'The *mise-en-scène* of suffering: French *chanteuses réalistes*', *New Formations*, 3 (Winter 1987), 107–128.

6   Paul Julian Smith, '*Blue* and the outer limits', *Sight and Sound*, 3:10 (1993), 18–19.

7   Anthologised in for example G. Mast and M. Cohen (eds), *Film Theory and Criticism* (Oxford, Oxford University Press, 1985), pp. 803–16.

8   For example, Richard Dyer, 'Don't look now', *Screen*, 23:3–4 (1982), 61–73.

9   Steve Neale, 'Masculinity as spectacle: reflections on men and mainstream cinema', *Screen*, 24:6 (1983), 2–16.

10 Sigmund Freud, 'On narcissism: an introduction (1914)', *Complete Psychological Works Vol. XIV*, trans. J. Strachey (London, Hogarth Press, 1937), pp. 73–102.

11 M. W. Alcorn, *Narcissism and the Literary Libido* (New York, New York University Press, 1994), p. 18.

12 K. Ross, *Fast Cars, Clean Bodies: Decolonization and the Reordering of French Culture* (Cambridge, Mass., MIT Press, 1995), p. 46.

13 'Feu James Dean', *Arts* (26 April 1956).

14 Interview in *Cinématographe*, 112 (July–August 1985), 20–22.

7

Beyond Almodóvar: 'homosexuality' in Spanish cinema of the 1990s

Santiago Fouz Hernández and Chris Perriam

In the mid-1990s the Spanish film industry experienced a modest explosion of gay-themed films[1] and this chapter looks at the four main examples: *Alegre ma non troppo* (*With Gaiety, Ma Non Troppo*, henceforth *Alegre*) (dir. Fernando Colomo, 1994); *Perdona Bonita pero Lucas me quería a mí* (*Sorry Sweetheart, but Lucas Was in Love with Me*) (dir. Felix Sabroso and Dunia Ayaso, 1996); *Más que amor frenesí* (*Not Love, Just Frenzy*) (dir. Miguel Bardem, Alfonso Albacete and David Menkes, 1996); and *Amor de hombre* (*The Love of Men*, henceforth *Amor*) (dir. Yolanda García Serrano and Juan Luis Iborra, 1997). *Perdona Bonita pero Lucas me quería a mí* (henceforth *Perdona*) and *Más que amor frenesí* (henceforth *Frenesí*) are comedies set in Madrid which engage with Pedro Almodóvar's Spanish-specific camp style, his liking for contrasts between strong and vulnerable women characters and his subversion of authority figures (in both films police officers). They deploy humour and transgression to challenge patriarchal values and are openly gay in content; nevertheless, one of our concerns here is whether they really signify a sea change in Spanish sexual politics or whether they are just an exploitation of the Almodóvar formula. The two other comedies of this mini-boom, *Alegre* and *Amor*, are less directly indebted to Almodóvar. Even if *Amor* was rightly introduced to its London audience in April 1999 with a mention of its 'nod to Almodóvar',[2] it owes as much or more to the global film market for its viability and appeal, with a feel-good factor comparable to *Tales of the City* (Alastair Reid, 1993) and a class setting akin to that of *Long Time Companion* (Rene Norman, 1990) or *Jeffrey* (Christopher Ashley, 1995) and, for the London audience, strong similarities to the Channel 4 series *Queer As Folk*. Colomo's *Alegre* is anchored by its director's reputation as a maker of urban comedies charting cultural

change in the post-Franco period;[3] at the same time it draws on international intertexts – Donen, Wilder, screwball comedy and the whole
subgenre of films about performers (here the musicians of the Spanish
National Youth Orchestra).[4]

The (substantial) history of the representation of homosexuality in
Spanish cinema is full of complex disavowals, repressions and revelations,[5] and this mix of qualities is part of the territory in which our four
films move. At a time when radical queer political interventions were
becoming visible in urban Spain,[6] and with an intellectual and artistic
capital accrued in films of the 1970s and 1980s which had directly
engaged with and politically contextualised questions of homosexuality,[7]
these films interestingly, perhaps frustratingly, but pragmatically, eschew
'politics'. Rather, they investigate gay and queer aesthetics, and go, in
differing degrees, for a paradoxically inflected and ultimately unstable
middle ground of inclusive, normalised, tolerant representations of men
desiring men. The tensions and the cinematic pleasures which arise out
of such preferences are ones which for our present readership we feel are
best explored with reference to what is arguably still Spain's most famous
and most homosexual film, Almodóvar's *Law of Desire* (1987). From the
late 1990s the film is seen by two influential commentators on Spanish
gay culture as a landmark because of its 'natural and spontaneous
portrayal of gay love'[8] and for the 'intellectual honesty and ideological
commitment' of the director in representing the 'reality' of the lives of
homosexuals.[9] Important too are perceptions in Anglo-Saxon cultural
spaces of Pedro Almodóvar as Spain's gay film director par excellence, 'a
hero of the gay movement from the Pyrenees northwards and the Atlantic
westwards' (in Ricardo Llamas's ironic terms).[10] And yet, if Aliaga is right,
it is precisely the quality he highlights which detracts from the values
Cortés identifies, since in many ways the film is extremely unrepresenta-
tive; and, as Llamas says, in Spain Almodóvar himself has never actually
come out. Furthermore his many lesbian and gay roles are not subversive,
just stridently 'modern', part of an apolitical hedonism, mere style
rebellion.[11] Indeed, complex structures erected by Almodóvar in
interview and in filmic practice disallow a ready identification of
'homosexuality' and 'Almodóvar'.[12]

Such (productive) contradictions are vital points of reference for the
1990s 'gay boom'. *Law of Desire* vacillates between representing radical
sexual alternatives and deploying an arguably reactionary politics of
representation, between affording its audiences the thrill of transgression
and allowing them joyfully to collude with comic strategies heavily

dependent on caricature and on that which is produced in the transgression, a sense of the normal. This was a film which had interpellated viewing subjects in the 1980s who were themselves perhaps shifting between a queer and a complacent reception, and those same theoretical subjects seem to us to have been interpellated anew at times in our four later films. However, these are grounded unequivocally by that earlier film's courageous making visible of the homoerotic, and, as Smith observes, in his filmic practice up to 1991 at least, Almodóvar anticipated 'in a number of ways a critique of identity and essence of a sort that subsequently would be taken up in queer theory'.[13] Readers will recall, for example, that an explicit homoerotic prelude specularises and commodifies a young male's body while playing with subgeneric and structural clichés: paid to play out a masturbatory fantasy of penetration, his scripted words – 'fuck me, fuck me' – are taken up by Antonio (Antonio Banderas) as he hurries from his viewing of the film to masturbate in the toilets. Though straight in both sexual orientation and social attitudes, he loses himself to the law of desire, becoming obsessed by, and eventually getting fucked (in Spain's first mainstream images of consenting anal sex between men) by the director, Pablo (Eusebio Poncela), whose film he has been watching. Antonio's elision with the prelude's fantasy object; his submission to his own obsession; a sex act classically disruptive of masculinity's self-definition through bodily integrity;[14] Pablo's need to script his own love life, writing to a boyfriend the words he wants relayed back to him verbatim: all deconstruct stable identity, the meanings of love, and, in Antonio, manliness. From the straight-acting, uptight gay husband, Antonio turns into an increasingly deranged jealous, wronged woman figure and is destroyed, melodramatically, by the staging of his own suicide at the end of the film. Pablo's transsexual sister Tina (Carmen Maura) – once a choirboy, now a mother – has an ostentatiously and therefore denaturalisingly feminine presence[15] and contradictory beliefs (she is libertarian, authoritarian, sensualist and a devotee of the Virgin Mary) which destabilise multiple sets of traditional values. Queer too is Pablo's sex life in its refusal to admit of monogamous 'love' and its exaltation of the private self constructed in domestic monogamy (even if it is possible to argue, as Smith has done, that his partners are 'defaced' by their interchangeability).[16] At the formal level too there is disruption of straight patterning: already self-parodic Hitchcockian sensationalist motifs and shots are evacuated of their meaning through an over-insistence on them; the plot is both blatantly absurd (Tina's back-history; Pablo's fortuitous amnesia) and elaborately crafted around precise timings and coincidences; the film ultimately refuses to take a stable interest in any one character or, indeed, character at all, despite its moments of intense personal crisis (even Tina, the closest one might get to a strong object of identification, is excessively coded, not only as feminine but as drama queen, the prey of fate and emotion).

However, the film also takes potentially reactionary, pragmatic short cuts through some issues it raises (transsexualism, lifestyle politics, class) and goes out of its way to avoid others, notably queerness itself, which the film 'straightens out' by effacing, displacing and abstracting homosexuality[17] through, for example, privileging the fraternal and the tender over the frantic and erotic and having ultimate recourse to traditional values in patterning personal relationships and narrative strategies.[18]

Almodóvar habitually uses the family, in his films of the 1980s, to get some straightforward serio-comic mileage out of the clash between a sexually polymorphous new generation (and class) of Spaniards and an older (or parallel) grouping strangulated by the incoherent imperatives of illiberal Catholicism and Francoist politics. In *Law of Desire* and *Matador*, for example, the Antonio Banderas character is given a caricature domineering mother as a half-explanation for his troubled sexuality. In part because of the stock comic capital to be exploited in the *topoi* of generation gap and family dynamics, all four of the 1990s films to which we will now turn place their homosexual subjects in real or alternative family relationships. In *Perdona* and *Frenesí*, as we shall see, although extra-filmic contexts pull away from queer commitment, radical possibilities as well as comedy and sexual intrigue arise out of the main characters' interconnectedness as a family of choice; in *Amor* the protagonists – heterosexual, single, and erotically unfulfilled Esperanza and her best friend Ramón, gay and sexually hyperactive – live in an extended family of gay men which encourages (but ultimately quashes) the construction and experience of new social and affective meanings with queer potential.

In Colomo's *Alegre*, again the family is central to a series of revelations in contrast to which there emerges a largely positive, if far from radical, queer position. Twenty-something musician Pablo (Pere Ponce), whose break-up with his Hockney-influenced artist boyfriend (also named Pablo) occupies the title sequence and first segment of the film, is constantly checked up on by a mother (Rosa María Sardà) whose very career choice – she runs a laundry and dry-cleaner's – offers her the perfect opportunity to fulfil the stock comic role of doing her son's washing in order obliquely to control and clean up his life. With a comical obviousness which both deflates and provisionally confirms the misogynist and heterosexist cliché of the smothering mother creating a nancy son, the reason for the collapse of the relationship is, as boyfriend Pablo says, 'you're like a mother, no, worse, like *your* mother'. The mother's role, and the meanings generated by family here, are however not in the end the simpler stock ones. Her vigilance – which means that she well knows but does not directly acknowledge that Pablo is not heterosexual – is one motivated not by the desire to de-gay her son, rather (comically) to avoid his coming under the influence of any rival woman. A depressed Pablo is persuaded by the dazzling girlfriend – Salomé (Penelope Cruz)[19] – of a straight hunk fellow musician (played by Jordi Mollá), whom Pablo thought he had seduced, to visit an analyst (later arrested for fraud) whose camp bad-taste flowery shirt, hairy chest and gold chain undermine his strenuous heterosexuality as well as the pat diagnosis that Pablo is looking for a father in order to resolve his mother's own emotional problems. Salomé seductively takes up where the analyst fails, and Pablo becomes convinced that he could begin to desire women, which appals his mother ('but of *course* you're homosexual' she objects when Pablo, complete with moustache and cigar, pretends at his grand-parents' golden wedding party to be going out with Salomé).

With traditional maternal control thus diverted, and psycho-sexology subverted, the film's key comic reversal of received ideas is in its refer-ences to and use of music. Pablo is represented visually as the weedy, sensitive, artistic type – 'musical', in fact, in the English euphemism[20] – and marked out as different through his ability to speak most clearly through music (sometimes imposed extra-diagetically on the representa-tion of his emotions, as in the break-up with his boyfriend, but mostly played on the French horn by him). But as is demonstrated in Ponce's acting – a well-judged mix of the soft-centred and the hard-headed[21] – music empowers him. When he gains a place on the orchestra's summer school at the northern coast resort of Santander, the arrival is persua-sively coded for Pablo as one of a homecoming which is also a coming out and a coming into his own: panoramic shots of wide maritime views, the grand Ivy-League-style buildings of the site, light-flooded rooms full of practising musicians are seen from his point of view, and reflected in his look, as marking a joyful personal breakthrough over and beyond the merely professional.[22] In an airy location scene set on the sunlit cliffs the brass players assembled for practice are urged to put an orgasmic energy into their playing and Pablo finds a sudden skill and voice as he plays his own deep-toned and strongly projected flourish which he dedicates, with horn brandished high, to a passing redhead with a gallant swagger reminiscent of the triumphs of the bullring. His playing of the horn makes of him a potent, heroic and romantic force (an association enhanced by extra and intra-diagetic inclusions of music by Borodin, Brahms and Tchaikovsky). It also allows him one night to seduce Salomé, and the film delicately allows him to come out of this first experience of sex with a woman still undecided and so, paradoxically, empowered anew: he does not have to play along to others' tunes and presuppositions.

His mother too interprets musicality against the grain, equating it with the uncontrolled male, heterosexual libido. Separated from Pablo's father (yet another Pablo – a further joke at the expense of psychoanalysis) because of his weakness for young women musicians, she blames his behaviour on an excessive interest in 'touching the keys' and on 'sensitivity'. At Santander, her views are borne out: the young male musicians are rampantly heterosexual and *machista*, and their representation generates a sharp, if lightly achieved, critique of conventional bragging and loudly homophobic masculinity.

In *Alegre*, then, we have a well-made comedy whose caricatures and exaggerations are turned towards a gentle but effective representation of plurality and ambiguity in sexual desire and gendered identity. If Pablo is reconciled in comfortable narrative closure with his parents in the end (Pablo senior is discovered to have slept with Salomé and is forgiven, and the mother's interference is laughed off), he nevertheless does not align with closed definitions of gay, straight or bisexual. From one point of view the film represents its homosexuality as no risk to a heterosexually hegemonic middle-class spectatorship with an interest in 'people' (Pablo comes out above all as a strong individual); also its strategies can be welcomed by integrationist gays as liberatingly normalising, democratic and tolerance-enhancing. From another point of view, however, it is precisely the eliding 'naturalness' of the representation[23] which makes possible a queer, reverse reading of Pablo in which he quietly, determinedly sustains his own difference from binary differentiations and categorisations, standing aside from the gay 'world', as represented in his boyfriend Pablo, and the straight, as represented by the raucous fellow musicians, from the terms of family and sexology, and even – in his musicality – from the entrapments of verbal language itself. In this way the film produces itself, and a certain audience, as queer: it coincides with a historic absence in Spain of identity politics and has a culturally specific tendency to avoid segregated social space and identity labels;[24] it also escapes what Óscar Guasch argues is the limiting and ill-fitting (if much adopted) 'gay model' of identity which attempts to redefine homosexuality in terms of an imported Anglo-Saxon-style politicisation and institutionalisation of homosexuality founded on the emergence of specifically gay spaces, and in terms of virility as a fantasy ideal.[25]

Amor is, by contrast, very much interested in separate physical and sentimental spaces for men loving men, and – a notable, safe absence in *Alegre* – men's (gym-toned) bodies, as its publicity posters and video cover suggest with their prominent naked male torso overwritten with the title words whose A and whose Os are quirky little heart-shaped cameo frames with the smiling faces of the focalising female character and the two lead hunks. Unlike in *Frenesí*, budget (and perhaps imaginative) restrictions leave the camera for the most part on the outside of the spaces of the clubs and bars which Ramón (Andrea Occhipinti) – a determinedly single, handsome young lawyer – frequents in a search for pleasure complicated only, and not greatly, by the desire he expresses to Esperanza – his best friend and the only woman with a substantial part in the film – to meet 'a man like you … or , I mean, like you but a man'.

Esperanza is simultaneously, and unresolvedly, radical and reactionary. She is independent, strong, clear on straight Spanish men – 'normal men aren't normal, I can tell you from experience' – and living on her own (a new if growing phenomenon for women in Spain). But others of her traits are far from modern: although she is a teacher, she has a markedly irrational world view which associates the suicide attempts she witnesses from her flat window next to a high viaduct and a supposed inevitable unhappiness in the gay men she knows; though pleased at, if jealous of, Ramón's successful sex life, she is disturbed by his preference for multiple partners and casual sex and attempts to set him up with the PE master from her school, Roberto (Jordi Mollá again); and when this goes uncomfortably well she tries both to defuse it by turning maternal procuress (bringing a monolingual Swedish boy home for Ramón) and to counter it by resolving to move to Alicante (in sentimental and superstitious response to a moment early in the film when she and Ramón had stood outside a travel agent's on Valentine's Night and pointed, eyes closed, each at a random destination). The fact that she ends up still in Madrid and back to the intense routine of friendship with Ramón emphasises, as much as the film's preference for domestic interiors, the containing presence of the boundaries of habit and normalisation.

On the other hand, there is a certain subversive agency in the flagrant presence of same-sex sex and eroticised male bodies in the film (Ramón's and Roberto's, and the occasional cruisy minor character's) and in the explicit sexual banter which invades everyday spaces such as middle-class homes, a hospital corridor or the neighbourhood bar. A further queer challenge to normalising discourses and spaces lies in the artificiality of the primary situation. Irritably, a distinguished critic, praising in principle the 'desire to show images of gay men on screen in a normal way', asks 'Does such an idyllic world exist? ... Is a character like Esperanza believable? A woman with no women friends and her only male friends gay?';[26] but this is wilfully to miss the point. By epitomising and abstracting its dramatic and affective situation and by refusing heterosexual verisimilitude, while far from adopting the formal and representational disruptions of queer film-making,[27] *Amor* at least attempts an emphatic statement – men live together as couples in Madrid – which is, in fact, more 'believable' for the non-heterosexual communities than Almodóvar ever was, and is in line with mainstream lesbian and gay politics of the 1990s in Spain, where a major issue has been the recognition in law of the rights of same-sex couples, the making visible of these alternative territories of desire.

On the same lines, both *Perdona* and *Frenesí* adopt Madrid's gay scene as a setting, subtly integrating gay territories into Spanish mainstream comedy and thus favouring gay visibility. One of our concerns here is to explore how the political potential of the comic genre is used. Comedy is, by its nature, anti-authoritarian. It favours a critique of the established social norm. By disrupting the social order and playing with social stereotypes it allows for a critical distancing from reality and provides an alternative representation of the values and behaviour normally uncontested in our everyday life. Yet, it can also be used to intensify oppression by presenting alternative values as ultimately undesirable.[28] The apparent onscreen sexual inactivity of the gay characters in *Perdona* contrasts with their overexposure to silly, absurd situations, thus pointing to an exploitative use of gayness as 'laughable', fitting the genre. This is confirmed by the use in both the film publicity and on the video sleeve of the word 'loca' (meaning in Spanish both 'mad' and 'queen' but also used to describe a hilarious, 'crazy' comedy) with 'loca, loca, loca' printed over the stills of the gay flatmates who, in further stereotypical representation, are shown with an exaggeratedly shocked expression on their faces and described as 'one fragile and depressive; one esoteric and hash-addicted; and one promiscuous and selfish'. *Perdona*'s story is strikingly similar to that of British hit *Shallow Grave* (Danny Boyle, 1994): the three gay characters – Carlos (Pepón Nieto), Alberto (Jordi Mollá) and Dani (Roberto Correcher) – advertise for a flatmate; a series of bizarre candidates are interviewed (or rather, as in the British film, auditioned) until tall, long-haired stud Lucas (Alonso Caparrós) appears at the last minute and decides to take the room. Lucas's presence in the flat generates intense competition between the three 'locas' for his attention and provides each of the three with a focus for their fantasies (and frustrations).

The marketing of the film as a 'mainstream' commercial comedy also has political implications of interest here. At one of a number of press conferences,[29] asked specifically about the relevance of their film to a putative Spanish 'queer' cinema, Ayaso replied that their only intention was to amuse, entertain and enjoy themselves and that the film had no hidden political agenda (queer or otherwise). When asked whether the stereotypical representation of the three gay men in the film was meant as a mockery of these types (and indirectly of gays in general) or as a recuperation of camp and effeminacy for the gay community (as opposed to the acceptance-seeking of 'straight-acting' types), both directors evasively suggested that they did not want to offend any social group or minority and (here confusing sexual identity with professional status) that all the characters were anyway stereotypes (the policeman, the cleaner and so on). The ostensible aim, then, was to make a traditional zany movie by throwing together a crazy cleaning lady, two crazy women police officers and three dizzy queens.

From these claims we can deduce that the film is directed at a mainly heterosexual audience who can accept the factual presence of gay life in Madrid as long as it appears funny, harmless and unthreatening. This is achieved, of course, at the expense of the queer audience's pleasure. The homoerotic visual pleasure of the film concentrates not on the gay characters' bodies but on heterosexual Lucas's, and sexual tension between him and the gay men is avoided by minimising their direct physical contact (except, very subtly, during the gay men's fantasy flashbacks during police evidence). Lucas's naked body is only shown when he is asleep or – when the film veers into being a murder mystery – dead. Interestingly, his corpse is fetishised both by the men, who still find him attractive (Carlos remarks on the extra-kinky appeal) and investigating police officer Mari Carmen who kisses him on the lips and enthusiastically takes the forensic photographs. For gay audiences, there is an extra factor involved: the iconography of the seven knives still stuck to Lucas's aesthetically bloodied, St-Sebastian-ised body, naked save for Calvin-Klein-style underpants.[30] Yet, none of the three gay men kiss him (alive or dead) on camera; most of the visual pleasure is mediated by the women;

and the gay men's sex lives exist only in conversation, their vivid, screened, accounts of their relationships with Lucas being revealed as wishful fantasies.

However, there are aspects of the film that can favour a 'queering' of the narrative. One of them is the music which constructs the film's queer space and atmosphere, marking it with specific gay, generational and national identities. The use of a karaoke bar ('Cocoon') facilitates the inclusion of Spanish popular music of the 1960s susceptible to camp readings and recuperations. The songs are performed, with great feeling, for an elderly audience (hence, in a nice film-buff joke, the name of the bar) by Estrella (Gracia Olayo), an 'excessive' woman (after Tina in *Law of Desire*) in her late forties who dreams of fame (her name meaning 'star'). Estrella's performances are at the centre of the camp setting of the film: the 1960s hits, popular with Spanish gay men (of all ages), make them and her markedly queer; as a queen of karaoke, she performs constantly on and off stage and is obsessed with youth, beauty, sex, excitement, her favoured 1960s clothes, extreme blond dyed hair and false eyelashes, all of which make her look like a drag queen, hinting strongly at the 'imitative structure of gender itself and its contingency'[31] and proving that drag is a phenomenon really beyond sex and gender identity (a woman can also impersonate a female 'alter ego' in drag).

Estrella's belated but intensively lived independence and sexual freedom ('nobody is worthy enough to give myself up for them', she says) is central to a queer reading of *Perdona*. Although initially presented as pitiable – a self-caricature of the crazy, discontented middle-aged woman – she has the most fun and, indeed, actually does have sex with Lucas, as we discover at the end. Depicted as if living in a world of fantasy (like the three gay men), she is the best at making her fantasies come true, until her fun is ended suddenly by her husband (an embodiment of the patriarchal system she was trying to escape), who kills Lucas in a grim reiteration of the traditional Spanish honour and revenge plays.

Like *Perdona*, *Frenesí*'s extra-filmic context is equivocal. A few months before the premiere of this film, directors Bardem, Albacete and Menkes gave an exclusive interview to one of Spain's best-selling magazines, *Cambio 16*. Once again, here were directors refusing to make reference to gay issues, their only (and secondary) mention of the gay characters in the film coming in the context of 'crazy comedy', and much being made of their main desire to make a film about their 'ideal women' ('comedia loca').[32] To a certain extent, these women – again flatmates – respond to the stereotypes represented in the three gay characters of *Perdona*: the sweet unsexy one, María (Beatriz Santiago), the over-sexed slut, Mónica (Cayetana Guillén Cuervo), and the virginal good girl, Yeye (Ingrid Rubio). The film playfully explores how these differences affect the women's love and sex lives. Mónica, who works behind the bar at a nightclub while trying to make it as an actress during the daytime, appears to enjoy no-strings-attached, often anonymous sex (even with Yeye's ex-boyfriend) and she is portrayed as lonely and unhappy, whereas Yeye – whose boyfriend Max (Nancho Novo) has ditched her – is presented as a morally immaculate creature who diverts her sexual energy into her friendship with Alberto (Gustavo Salmerón), her gay confidant. It turns out that Max is at the centre of a murder investigation unofficially carried out by a lurking homophobic ex-policeman who thinks Max murdered his wife. In the meantime, Alberto's sex life is cut short by the fact that both the men he fancies – Alex (Javier Albalá) and David (Liberto Rabal) – turn out to be, respectively, married and straight.

As in the other three films, the presence of gay characters and a constructed queer space offers an empowering visibility unusual in mainstream productions. Here, the music is more recent and belongs to an Anglo-Saxonised 'techno' scene that makes it recognisable as 'gay' for a wider, young audience also outside Spain. It provides a perfect background for a last-reel fancy dress party at the Frenesí club which invites sex and fantasy-role playing. Yeye abandons her usual naivety and appears dressed up as a femme fatale (in a dress inspired by the grotesque Gaultier creation worn by Victoria Abril in Almodóvar's *Kika*) and takes the butch role when dancing with Mónica (dressed up as a hyper-feminine dame); also, an unexpected passionate kiss and their toast to 'a world without men' offers the possibility of an anti-patriarchal ending. Alberto, the gay man, dresses up as Cindy Crawford and takes on the 'strong woman' position to reject his bisexual ex-lover Alex after finding out that he is a closeted married father.

Frenesí's drag queens offer contradictory meanings. Like Estrella in *Perdona*, they seem to function as a metaphor for the tragi-comic life of queers (inevitable loneliness and the end of partying are frequently alluded to by characters): they *perform* happiness, and their masks seem to hide sadness, as is clear from a comic *Priscilla*-like dance routine to the song 'Estoy llorando por tí' ('I weep for you'), which itself mixes cheerful pace and rhythm with grave, depressive lyrics. On the other hand, the gay hymn 'A quién le importa' ('Whose business is it?'), in a dance version by La Baker, marks the moment of triumph for a group of drag queens (regulars at the girls' parties) who accidentally give a fatal blow (with the toilet door) to the ex-policeman moments after his frustrated attempt to rape María. The song is affirmative of transgressive personality and lifestyle, a challenge to the intransigent majority, and originally performed as a liberating manifesto by gay icon Alaska, one of Spain's most controversial artists of the 1980s.[33] The empowering key statement of the lyrics – 'I will never change' – facilitates a queer 'proud' ending of the film, and signifies an important step forward in the narrative, since the idea had been used before deterministically in relation to heterosexual Max to denote powerlessness. In this musical context, the film gains a partly subversive happy ending in which the homophobe tyrant is finally killed, inability to change is turned into assertive refusal to conform, and various characters realise their dreams. However, the effects of this are equivocal: plain, sweet María's fantasy of dating her pretty-boy neighbour comes true, Alberto recovers his self-esteem, and Max and Yeye reunite, walking back home together as day breaks marking a happy but conservative and reheterosexualising move away from the nightlife of corruption and unorthodox sex.

If in *Perdona* Estrella was the character with the strongest queer potential, in *Frenesí* it is Cristina, the lesbian madam of a male brothel, played by Bibi Andersen, an out transsexual television presenter and actress of considerable fame and presence (a regular in Almodóvar films) who has long been identified in Spain with sexual transgression and rule-breaking. Thus, what is represented as 'transgressive' same-sex attraction is, in fact, more radical and dismantles boundaries between screen and star personae, between gender and sex.[34] The fact that one of the drag queens is a woman (Paloma Tabasco as Jacky Kennedy) also adds to this effect. Mónica too is empowered by performance (she is an aspiring actress), constantly evoking drag in her frequent use of fancy dress for casting sessions. She is also, as mentioned above, the most sexually active character in the film and often videos her sexual experiences. In filming and archiving her sex encounter with Max (as with other men before), she not only converts her own sex life into a narcissistic performance, watching herself on huge monitors around the club, but like Mari Carmen with her photos of Lucas in *Perdona*, she appropriates men's bodies.

However, the use of video within the film also contributes to the same sense of mediated visual pleasure that we observed in *Perdona*. A video camera is also used to show the guests arriving at one of the girls' house parties, and a mirror is used as one of the visual vehicles of the only gay sex scene in the film, between Alberto and Alex (in the shower, echoing a similar, less up-front scene in *Law of Desire*). The scene, which starts with a series of direct close-ups and medium shots of the men's toned bodies under beautiful, gentle blue lighting, ends with penetration reflected in the mirror. This reflection partly mitigates the sense of pleasure, creating a barrier between film and audience, suggesting that this is a mirage, a brief encounter destined to failure, in bitter anticipation of the plot's development to this end (as is also the case when mirrors feature similarly in scenes of Yeye's deception-strewn relationship with Max).

Jordan and Morgan-Tamosunas speak of a series of recent Spanish films of gay narrative which 'promote strong identification with their protagonists and facilitate the effective representation of their particular perspective and subjectivity', arguing of *Perdona* that 'rather than positioning the characters' homosexuality as [its] subject of scrutiny [it] avoids turning homosexuality into an issue, representing gay identity as just another option in the contemporary social collage'.[35] *Perdona* seems, rather, to avoid such subject positioning, and both it and *Frenesí* reinforce misconceptions and myths of homosexuality constructed from a heterosexual (perhaps even heterosexist) viewpoint. The supposition that gays fall in love with heterosexual men and try to seduce them, often ignoring the unavoidable tragic consequences, applies to Alberto's advances to straight nude male model Pablo in *Frenesí* or, in *Perdona*, to the teasing of the gay characters (and audiences) with the ambiguously mysterious sexual identity of Lucas (the belated revelation of whose heterosexuality is strongly anticlimactic). Both tend to heterosexist stereotypes of gay men as hysterical, unhappy (especially in *Perdona*, where Carlos is in therapy and Alberto relies on relaxation tapes), frivolous, vain (preening Dani in *Perdona* reminds Carlos that as a fat guy he will never be happy on the gay scene) or hooked on drugs (in *Frenesí*). In both films, the gay men put their impossible sexual-romantic fantasies with straight men before their friendship with the female characters (Estrella and Yeye). While they introduce sexualised gay images and a (limited) range of gay characters into the narrative of mainstream films, and while they activate intermittently the subversive potential of gender and identity instability, of overdetermined visual and dramatic styles, these two movies at least are far from 'queer'. They can be said to be (perhaps by accident) as gay integrationist as is *Amor*, conforming to the norm, rather than challenging it. The representation of gay characters as victims or as 'funny', harmless, asexual characters in order to be accepted contrasts with Anglo-Saxon notions of queer positive images which highlight the dangers of 'weak and apologetic' self-representations which allow the heterosexist status quo to be maintained. Far from creating 'positive images of homosexuality to spread around the world' (a role that Todd Haynes has claimed as a queer director),[36] these films seem to reinforce gay stereotypes, and not particularly positive ones.

None the less, the four films we have been discussing still invite queer viewings which can identify genuinely new and challenging territories of desire within Spanish contexts, can usefully reveal the apparently radical to be sanitised, and make the avowedly safe destabilising. *Frenesí*'s representation of homosexuality and sex in the city is queer in style and yet not necessarily so in effect; *Perdona*'s camp attitude has it collude with and break from normalising structures of patriarchy and traditional narration; *Amor* is gay in the sense that it insists, tacitly, on a form of identity politics, on equality and integration (men loving men is special and defining but not different, is its argument); *Alegre* normalises its queer content through polished cinematic and comic technique while simultaneously becoming queer in as much as its wit subverts traditional structures and mores, allowing its protagonist (and audience) to evade normalising identifications.[37]

Notes

1   When foreign imports are added in, this is seen as an 'avalanche' in *Fotogramas*, 50:1,842 (April 1997), 30. All four films rank in the top fifty of the Spanish Ministry of Culture's figures on box office takings and viewing figures for their respective years of release *Perdona*'s respectable viewing figure of 276,125 to the end of 1997 placed it thirteenth of ninety-one Spanish production releases, and ahead of *The Return of the Jedi* (Special Edition), *Michael* and *Secrets and Lies*. *Frenesí* was seen by 251,865 by the end of 1996 (and some 50,000 in 1997); *Alegre* reached 201,672 in 1994; and *Amor*, more modestly, was seen by 34,626 in the last three months of 1997. Source: Ministerio de Cultura, *Boletín informativo: anexo cultural en cifras. Películas. Reacaudaciones. Espectadores* (Madrid) (for 1994, 1996 and 1997: figures for 1998 unavailable at time of going to press).

2   R. Baker and B. Hanson, [Brochure copy for] thirteenth London Lesbian and Gay Film Festival (18–22 April 1999), 6. The sub-titled version has been released with the unhappy title *Excuse me duckie, but Lucas loves me!*

3   See B. Jordan and R. Morgan-Tamosunas, *Contemporary Spanish Cinema* (Manchester, Manchester University Press, 1998), pp. 68–71.

4   As noted by V. Molina-Foix, '*Alegre ma non troppo*: Colomo no está en crisis', *Fotogramas*, 47:1,809 (1994), 17.

5   See J.-C. Alfeo Álvarez, 'La imagen del personaje homosexual masculino como protagonista en la cinematografía española', Doctoral thesis (Univer-

sidad Complutense de Madrid, Facultad de Ciencias de la Información, 1998), and 'La representación de la cuestión gay en el cine español', *Cuadernos de la Academia*, 5 (May1999), 287–304.

6   See R. Llamas, *Teoría torcida: prejuicios y discursos en torno a «la homosexualidad»* (Madrid, Siglo XXI, 1998), pp. 371–82.

7   See P. J. Smith, *Laws of Desire: Questions of Homosexuality in Spanish Writing and Film 1960–1990* (Oxford, Clarendon Press, 1992), pp. 129–62.

8   J. V. Aliaga, 'Cómo hemos cambiado' in Aliaga and J. M Cortés (eds), *Identidad y diferencia: sobre la cultura gay en España* (Barcelona and Madrid, Egales, 1997), pp. 19–107, p. 83.

9   J. M. Cortés, 'Acerca de modelos e identidades' in Aliaga and Cortés (eds), *Identidad y diferencia*, 109–96, p. 131.

10 J. V. Aliaga *et al.*, 'Voces y ecos de la comunidad gay en España' in Aliaga and Cortés (eds.), *Identidad y diferencia*, 201–37, p. 206.

11 R. Llamas and F. Vila, 'Spain: Passion for Life. Una historia del movimiento de lesbianas y gays en el estado español' in X. Buxán (ed.), *Conciencia de un singular deseo: estudios lesbianos y gays en el estado español* (Barcelona, Laertes, 1997), pp. 189–224, p.213.

12 P. J. Smith, *Desire Unlimited: the Cinema of Pedro Almodóvar* (London and New York, Verso, 1994), pp. 80–2.

13 *Ibid.*, p. 3.

14 As summarised, for example, in Llamas, *Teoría torcida*, pp. 11–21, and E. Jackson Jr, 'Scandalous subjects: Robert Glück's embodied narratives', in T. de Lauretis (ed.), *Queer Theory: Lesbian and Gay Sexualities*, Special Issue of *differences: a Journal of Feminist Cultural Studies*, 3:2 (1991), 112–34.

15 See Smith, *Desire Unlimited*, pp. 85–6.

16 *Ibid.*, p. 81.

17 *Ibid.*, pp. 81–3.

18 J. Arroyo, '*La ley del deseo*: a gay seducion' in R. Dyer and G. Vincendeau (eds), *European Popular Cinema* (New York and London, Routledge, 1992), pp. 31–46.

19 The name may be a gesture not only to her Biblical namesake but to the Spanish 1960s artiste of that name, still a gay icon.

20 The precise equivalent is not, however, available in the Spanish language, which contents itself with *artístico* or *creativo*.

21 As observed in E. Rodríguez Marchante, '*Alegre ma non troppo*: para reir', *Cinerama*, 3:25 (1994) 29.

22 An Oxbridge setting and a classical music soundtrack similarly enhance a moment of emotional, homoerotic discovery in *Maurice* (dir. James Ivory, 1987).

23 A key point in favour for both Molina Foix, 'Colomo no está en crisis', and Rodríguez Marchante, 'Para reir'.

24 A typology suggested in E. Bergmann and P. J. Smith, 'Introduction', in

Bergmann and Smith (eds), *¿Entiendes? Queer Readings, Hispanic Writings* (Durham, North Carolina and London, Duke University Press, 1995), pp. 1–14.

25   *La sociedad rosa* (Barcelona, Anagrama, 1991), pp. 43–89.

26   R. Freixas, '*Amor de hombre*: la vie en rose', *Dirigido*, 262 (November 1997), 25.

27   See J. Wyatt, 'Cinematic sexual transgression and new queer cinema', *Film Quarterly*, 46:3 (1993), 2–8, and Bad Object Choices [collective] (eds), *How Do I Look: Queer Film and Video* (Seattle, Bay Press, 1991).

28   See A. Doty, 'Queerness, comedy and *The Women*' in K. Brunovska Karnic and H. Jenkins (eds), *Classical Hollywood Comedy* (New York and London, Routledge, 1994), 332–47, and K. Rowe, 'Comedy, melodrama and gender: theorizing the genres of laughter', in Karnic and Jenkins (eds.), *Classical Hollywood Comedy* 39–59, pp. 39–56.

29   Held on 8 August 1997 within the XXXIV Curso de Cinematografía at the University of Valladolid (Spain); questioner S. Fouz Hernández.

30   Ayaso insists that there were seven knives simply because seven were included in the set purchased for props.

31   J. Butler, *Gender Trouble: Feminism and the Subversion of Identity* (London and New York, Routledge, 1990), p. 137.

32   See P. Leyra, 'Todos para uno', *Cambio 16* (8 July 1996), 76–7.

33   On Alaska, see Aliaga, 'Como hemos cambiado', pp. 57–8.

34   On Andersen's lesbian role in Almodóvar's *High Heels* and the interconnectedness of performance and real life, see M. Kinder, *Blood Cinema: the Reconstruction of National Identity in Spain* (Berkeley and Los Angeles, University of California Press, 1993), pp. 257–8.

35   Jordan and Morgan-Tamosunas, *Contemporary Spanish Cinema*, p. 152.

36   In Wyatt, 'Cinematic sexual transgression', p. 8.

37   Our focus on Castilian-language light/comic dramas leads to obvious exclusions: shorts (usually with festival exposure only), and the work of Catalan director Ventura Pons (showcased at the ICA, London, in March 1999). *Caricies* (*Caresses*, 1997) and *Amic/Amat* (*My Friend, My Beloved*, 1998) suggest the emergence of a more serious queer movement in the cinema of the Spanish nations.

8

'It's not that I can't decide; I don't like definitions': queer in Australia in Christos Tsiolkas's *Loaded* and Ana Kokkinos's *Head On*

Deborah Hunn

A question which has preoccupied queer theory and queer aesthetics as both have developed over the last decade has been whether, and to what extent, the discourses of regulatory regimes – the language and images that penalise and marginalise gays, lesbians, bisexuals and transsexuals – can be occupied and refigured so that they may yield transgressive potential. Judith Butler, for instance, has focused on the newfound currency of the word *queer* as a signifier of pride and resistance. Can queer, densely embedded as it is in a history of homophobic abuse, 'a paralysing slur' functioning through ritualised and repeated use 'as the mundane interpellation of a pathologised sexuality',[1] be appropriated, turned against its customary usage? While arguing that such moments of 'affirmative resignification'[2] are indeed possible, Butler advocates a critical practice which maintains a scrupulous awareness that words that wound can, in certain contexts, with certain uses, work to reinscribe the ideology which they seek to transgress. Queer theory, then, must address the production of new queer identities at the same time as it critiques old ones. Grounded in post-structuralist theories of the subject as constructed within discourse and Foucauldian politics of resistance, it opposes essentialist understandings of sexuality and identity, working instead to trace what Lisa Duggan has termed 'multiple marked identities'.[3] While maintaining a firm focus on same-sex desire, the critical and aesthetic trend in the 1990s towards queering sexuality has led also to the disarticulation of the hetero/homo binary in favour of fluid models of desire. In regard to sexual identity, dialogues about outness and about the speech acts of disclosure have emphasised a politics of difference. As Butler notes of the demand for 'outness': 'Who is represented by *which* use of the term, and who is excluded? For whom does the term present an impossible conflict between racial, ethnic and religious affiliation and sexual politics?'[4]

In Australia the queer moment has coincided resonantly with a shift in more general debates about what constitutes Australian identity. Robert Reynolds comments that, under the Hawke and more specifically the Keating labour governments of the late 1980s and early 1990s, 'the official story of Australian identity was built around the idea of a multicultural, cosmopolitan and tolerant society embracing and invigorated by change',[5] a move which led to a degree of inclusiveness towards gays and lesbians and some recognition of sexual identity as a legitimate area of concern in the dialogue that was reshaping national identity.[6]

Debates about the role of sexuality within more general reformulations of identity have provided a vigorous context for critical theorists and cultural producers who have sought to queer and query fixed understandings of both what it means to be Australian and what it means to be queer *in* Australia. The drive to articulate new configurations of sexual identity and desire has often involved astringent tactical disarticulations of fixed ones – whether these be found in heteronormative and homophobic discourses within the dominant culture, in the deradicalising conformity implicit in strands of tolerance and inclusiveness legitimated by the dominant, or in the homogenising tendencies of the established gay and lesbian subculture. The texts produced through this engagement have been characterised by a rich vein of experimentation with language, genre and technique – aesthetic play which has frequently, and sometimes problematically, skirted the borders between transgression and reinscription and which has often located itself firmly at the intersection of difference.

What I want to do here, then, is to consider this aspect of Australian queer culture by focusing on two interrelated texts which – whether in their own right, or as they interact – usefully exemplify the pleasures and dangers of this body of work: gay writer Christos Tsiolkas's 1994 novel *Loaded*[7] and lesbian director Ana Kokkinos's 1998 translation of *Loaded* into film, under the new title *Head On.*

Loaded has been classed as an example of 'grunge' or 'dirty realism'. Popular in Australia in the 1990s, the genre has been critiqued as a vehicle for legitimate social comment by those concerned with its postmodern predilections for surface over substance and esoteric subject matter. But the focus on 'performance[s] of semi-exotic subcultural styles'[8] has also been defended as exploring 'the psychosocial and psychosexual limitations and excesses of young sub/urban characters in relation to imaginary and socially constructed boundaries defining notions of self and other'.[9] *Loaded*, certainly, is an eloquent exploration of the bleakness and alienation that underpins performative surfaces, transcending the monotone banality or gratuitous excess which sometimes plague the genre through bursts of hyperrealism, an inventive poetic seam and considerable complexity of characterisation.[10]

Loaded tracks approximately twenty-four hours in the life of Ari, the central character, as he traverses the suburbs and city of Melbourne. He is nineteen, a working-class Greek-Australian. His father is a Greek immigrant, his mother born in Australia of Greek parents. He is angry and alienated, cruising the streets tuned in to his walkman, looking for action and frequently high on a cocktail of drugs. Although he lives with his family, he is radically estranged from them and the traditions of Greek culture to which they maintain what he perceives to be a crippling allegiance. While shocking and angering them with displays of defiant and undutiful behaviour, he retains a wall of secrecy around issues of sexuality. Ari is a voracious consumer of casual sex, occasionally with women, but mostly, and covertly, with innumerable men whom he picks up in clubs and beats.

Ari, then, is gay. Or is he? The back cover of the 1995 Vintage edition presents the reader with the story of 'a poofter who doesn't want to be gay'. The phrase suggests that any resistance to categorisation demonstrated by the central character – and there is plenty to be found – can be understood as one individual's denial of the 'truth' of a sexual identity, the terms of which remain beyond query. Indeed, there is much to suggest that Ari is struggling with internalised homophobia – most notably in the belief that emotional commitment to another man will feminise him. And yet there is also evidence that the narrative is employing Ari's defiant personality to work through questions about the construction and coherence of identity that are a little more complex.

Loaded is divided into four sections – East, North, South, West – and Tsiolkas uses Ari's commentary to produce a map of the suburbs and city which reflects an acute awareness of hierarchies of class, race, ethnicity and sexuality.[11] Of the East: 'I detest the East … The whitest part of my city, where you'll see the authentic white Australian …'; 'East are the brick-veneer fortresses of the wogs with money. On the edge, however, bordering the true Anglo affluence, never part of it.'[12] Of the West: 'an industrial quilt of wharfs, factories, warehouses, silos and power plants. And the endless stretch of housing estates. The West is a dumping ground; a sewer of refugees, the migrants, the poor, the insane, the unskilled and the uneducated.' Ari insists that 'I don't belong to the West',[13] but he vehemently rejects his appointed destiny in the North: 'The North is a growing, pulsating sore on the map of the city, the part of the city in which I, my family, my friends are meant to buy a house, grow a garden, shop, watch TV and be buried in. The North is where the wog is supposed to end up. And therefore I hate the North …'[14]

Ari's politically loaded mapping of Melbourne is inflected through a cartography of desire. He expresses his 'contempt' for the North in forays for casual sex with Greek men who symbolise his destiny: 'I roam the North so I can come face to face with the future that is being prepared for me. On my knees, with hate written on my face, I spit out bile, semen, saliva and phlegm, I spit it all out. I spit out the future that has been prepared for me.'[15] Sex with men – rough, anonymous and stylised – seems at times to function for Ari as a politics of resistance enacted through the body. Such rituals, however, serve also to deflect him from the possibilities of a more sustained transcendence. Ari's ultimate desti-nation, if he chooses to take it, is in the opposite direction, in the bohemian South: 'To the South are the wogs who have been shunted out of their communities. Artists and junkies and faggots and whores, the sons and daughters no longer talked about, no longer admitted into the arms of family.'[16] What remains unclear at the point of narrative closure is whether he is prepared to make this choice.

In the South, towards the end of his journey through a day of arguments with family, cruising and partying with friends, Ari is confronted with an opportunity to move towards a serious relationship with a man he genuinely cares for – George, a friend of Ari's student brother. However, after sex they fight and part on seemingly irreconcil-able terms when George challenges Ari over what he perceives to be Ari's immature attitude to his parents regarding his sexuality: 'You just have to tell the truth once … Just once, Ari, once you tell them the truth, one argument, no matter how brutal and you never have to lie again.'[17] Ari responds angrily: 'Truth they use against you … never tell a wog anything about yourself. The truth is yours, it doesn't belong to no one else.' The episode closes in such a way as to suggest that Ari's refusal to come out of the closet to his family cannot be excused purely in terms of ethnic speci-ficity but works rather to entrap him in the more 'fucked up' aspects of his personality – specifically it protects him from emotions and locks him into a solipsistic politics of resistance: bleak nihilism and private acts of defiance which will change little in his own life or that of others. As George walks away, Ari rigidly refuses to disclose openly what he admits internally: 'I love you. I want to say the words, but they are an obscenity I can't bring myself to mouth. I've never said those words, I'm never going to say those words.'[18]

Ari's defiance is pathetically self-defeating, but his closet is one of complex dimensions. Differences of socio-cultural location *are* crucial in his attitude to 'truth' and to disclosure. In conflict with the Anglo George, he spits out: 'You talking about your parents or my parents?'[19] Tsiolkas himself argues that Ari's experience is:

> specific, I think, to a lot of Greek-Australian experience ... he thinks it will force him into a position where he will be in danger, whether that danger comes from his family, whether that danger comes from his peers, or from the community. *I suppose in some ways it was a reaction to some of the easy positions that the gay and lesbian community can take about issues like coming out or expressing their sexuality.*[20]

Such comments suggest a useful comparison with Butler's engagement with the identity politics of outing. Noting the fallacy of assuming the transparency of language in the act of disclosure, Butler queries what it means to say one is a lesbian? One is gay?: 'If I claim to be a lesbian, I "come out" only to produce a new and different "closet." The "you" to whom I come out now has access to a different region of opacity. Indeed, the locus of opacity has simply shifted: before you did not know what I "am," but now you do not know what that means ...'[21] One does not, she suggests, come out of the closet into some 'unbounded spatiality' but rather into a range of interpretative locations which inflect the lesbian or gay signifier with different specificities. Whilst insistent that she is not 'legislating against the use' of terms such as lesbian or gay, Butler nevertheless argues for a critical engagement which consistently queries 'which use will be legislated ... what play will there be between legislation and use such that the instrumental uses of identity do not become regulatory imperatives?'[22]

Interpretations of the text have viewed the character of George uncritically as more mature, more in touch with his sexuality, but his response to Ari's closeting is intolerant in regard to questions of difference. He can understand Ari's situation only in terms of the context of his own experiences of disclosure, his own socio-cultural specificity. Whilst his criticisms of Ari's evasiveness do form an important part in the dialogue about disclosure and outness in the novel, his role is ambivalent and he can be seen as also representing the 'easy positions' which Tsiolkas seeks to critique.

The tendency to efface intersections of subcultural or minority identities by singling out one strand of identity at the expense of another has been the subject of critique in recent work on sexuality in Australia. Audrey Yue, for instance, in her work on the marginalisation (in both straight *and* lesbian discourse) of Asian lesbians in Australia, argues that: 'mapping identity requires interrogating the hegemonic circuits that articulate "natural" subject positions … a politics of difference must imagine new political subjects and terrains for multiple points of resistance that challenge the multiple and interweaving axes of domination.'[23] In *Loaded*, Tsiolkas's play with language queers 'hegemonic circuits' through a juxtaposition of sexuality, ethnicity and gender which unsettles the 'natural subject positions' set in place by regulatory regimes, and attempts, somewhat ambivalently, to imagine 'new subject positions' through transgressive resignifications of 'loaded terms'.[24]

A scene in which Ari responds to a burst of homophobic abuse upon leaving a gay club and entering 'another world' on the street outside provides a key instance of sexual/textual resistance:

Fucking Faggot

Fucking faggot rings in my ear. Faggot I don't mind. I like the word. I like queer, I like the Greek word *poutsi*. I hate the word gay. Hate the word homosexual. I like the word wog, can't stand dago, ethnic or Greek-Australian. You're either Greek or Australian, you have to make a choice. Me, I'm neither. It's not that I can't decide; I don't like definitions.

If I was black I'd call myself a nigger. It's strong, scary, loud. I like it for the same reasons I like the word cocksucker and wog. If I was Asian I'd call myself a gook, but I'd use it loudly and ferociously so it scares whitey. Use it to show whitey that it's not all yes-sir-no-sir-we-Asians-work-hard-good-capitalists-do-anything-the-white-man-says-sir. Wog, nigger, gook. Cocksucker. Use them right, the words have guts.

Her words, fucking faggot, they ring in my ear.[25]

Just as the novel is divided up into four sections – East, North, South and West – so too these section are split into a series of discrete scenes. Each scene is prefaced with a short title which is taken from its first words. These title words are then developed into a sequence in the story – with initial meanings often elaborated, interrogated, wrenched from context, and flipped around, transposed and transformed. In considering such juxtapositions Beth Spencer notes Tsiolkas's intertextual integration of music and cinema, commenting on his narrative approximation of montage and noting that what links these scenes together are certain key words – 'wog', 'faggot', Greek', 'Australian' – whose meanings are constantly reworked 'like a sampled phrase or a good piece of techno music'.[26] Such techniques may be seen as an attempt to prise away these terms from fixed meanings and open them up to the possibility of resignification, although the narrative is somewhat ambivalent about the complete efficacy of such transformative wordplay.

'Fucking faggot' is, perhaps, one of the most condensed and internally unified of these scenes. Its intense precision may, I think, owe something to its crucial positioning in the narrative's map of desire. 'Fucking Faggot' is the second scene in 'South' and is a response to events in the last scenes of North. Spatially it occupies a border position between 'North' – Ari's appointed destiny should he take up the role of good, ambitious Greek-Australian, sublimating his sexual need to forays of beat sex – and South – the space of open sexuality and familial rejection. In this highly charged narrative space – the site of a possible border crossing – we are given one of the most extended developments of Ari's views on his sexual identity. Ari's 'It's not that I can't decide; I don't like definitions' may be a resistance to commitment, yet it may also signal that changing spaces will force him into definitions which are by no means unproblematically liberatory; which may, indeed, remain implicated in the regulatory discourses of the dominant.

The abuse comes from a drunken teenage girl and is directed specifically at Ari's transvestite friend Johnny, who is dressed in full drag as 'Toula'. Initially, 'the girl goes on a rave about how much she likes dancing with gay men. Australian men can't dance, she tells the hot-dog man and his driver friend, they can't fucking dance for shit. Poofters can dance.' She then 'starts giggling at Johnny. Honey, you're beautiful, she jeers. Johnny gives her a dagger look. Honey, you're a mess, he replies. Fucking faggot, she calls out and nestles under her boyfriend's arm.'[27]

'Poofters can dance.' Perhaps the overt abuse here – 'Fucking faggot' – is less offensive than the domesticated and patronising crossover stereotype. Ari's comments about racial and ethnic assimilation provide a useful supplement to the less developed comments about sexuality: 'If I was Asian I'd call myself a gook, but I'd use it loudly and ferociously so it scares whitey. Use it to show whitey that it's not all yes-sir-no-sir-we-Asians-work-hard-good-capitalists-do-anything-the-white-man-says-sir.' Ari's use of racist terminology (here and throughout the novel) is blown to such a point of excess that it is presumably meant, like many of the character's more extreme statements, to function as a critique of his residual immaturity. However, coupled with the excess is a relatively shrewd political commentary on the seamier ideological underside of official discourses of multiculturalism and tolerance: the price of acceptance and assimilation is to become a cog in the capitalist wheel, a producer and consumer of commodities, subservient to a dominant culture which remains homogenising, even racist: 'yes-sir-no-sir-we-Asians-work-hard-good-capitalists-do-anything-the-white-man-says-sir.'

Ari's embrace of the words 'faggot' and 'queer' may be seen as attempts at a transgressive resignification of such abject identifications – a refusal of the ideological complicity with bourgeois life signified by such safely domesticated and respectable words as 'gay' or 'homosexual'. In this sense the structural play which repeats 'fucking faggot' at the end marks that the term has turned full circle as it rings for a second time in Ari's ear, inverting its initial abusive usage and transforming into a term of tactical engagement.

Extrapolating from issues of ethnicity and race to issues of sexuality I think it is possible that, in a tentative and somewhat covert way, the narrative is using Ari's tirade to flirt with an oppositional use of 'queer' and to tease out some of queer's currency as a term of radical engagement with fixed categories of sexual identity signified via entrenched terms like 'gay' and 'homosexual'. Certainly Ari's resistance to definitions, and the possible uses to which the novel may be putting 'queer' invite comparisons with other articulations of queer by Australian writers and critics. Poet Ian MacNeill, for instance, offers the following observations in his 'Some notes towards a definition of queer':

> Queer embraces all but straight. And gay.
> It attempts to speak for a whole range of behaviours that do not embrace straight or gay.
> It refutes identification.
> Queer is bisexual in theory; it thus feels it avoids limiting itself.[28]

And yet the status of 'queer' as a resignification of identity which resists definitions is ambivalent in the Tsiolkas text. While drawing on queer's power to query the reductive possibilities of identification, the narrative also critiques Ari's nihilism as excessive. Arguably, indeed, it uses it to illustrate the dangers of taking queer too far. The repetition of 'fucking faggot' may also be seen as a structural rearticulation of Ari's closet. His wordplay is purely interior; there is no actual verbal engagement, no talking back. The circle of language closes around him, trapping him in silence and anger. In a pointed irony, talking back is left to Johnny/Toula, the feminised male who represents everything that Ari, with his hyper-masculine posturing, fears about homosexuality.

The contrast is particularly telling given that only a few pages earlier there is a graphic account of the distorting effect of Ari's internalised homophobia. In the club Ari picks up Con, a Greek guy 'hard and handsome' like Ari. During a brief sexual encounter Con asks Ari for anal penetration, commenting afterwards:

> You're one of the few people I've ever let fuck me. He sits beside me again. It's because you're a man, he adds. I look over at him. He no longer seems quite the masculine Greek man I met a short while ago. His voice sounds an octave higher, he is waving his arms around. Fucking him has feminised him in mind. It could be the drugs.[29]

The hyperreal distortion of perception facilitated by Ari's voracious drug consumption is a useful vehicle for conveying the extent to which the body itself is constructed through culturally loaded narratives of desire. Con undergoes metamorphosis, is feminised. Ari himself rarely submits to penetration, preferring oral sex and choreographing his sexual acts as struggles for dominance. The narrative both endorses and critiques the complex implications of the trajectory of Ari's desire. His need to 'have a man and be a man'[30] certainly produces a queer disarticulation of one of the dominant binaries which structures the notion of a unified sexual identity – identification and desire are, in normative discourses of desire, opposites; the desire to be and the desire to have cannot be located on the same object. In this way Ari's desire to have and to be a man challenges homogenising constructions of homosexual desire which structure male/male, or female/female relations, as inversions of normative hetero-sexuality. Yet some of Ari's psychological and physical posturing verges towards the hypermasculine, and indeed, towards 'straight acting'. As David Buchbinder notes,

> Straight acting, which presumes heterosexuality, becomes the social and public demonstration of gender normality, and is articulated – in Butler's terms cited – through a particular repertoire of verbal and gestural signs which are understood to be tokens of heterosexual masculinity. Such behaviour is both reinforced and enforced by the structure of patriarchal masculinity, which in turn produces a sort of undeclared police-state mentality among men, establishing guidelines of attitude, behaviour and other sorts of practice in order to assure the culture that its males will act in required, approved ways; and to warn those males who are unable to do so, or who refuse those guidelines, that there will be punitive consequences for their noncompliance. In this way, heterosexual masculinity takes on the guise, not merely of normality, but of essence. Men who conform, whether they are homosexual or heterosexual, to the dictates of the discourse of

patriarchal masculinity thus seem *essentially* masculine and therefore apparently heterosexual.[31]

Buchbinder's reference to Butler's notion of performative or citational identity is particularly useful for *Loaded*. For Butler, gender is not an expression of essence but 'an identity tenuously constituted in time, instituted in an exterior space through a stylized repetiton of acts'.[32] In effect Tsiolkas plays with the performativity of gender identity to undermine heterosexuality and masculinity as essences through tracing a cartography of desire which explores the underworld of straight-acting men. Ari's pick-ups are frequently not gay or even bisexual men, but rather men who have sex with men, men who pass as heterosexual (as Ari himself sometimes does) and may even classify themselves as such.

Gender performativity comes to the fore in the film version of *Loaded*, retitled *Head On* and released in 1998.[33] Director and co-scriptwriter Ana Kokkinos streamlines the complex and diffuse first-person monologue of the novel into a plot which, through a series of stylised scenes, culminates in a face-off between Ari and Toula – who replaces George (here renamed Sean) as the ethical centre of the narrative – over the issue of sexual politics. If the dazzling wordplay and tense interiority of Tsiolkas's technique – so suggestive of closeted space – never quite find filmic equivalents, then the visual elements of cinema are exploited to allow for a richer development of gender performativity and, through this, for the deconstruction of the masculine/feminine binarism offered by the Toula/Ari juxtaposition.

The new line of narrative locates Ari's ambivalence about sexual identity in a mixture of tenderness and embarrassment towards Toula – a considerable embellishment on the subtextual resonances of their relationship in the novel and one, it might be noted, which tends to tip the balance of sympathy in favour of the feminised male. Indeed, the factoring of male homosexuality through the lens of a lesbian director might be seen to give the film a doubly 'queer' emphasis, mixing a focus on same-sex desire with a textual translation effected through a complex cross-identification between lesbian and gay male concerns. Although Tsiolkas's anti-hero Ari (Alex Dimitriades) is still a compelling and central force, it is Toula (Paul Capsis) who becomes Kokkinos's hero(ine). Conflict in the film builds around a proposed visit to the Greek club The Stekki. Ari manipulates his friend Joe and Joe's girlfriend, Dina, into visiting the club because he knows that Sean will be present. An early scene shows Ari in Johnny's darkened bedroom as Johnny sits in front of a mirror slowly putting on make-up, constructing himself as Toula. Ari is at ease, lying back on the bed and seeking advice about love from Toula, although not revealing his feelings about Sean. Toula teases him and then rolls on to the bed, tenderly covering Ari with kisses which leave the marks of freshly applied lipstick. Toula suggests to Ari that they go dancing together that evening but Ari refuses, as he is determined to go to the Greek club, a place where Toula would be unwelcome. They are interrupted by the arrival of Johnny's brutal father, who shouts from the next room and bangs on the door asking whom Johnny has in the room with him. He is delighted to hear that it is Ari, of whom he is fond, seeing him as the kind of son he would like, and not realising that Ari, like his own son, is gay. The father yells for Ari to join him for a drink. Hailed by the law of the father, Ari is instantly interpellated back into the symbolic register of patriarchal masculinity. He looks in Toula's mirror before he leaves the room and wipes the marks of gayness – the lipstick smudges from Toula's tender kisses – off his face in horror, hurrying from the room. The father engages him in sexual banter: 'You fuck a few girls for me tonight Ari.' Ari's macho image is compromised by the audience's knowledge of the sexual secrets Ari has left behind in the safely closeted space of Toula's bedroom, and thoroughly undermined when Ari fails to defend Toula who comes out of the safe space of the bedroom and continues her defiance. S/he confronts the father, calling on the name of the dead mother from whom s/he takes the name Toula, and whom the father has brutally abused: 'Toula's back Papa.' The father pours out abuse, drawing in Ari, his arm tight around his neck: 'Would you smash plates for her?' or 'pay to watch her dance'. Ari does not respond, but looks guiltily at Toula. Toula's courage and isolation is emphasised through tight editing, which cuts between shots of the two men together, Ari locked in the embracing arm of the patriarch, and Toula alone, dignified and defiant, slightly shaking her head. Bravely 'out', but not stooping to out Ari, despite his failure to defend her, the feminine-identified Toula makes the masculine-identified Ari seem cowardly – a comment on the essentialist models of gender and sexuality which the father draws upon to rebuke the 'unmanly' son in favour of a preferred 'manly' son substitute.

Later Ari, during dinner with his family, does defend Johnny's right to live as he pleases when his own father expresses disgust that he is still seeing 'that *poutsi*' (poofter). The rigidity of family life is stressed here with fights breaking out over the father's attempts to insist that Ari and his sister attend a family gathering rather than party with friends. At the same time, Ari's need for his father's love and approval is apparent in a scene where the two perform the complex moves of a Greek dance together, the father complimenting the son's recitation of his own steps; suggesting he is 'almost' as good. In the ritualised acts of Greek dancing, Kokkinos finds a medium for suggesting that masculinity and femininity are citations.

In a bout of 'straight acting', Ari attempts to seduce his straight friend Joe's fiancé Dina (largely to undermine Joe's capitulation to family pressure to settle down). Ari employs the techniques of a sleazy stud. Ari's selection of background music, Isaac Hays's theme song for *Shaft*, injects an element of parodic excess – 'Who's the sex machine to all the chicks' – of which Ari is not wholly unknowing. However his macho posturing when delivering his younger sister to her Lebanese boyfriend's house, strutting away from the boyfriend's gang and then stopping in silent menace, muscles taut to quiet their heckling, is deadly serious. Later in the evening, when he breaks up a sexual encounter between the young couple, the sister complains tellingly that he is behaving no better than their father – a reminder that Ari's model of masculinity runs the risk of tipping over into a (re)citation of the Greek patriarch he both fetishises and despises. In The Stekki Ari flirts with a woman, Ariadne, although this is partially to attract the attention of Sean. Dancing with Ariadne he vigorously performs the role of dominant male, but his eyes are on Sean. Ari himself is the object of the competing gazes of both Sean and Ariadne. Through this brief triangulation of desire the film evokes some of the bisexual possibilities hinted at in the novel.[12]

In the film the dance scene is interrupted when Toula enters the bar. Greeted by sniggers from the crowd, she approaches Ari: 'Sugar you're so beautiful when you dance.' Ari looks aghast and when someone shouts, 'Hey mate, who's your girlfriend?' he begins to slink away into the crowd. The music starts and Toula begins to dance – a performance as assured and stylish in its femininity as Ari's has been in its masculinity. Cuts to the crowd show a mixture of disdain and then growing interest and appreciation. As the crowd begins to clap in time to the music, an embarrassed Ari, his eyes drawn to Toula, heads towards the door. Toula is defying patriarchy, bent on disproving her father's claims that no one would want to watch her dance.

Sean follows Ari out of the club. The conversation begins to develop their relationship, but Toula interrupts, rushing from the club to squeal 'they loved me'. Ari's surly response is to introduce her as Johnny, but she corrects him, noting 'Johnny's not here. It's Toula.' Sean is comfortable with Toula. Kissing her hand in a courtly gesture he plays along with the high camp mix of gentility and crudeness. Toula infuriates Ari by feminising him, telling Sean it is a 'a girl's night out'. When Ari shouts at Toula that the Stekki episode is 'too much', Toula responds: 'never say anything is too much'. The scenes which follow are designed to externalise and dramatise the threats of homophobic violence only subtextually apparent in the novel. Sean, Ari and Toula agree to go to a gay club. Ari and Toula jump in a taxi. Sean says he will meet them later. His absence from the film's most polemically charged scenes works to further Kokkinos's/Toula's appropriation of his political role in the novel. Their dope-smoking Turkish driver is stopped for running a red light and, as the policeman approaches the vehicle, Toula incites trouble, slipping Ari some pills ('A cocktail, Sugar. Something to make you fly') and then rolling down the window to hail the police in mock hysteria: 'Is there a problem here, officer?' The two proceed to giggle and Ari, high, makes pig snorting noises. The film cuts to a stark white police cell. Ari and Toula are detained on suspicion of possessing drugs. Toula's defiantly frivolous attitude is brutally punished by a vicious police sergeant. Ari's initial attempts to stand up to him are broken down when the cop puts him in a headlock and draws a gun, threatening to shoot him, then put the gun in Ari's hand, claiming self-defence. The close-up of Ari locked in the grip of the cop ironically rearticulates the earlier scene in which Ari is caught in the embrace of another patriarch, Toula's father. The Sergeant then orders a strip search – a humiliating procedure for Toula as exposure forces a psychic conflict between his/her feminine identification and a still masculine body. When s/he refuses to remove underwear, the Sergeant baits his nervous young Greek-Australian subordinate into bashing Toula. The Sergeant, who has earlier antagonised the younger cop by asking him whether Toula is not also his wife's name, proceeds to mix racism with homophobia, ordering the younger cop to physically force Toula to strip, seeing 'you know them so well'. When Toula remains defiant and screams abuse in Greek, the younger cop, in a frenzy, rearticulates abuse directly similar to that of Toula's father and bashes and kicks her. Ari looks on in tears but is bolted to the spot by the Sergeant's taunting menacing gaze. Buchbinder's trope of an 'undeclared police-state mentality among men, establishing guidelines of attitude, behaviour and other sorts of practice' is here given graphic symbolic realisation.

The film cuts to a battered Toula leaving the station, followed by Ari. He tells Toula that she should have kept quiet. Enraged, s/he responds: 'Haven't we always said that what we hate about the wogs is that they keep their mouths shut.' S/he then orders him on his knees (the debasing position to which, in sexual encounters with other Greek men, he must be forced) and comments: 'every time you keep quiet that's where you stay'. Ari argues that he has 'his own truth'. Toula chastises him: 'you have to stand up against all the shit and all the hypocrisy, that's the only way to make a difference'. Ari seems chastened and wants to accompany Toula, but she refuses the offer, saying that 'Toula can take care of herself'. In a telling deconstruction of gender binarisms, the feminine-identified Toula emerges as hard and courageous; the masculine-identified Ari as soft and timid.

Many of the confrontational political lines in Toula's key scenes are reworked recitations from the novel – including, most significantly, a key section in which Ari recollects the occasion when Johnny performs 'Toula' for the first time:

> He went off into the bathroom and emerged, twenty minutes later, in a red dress, thick make-up, his hair in a bun, looking like a woman in a black and white photograph, a scared young woman on foreign soil. What do you think? he asked me. I groaned. Johnny, Johnny that's too much.
>
> I'm disappointed in you Ari, he retorted. Never, ever, ever think anything is too much … Haven't we always said, he continued that what we hate about the wogs is that they are gutless? … Don't die on me Ari, he implored me, don't become like the others. I took his hand and led him out of the lounge room and his father stood up and started yelling at him. Johnny ignored him and I tried to hide in a corner … Yianni, he screamed, you go out like that, you go out like that you slut, and I promise you, Yianni, I'll fucking kill you. Johnny didn't flinch, didn't make a sound as the bottle smashed on the wall next to him. I'm not Yianni he told his father, slowly, deliberately, Toula is back. He spat at his father. Toula is back from the grave papa … I waved goodbye to Johnny's father, wanting to say something to wipe away the man's shame, staying silent because there was nothing I could say; and walking out into the twilight, Johnny on my arm.

For Ari walking out of the house with Johnny dressed as Toula is one of 'Five transcendental moments in my life'.[34] Tsiolkas's Ari, even if ambivalently positioned, is braver than Kokkinos's Ari, who is overpowered for the rest of the film by Toula's gutsy exit. In the film, the confrontation with Sean is rendered in an almost wordless, failed sexual encounter ending in a fist fight, with Sean kicking Ari out of his flat, angry at his failure to commit fully to the encounter he has prompted.[35] This rewriting of a more vocal novel scene, although powerful, gives further emphasis to Toula as the film's ethical centre. It also undermines some of the novel's concerns with the tension between sexuality and ethnicity in regard to disclosure.

Instead of turning full circle and returning Ari to his home in the early morning, the film closes as he dances in front of the bay – a scene reworked from the section 'South' – proclaiming that he is 'sinking into the sewer', that he is 'a sailor and a whore and will be till the end of the world'. During this scene Kokkinos interpolates (as she has done on several earlier occasions) old black-and-white documentary footage of Greek migrants disembarking in Australian ports. Ari's voice-over continues: 'I'm going to live my life. I'm not going to make a difference. I'm not going to change anything. Nobody is going to remember me.' Part of the documentary footage includes a young mother and child. A still of this pair has been highlighted earlier in the scene in Johnny's bedroom where he has been transforming himself into Toula. The repetition emphasises that Toula, unlike Ari, will make a difference.

The mother/son portrait gives a visual realisation of the image used to liken Johnny to his mother in the novel: 'looking like a woman in a black and white photograph, a scared young woman on foreign soil'. One of the dangers of Johnny's recitation of his mother Toula is that he will also be a victim – trapped in a destructive cycle of deference to patriarchy. Instead Kokkinos draws out Tsiolkas's initial use of the son who re-enacts his mother to effect something akin to what Dollimore has termed a transgressive reinscription: 'a turning back upon something and a perverting of it typically if not exclusively through inversion and displacement'.[36] But such inversion and displacement of the mother/Madonna continues Tsiolkas's play with loaded words. 'Madonna' is one word which undergoes affirmative resignification through repeated use in the novel. Ari recollects visiting Joe's mother after she has gone mad roaming 'the streets of Burnley screaming the Antichrist was coming'. Looking at an icon of the Madonna, he connects the suburban migrant mother with the holy Madonna, arguing that the story of the immaculate conception must have once been considered madness: 'The Madonna was mad.'[37] Eventually Ari cites his own queer Madonna, and through this citation weaves a new map suggestive of territories of desire that cross race, religion, gender and sexuality:

> Everyone has Madonna. Call her a tramp. My mum does. Call her a slut. All the boys at school did. Call her a bad singer. As if it matters. But everyone has a Madonna record. She was the first woman I saw who showed off her cunt with as much pride and bravado as a man showed off his dick. Bootlegged Madonna tapes, sent over by penpals from Australia must be

like hard currency on the streets of Tehran. I keep thinking of some young girl in full chador, her veil covering her Walkman, walking down a street, ignored by all these Muslim men, and she's listening to *Like a Virgin*, or *Justify My Love*. And going home, alone in her bedroom, touching her cunt, liking it. Bless the Madonna.[39]

Kokkinos's filmic reworking of *Loaded* carries with it the queer energies of popular culture's transgressive Madonna. Certainly the focus on Toula effects a complex criss-crossing of desire and identification not dissimilar to Judith Butler's discussion of the lesbian gaze in Jennie Livingston's *Paris Is Burning*: 'What would it mean to say that Octavia is Jennie Livingston's kind of girl?'[40] However Butler's use of *Paris Is Burning* to signal that gender performances are a risky business which may work to reinscribe the dominant is also relevant here. Like the tragic murdered drag queen Venus Extravaganza in Livingston's film, Kokkinos's Toula is subject to violence. And, more dangerously like Venus, Tsiolkas's Toula *is* possibly still partially trapped in her mother's role. In the novel Toula does not walk defiantly away but returns home to more abuse (physical and probably sexual) from the father. For Tsiolkas perhaps more than Kokkinos the possibilities of affirmative resignification must be tempered with the recognition of possible hegemonic reinscription.

It may be that the celebration of Toula carries with it the force of queer desire – to paraphrase Butler, we may consider whether she is Kokkinos's kind of girl. Here, however, we should remember that the most powerful site of tensions between sexuality, ethnicity and gender in *Head On* and *Loaded* is intergenerational conflict. If the interpolated documentary footage of migrants in *Head On* suggests a continuity between generations which bridges difference, then perhaps for a Greek-Australian lesbian director Toula provides a way of queering the mother/son relationship so that it may stand, also, for mother/daughter. The small baby clasped in the mother's arms, clad in a white smock, is after all genderless. If both *Loaded* and *Head On* offer, in differing ways, powerful realisations of contemporary queer life in Australia, then perhaps the richest queer space the two texts map out is that demarcated in the translation across media, and, through this translation, in the disarticulating leap, to borrow Sedgwick's words, 'across gender, across sexuality'.[41]

Notes

1   Judith Butler, *Bodies that Matter: on the Discursive Limits of 'Sex'* (London and New York, Routledge, 1993), p. 223.

2   *Ibid.*, p. 223.
3   Lisa Duggan, 'Making it perfectly queer', *Socialist Review*, 22:1 (1992), 18.
4   Butler, *Bodies that Matter*, p. 227.
5   Robert Reynolds, 'Living the gay life: identity and politics in twentieth century Australia', *Island*, 77 (summer 1999), 58–9.
6   Although Reynolds argues that the gains of the earlier period are too substantial for the election of the conservative Howard government in 1996 (and again in 1999) to cause significant setbacks, a somewhat blacker tone prevailed in the late 1990s. Here it is perhaps worth noting that Kokkinos's *Head On* stands on the other side of the decade form Tsiolkas's *Loaded* and hypothesising whether the addition of new scenes showing specific official brutality to gays may perhaps be interpreted in part as a reflection of concerns about less sympathetic trends.
7   Christos Tsiolkas, *Loaded* (Sydney, Vintage, 1995).
8   Karen Brooks, 'Shit creek: suburbia, abjection and subjectivity in Australian "grunge" fiction', *Australian Literary Studies*, 18:4 (1998), 87.
9   Margaret Henderson and Shane Rowlands, '"Clubs, drugs and other four letter words" : a survey of "grunge fiction"'. *Australian Women's Book Review*, 8:1 (1996), 4.
10 See Beth Spencer, 'Loaded terms', *Australian Book Review* (October 1995), 46–7, for a useful problematisation of the novel's relation to the 'dirty realism' genre, in particular in regard to the poetic use of language. Tsiolkas himself places his work more within the context of hyperrealism. See his interview with Nicola Robinson in *Australian Book Review* (October 1995), 47–8.
11 See Joan Kirby's 'The pursuit of oblivion: in flight from Suburbia', *Australian Literary Studies*, 18:4 (1998), 11–16, for an excellent account of Ari's map of Melbourne.
12 Tsiolkas, *Loaded*, p. 41.
13 *Ibid.*, pp. 143–4.
14 *Ibid.*, p. 82.
15 *Ibid.*, pp. 83–4.
16 *Ibid.*, p. 132.
17 *Ibid.*, p. 129.
18 *Ibid.*, p. 131.
19 *Ibid.*, p. 129.
20 Robinson, 'Interview with Christos Tsiolkas', p. 48. My italics.
21 Judith Butler, 'Imitation and gender insubordination' in Diana Fuss (ed.) *Inside/Out: Lesbian Theories, Gay Theories* (New York and London, Routledge, 1991), pp. 15–16.
22 Ibid., p. 16.
23 Audrey Yue, 'Colour me queer', *Australian Queer*, a special edition of *Meanjin*, 55:1 (1996), 89–90.

24 I am indebted her to Beth Spencer's recognition that Tsiolkas's play on the title word 'loaded' extends to the way in which words are 'loaded terms'. See Spencer, 'Loaded terms', p. 46.

25 Tsiolkas, *Loaded*, p. 115.

26 Spencer, 'Loaded terms', p. 47.

27 Tsiolkas, *Loaded*, p. 114.

28 Ian MacNeill, 'Some notes towards a definition of queer' included in Chris Berry and Annamarie Jagose's 'Introduction: Australian queer' in the *Australian Queer* special edition of *Meanjin*, 55:1 (1996), 8.

29 Tsiolkas, *Loaded*, p. 107.

30 *Ibid.*, p. 101.

31 David Buchbinder, *Performance Anxieties: Reproducing Masculinity* (St Leonards, NSW, Allen and Unwin, 1998), p. 131.

32 Judith Butler, *Gender Trouble* (London and New York, Routledge, 1990), p. 140.

33 *Head On* (1998): a Great Scott production in conjunction with The Australian Film Corporation. Tsiolkas was not listed on the script-writing team, although co-operative with the project.

34 Another example of this is a scene in the film between Ari and Joe's sister Betty in which Ari performs oral sex on Betty but is unable to respond sexually himself. The couple fight, Betty calls Ari a poofter and he responds by calling her 'dyke' and 'lesso', but the argument is more playful than serious as the couple are close friends. The possibility that Betty is a lesbian is never developed. Here the film also touches on but does not develop, some interesting scenes which employ Ari as a focus for explorations of a broader queer subculture – in particular involving discussions between Ari and a lesbian, Serena, whom he meets at a nightclub, and whose position somewhat replicates his own.

35 Tsiolkas, *Loaded*, p. 100.

36 In an early scene where Sean and Ari drink coffee after meeting at Ari's brother's house, Sean queries Ari about the dissimulations which he and his brother employ towards their parents, thus rearticulating George's comments in the confrontational novel scene. However, as Ari has not yet revealed his sexuality to Sean, the comments are more general in tone.

37 Jonathan Dollimore, *Sexual Dissidence: Augustine to Wilde, Freud to Foucault* (Oxford, Clarendon Press, 1991), p. 323.

38 Tsiolkas, *Loaded*, pp. 67, 69.

39 *Ibid.*, p. 123.

40 Butler, *Bodies that Matter*, pp. 135.

41 Eve Kosofsky Sedgwick, *Tendencies* (London and New York, Routledge, 1994). Chapter 1 provides a good explication of the queer cross-identifications denoted in the phrase.

9

'Hypothetical hills':
rethinking northern gay identities
in the fiction of Paul Magrs

James Knowles

When your lover is so much older than you, older than the hills, and really,
you had no idea, no conception, that you had been hoodwinked by a flesh
that is vellum and rich in a manner you thought only youth could possibly
be, you feel ... a little dwarfed in the complex shadows cast by these
hypothetical hills.

Surely in science fiction the wildly outlandish is permitted existence?
Couldn't they have come to some kind of settlement up on that mountain;
faced the truth, in the teeth of the tempest, about their feelings for each
other?

Paul Magrs, *Marked for Life*[1]

The issue of space has been one of the most pressing concerns of gay
politics during the 1980s and 1990s as debates over identity and
community have fused with the specialisation of urban spaces and the
creation of highly visible, confident, economically powerful popula-
tions.[2] Urban capitalism has shaped our identity to such an extent that it
sometimes seems that sexual citizenship has become largely a matter of
consumption, prompting questions over a problematic imbrication in
commodity capitalism, especially the 'market-mediated' cultural forms
which have produced 'institutions of queer culture ... dominated by
those with capital'.[3] Even as urban zones such as Old Compton Street
(London), the Gay Village (Manchester), the Pink Triangle (Edinburgh)
have literally and apparently concretised a visible presence in many cities,
the nature of the identity they embody has been questioned. Some critics
regard these as 'colossal closets' rather than affirmative gay spaces while
others, associated with, broadly, 'queer' politics, celebrate the possibility
of more dispersed, radicalised spaces of the 'queer (kind of) city (or
better yet kind of, cities)'.[4] These differing perceptions suggest an

economy of mutually reinforcing definitions whereby sexual identities are coded into interpretations of urban space. If gay identity and essentialism produce 'the' gay space, queer politics and constructionism produce a diverse 'perverscape' in which specific (queer) acts disrupt ordered, capitalist, civic geography.[5]

Representations of gay identities have similarly been dominated by cities from Sodom to San Francisco, and until the late nineteenth century the most pervasive sexual descriptor, *sodomite*, figured us as inhabitants of an imaginary city of the plain. Much of our fiction, especially the coming out novel (the dominant literary mode of gay writing), has depicted a sexual pilgrim's progress, from the Cave of Care to the Heavenly City, requiring the negotiation of Apollyon and Vanity Fair to find salvation in an 'out' gay identity.[6] Although these fictions have played an important part in both individual and communal identity formations, they clearly have their limitations, like the gay spaces of urban cities, leaving unrepresented those marginalised by geography, economics or ethnicity from (or within) the city. In British or, more properly, English versions these marginalisations become markedly more problematic as, despite the social reality of numerous northern gay spaces, typical English gay novels focus upon an inexorable move southwards to London.

This southwards orientation feeds upon a collocation of upper-class images which have dominated English conceptions of homosexuality. English culture is heavily marked by the association of gay sexuality with cultural 'sophistication', dissipation and decadence, aristocracy, public schools, 'Oxbridge' and, generally, elite mores. This class culture, epitomised by Forster's *Maurice*, especially as popularised in Merchant Ivory's 'white flannel' film, continues in the nostalgic, pastoral vision of modern writers such as Alan Hollinghurst. These images and ideas, which partially have their root in the nineteenth-century dandy and his Wildean appropriation, assimilate other, complex political and cultural indicators which figure London as the centre of English culture and institutions with regions, such as 'the' Midlands and 'the' North acquiring 'mythopoetic positions' as margins to that centre.[7] The association of homosexuality with elite culture and London accounts for the magnetism of the city, its more complex social structure allowing escape from 'oppressive' close-knit communities of the north. These powerful and pervasive myths of North and South encode a class politics which effectively disappear large sections of the community they purport to represent.

There are, however, alternative voices in English gay writing, in particular 'regional' voices which unpick the place myths of English society, articulating the views of those marginalised by the dominant class politics of gay images. This chapter concentrates on the work of one contemporary novelist who recovers some of the marginal voices within gay England, questioning the dominant political and cultural categories of English gay writing. The novels of Paul Magrs explore questions of identity, space and politics, complicating our awareness of the variety of identities and spaces for gay men and women. This more diverse vision is embodied in two interconnected elements in his fiction: northernness and a radicalised queer style. Northernness is used to disrupt ideas of space associated with conservative politics (the abandonment of the North) and with gay politics (the creation of gay spaces) and to critique both approaches to national and sexual identities. The second complicating strand aligns re-radicalised queer political strategies and style. The novels strikingly combine the fabulous and the mundane, interweaving fairy tale, myth and magic realism to furnish a fantastic northern landscape, the 'intense north-country light' which pervades the writing. Through this volatile combination of diverse elements Magrs fashions a politically and formally radical northern queer style: queer northern magic realism.

'Surrounded by exotic things': some contexts for Magrs's fiction

Born in Newton Aycliffe, County Durham, in 1969, Magrs has produced three novels, *Marked for Life* (1995), *Does It Show?* (1997) and *Could It Be Magic?* (1998), along with a collection of short stories, *Playing Out* (1997).[8] Deploying interlinked settings and characters (who enter and exit the diffuse narratives much like the soap-opera characters they often mention), the episodic plots explore events through their impact upon the life of a community and its members. The novels concentrate upon north-eastern settings (mainly Newton Aycliffe, Darlington, South Shields, Newcastle) although *Marked For Life* and *Could It Be Magic?* include scenes in Leeds and Edinburgh. These overlapping settings create a more nuanced sense of the north and north-east, providing a complexity which stands against the simplistic views of many depictions of 'the' North. The monolithic north of southern mythology is replaced by a textured North, reinforced by the reappearances of characters in new roles in later books, invoking northern society as a huge network of relations and filiations. Thus in *Marked For Life* the baroquely tattooed Mark and his relationships, first with Tony and then with Mark's wife

Sam, provides the main focus of the novel, which tells of Tony's kidnap of Mark and Sam's daughter Sally and her rescue from a strange household in Victorian Leeds. These main characters are supplemented by Sam's nudist mother, Peggy, and her lesbian lover, Iris (Wildthyme), as well as, on the fringes of the story, the figures of Liz the transvestite and her daughter Penny. The overlapping of characters continues in *Does It Show?*, where Liz and Penny become the central figures, and Vince North-spoon, Penny's English teacher, and his sometime lover Andy are woven into the narrative, and then in *Could It Be Magic?* Penny fades out as the novel focuses upon Andy and his journey to Edinburgh after his 'impregnation' by Mark and the birth of their leopard-furred child in the toilets at CC Bloom's, a gay nightclub.

Many of Magrs's fictional concerns are framed by his academic study of Angela Carter, which explores Carter's subversion of the twentieth-century male subject and male modernism as constituting 'masculinist hegemony's last stab at privileging its experience over all others'.[9] In contrast to the 'hasty patching-up of fragmented subjectivities … as objectivities' typical of male modernism, Magrs argues that Carter creates heroes who are 'precarious, contingent, self-improvising creatures who expose the performance that constitutes modern masculinity'.[10] Carter's emphasis upon performativity reinvents the gay/straight binary as a 'natural'/'unnatural' binary, just as transvestism and drag 'open up crises in categories', using gender fluidity (Carter's 'outing' of 'a self-deluding masculinist world') to question masculinity.[11] Importantly, Magrs isolates the 'plurality of worlds' in Carter's fiction, connecting style, 'the vertiginous impossibilities of the postmodern text', with her explicit political challenge to modernism and the modernist hero's fictions of objectivity and naturalness.[12]

Most importantly, Magrs's isolates the 'apocalyptic thresholds', which Carter adapts from Lawrence, as 'invitations to deconstruction and reinvention' and appropriates these liminal moments for his own fiction, as people, events and places shatter their norms and categories, reinventing themselves and their surroundings. Indeed, much of Magrs's fiction places figures in situations which subvert normative categories, as in *Marked For Life* when Sam's view that 'life was clear cut and dreams did not impede' is shattered as she finds herself, snow-bound in Leeds 'on all fronts, between states'.[13] Key narrative events occur at Christmas or New Year. For example in *Could It Be Magic?* the conception of the leopard child occurs at New Year, the moment when Liz chooses to reappear 'magically' after her absence with her bus-driver lover, Cliff. These 'spots

of time' are the moments when consciousness and events radically shift:
'It is coming on to midnight … It is the focus of the night. It is time to
think about the way the year will turn. Time concentrates the main events
as they go off – one, two, three – around the chimes.'[14]
The double allusion in this passage to both *The Winter's Tale* (the intervention of Time) and *Cymbeline* (Iachimo's nocturnal prowlings in
Innogen's bedchamber interrupted by the clock's chimes) suggest the
ways in which Magrs borrows from romance structures, with losses,
discoveries, recognitions, misrecognitions, magical interventions,
dreams, prophecies, families fragmented and reunited, strange lands,
seascapes and journeys.[15] Rather than the sea coast of Bohemia, Magrs
relocates these magical lands to the north-eastern coast, drawing upon
their mythic structures and dense, allusive style to reinvent the North.

This reinvention of North develops from both Carter's work and
Foucauldian emphases upon spatiality.[16] Carter's work is full of liminal
spaces (for instance the tundra, the circus ring, the music hall and
theatre) as well as enchanted places derived from fairy tale (the wood, the
secret chamber, the castle) and sophisticated urban geographies, such as
the complex, labyrinthine, mirage-laden city of *The Infernal Desire
Machines of Doctor Hoffman*. Carter's gendered, magical and enchanted
spaces of beauty and horror provide an important subtext to Magrs's
writing, and his understanding appears to have been influenced by her
Foucauldian spatial preoccupations and neo-Foucauldian social
geography.[17] Yet, whereas Carter's spaces tend to be mythical or historical, Magrs infiltrates greater radicalism by using real places figured in
what can only be described as a queer northern, magic realist pastoral
which disrupts the categories of north/south as part of a wider queering
of categories, straight/gay, and a deep questioning of identity politics.

Intense northern light: rewriting the North/South myth

'You haven't been to London much,'…

'No,' I say knowing full well that Nanna Jean can't see the point of
London or the south of England at all. The south is where she has to pass
through on her way to travel the world. Gatwick, Heathrow, these are the
south to her and they are just waiting rooms, stepping stones. Everything in
the whole world, she says, you can find here in the northeast.[18]

This exchange between Andy and Nanna Jean in *Could It Be Magic?* establishes the connections between sexual identity and topography, associat-

ing 'queer fellas' and out sexuality with London, while questioning the very assumptions upon which such associations are founded. The 'south' represents not only 'out' sexuality but a hegemonic geography of centre and margin, figuring the north as marginal, uncivilised and unliberated, part of a Cartesian spatial politics of categories and hierarchies. The passage decentres this geography by Andy's admission that 'I have thought about moving to somewhere bigger', but northwards to Edinburgh rather than towards England and the South. This refusal of the 'place-myth' of the North also marks an uncertainty about gay identities which have grown up within this geography. Andy's own selfhood is not posited as closetedness (he is 'self-evident' as he puts it), but as an unwillingness to deracinate, to simply accept the alluring idea of 'gay village' and 'tight T-shirts, dancing every night'.[19] It is an uncertainty about the implications of gay identity politics, a sense of a different community in the north-east, full of possibilities and not simply repressions, which complicates his response.

In *Places on the Margin*, Rob Shields summarises the 'place-myth' of the North which he traces from the Darkshires and Coketowns of nineteenth-century fiction through the kitchen-sink realism of British film of the 1960s, soap opera (*Coronation Street*), to 1980s political rhetoric of the north/south divide.[20] In these differing discourses the North is imagined as homogenously industrialised and working-class, its bleak rural landscapes a foil to the tamed pastoral of the South, the home of mythical organic communities which provide a semblance of emotional support against urban and industrial anomie, and which is associated with an 'authentic' Englishness. Magrs takes many of these elements and redefines them, so that the South is no longer central (especially in the sexual geography of the novel), undercutting the image of a monolithic North and refiguring the idea of community and identity which are so central to the mythic North.

The figure most clearly associated with the South, Vince Northspoon, appears in *Does It Show* and *Could It Be Magic?*, first as Penny's English teacher and then as Andy's lover. In *Does It Show?* he introduces Forster's *A Room With a View*, a novel which embodies not only the sexuality of the Italian south but also a southern English viewpoint. He views Aycliffe as 'circumscribed' and stuck in the 1950s, encouraging Penny to escape to college, and viewing his own return as a failure.[21] In the later *Could It Be Magic?* this desire to leave becomes more insistent ('I do have to go south'), and Vince reappears only as a disembodied telephonic voice from Paris. This Paris is stripped of its romantic associations, becoming a 'smart art-house movie with subtitles', linking Vince firmly to elitist cultural views, only confirmed by his new lover's status as 'a Jane Austen expert'.[22] The literary references both locate Vince as someone 'happier with his lover inside the book', and by combining Austen and Forster suggest an enclosed, claustrophobic, repressed emotional and social landscape.[23] Through these literary co-ordinates, neatly encapsulated by Virginia Woolf as 'beauty imprisoned in a fortress of brick and mortar', Magrs distances his writing from the tamed pastoral of southern England, and more particularly from the gay culture associated with Forsterian fiction.[24]

Vince's position as an English teacher links him to the authorised, literary myth which associates the South with culture and the North with industry and labour. Yet the novels' careful treatment of different northern locations – Leeds, Darlington, Newton Aycliffe, Durham – giving each a particular identity rather than a generic northernness, critiques this cultural myth of northern homogeneity. Indeed, in *Could It Be Magic?* this homogenised view is associated with the schizophrenic religious education teacher, Tom:

> I'm not even from Newton Aycliffe, he thought, but he recognised it as a place that always drew him back. No one actually came from that town … It was too young. It was a place that took people in and made them all the same. You had to go to the same shops. It made no one better than anyone else. It dulled the goodness out of people.[25]

Tom embodies the authoritarian, hierarchicised view which produces 'the North', associated with religion, the education system and vocabulary used to control.[26] In contrast, Fran (one of the figures in *Could It Be Magic?* who bridges the modern new town and the old country life) perceives Newton Aycliffe in more complicated terms which unpick the homogenising voice of the northern place myth. Her Aycliffe oscillates between the present and the past, illusion and reality:

> Newton Aycliffe was an illusion. It only looked urban. You could walk off the edge of the estate, through the trees, and then you were in the middle of a blond, green, leafy nowhere. The sky was huge. Aycliffe came from Aclea, a clearing in an oak wood … The old village of Aclea, a thousand years old, lay underneath Aycliffe town centre, which had lasted only fifty years. They had roots here after all.[27]

Fran's awareness of the older community beneath the new and the sense of 'rootedness' reveals Aycliffe's history, encompassing a distinctly magical past, which subverts the modern 'illusion' of urbanism.[28] Instead of the homogeneity of modern urbanism, the 'leafy nowhere' reveals a complex layering of the past reminiscent of Lawrence's sense of Nottinghamshire in the 1930s as 'still the old England of the forest and the agricultural past ... the mines ... were an accident on the landscape, and Robin Hood and his merry men were not very far away ... life was a curious cross between industrialism, and the old agricultural England, Shakespeare and Milton, and Fielding, and George Eliot'.[29]

In *Marked For Life* the multiple inhabitants, functions and meanings of Aycliffe are also invoked (Roman conquest, Tudor agrarianism, Victorian industrialisation), but in a fashion which prevents simple nostalgia as the Roman zone of military occupation, becomes 'bleak pasture' and then industrialises, the 'inadequate mechanism' and 'inauthentic ticking' of a malfunctioning alarm clock inserted into the landscape.[30] Unlike Lawrence's vision of the Midlands which focuses on a utopian nostalgia for past organic community (invoked in the literary tradition), Magrs avoids either nostalgia or progressivist adulation of the present ('This is now, and it's terrifying enough'), creating, instead, an awareness of a layered space, full of complexities and contradictions, in which traces of past spatial semiotics supplement current, reductive meanings and functions. Most importantly, the energies of the landscape, like those which seep out of the Tube station in Woolf's *Mrs Dalloway*, 'bubbling up from somewhere' in *Could It Be Magic?*, disrupt the categories imposed by urbanisation, by the planning authorities and cartographers. They are all 'illusion'.[31]

The subversion of northern space myths through the creation of a multiple, layered, complex location is developed by the use of Aycliffe to challenge the mythic organic communities of soap opera and northern realism.[32] As a new town built in the 1950s and 1960s, initially to provide labour for armaments production and then supplement the declining coal and steel industries, it encapsulates the utopian and socialist ideals of planned communities promoting equality, while their social reality, especially after the Thatcherite deflation of the early 1980s, is more mundane, with the ever-looming threat of low wages and unemployment.[33] These threats are all registered in the novels, but the Phoenix estate retains a communal sense, though shorn of the idealist rhetoric of the northern myth. Like Fran many of the characters either half-realise or articulate how 'something ties me here'.[34] This movement away from the mythic organic community is perhaps best embodied in the reassessment of the family as a symbol of local community as Magrs constantly undermines the 'ideal' of the normative, natural family: 'I hate to tell you there's no such thing as a normal family.'[35] Indeed, the assumption that

normative families will reproduce a stable society is questioned, both by
the economic reality shown to cripple many families and by the violence
of the nuclear family which produces alienated, thuggish youth.[36] In
contrast, a more diverse and inclusive sense of family pervades the novels,
and in *Marked For Life* the 'postmodern Valkyries', Peggy and Iris, 'rig up'
a Valhalla, a northern alternative to the Christian heaven restricted to
'legitimate family', which includes 'family members of the most illegitimate kind. Old dykes, tattooed faggots, divorcees, co-opted coppers, the
lot'.[37] Similarly, Nanna Jean, a recurrent figure throughout the novels and
the short stories, deploys a fiercely protective supportive maternity, so
that Andy comments, 'Even though an orphan, how well I was parented'.[38]
These extended, constructed, and non-natural families operate more
successfully than the more apparently 'normal' nuclear families,
imagining the possibility for families built upon bonds of kindness and
affection rather than blood.

These versions of the North refuse the myths of homogeneity, of
organic community, of marginal position and cultural subordination,
but they also represent Tyneside and Teesside as ambivalent places. *Does
It Show?* includes a graphic queer-bashing and all the novels refuse to
gloss over prejudices such as Elise's, who refers to 'ponce[s]' and 'shirt-
lifter[s]'.[39] Yet the novels are also full of strange alliances and moments of
unexpected beauty and tenderness. Thus Craig, a figure who symbolises
disaffected, potentially violent youthful masculinity earlier in *Could It Be
Magic?*, journeys north to see Andy and his leopard-child, fitting into
Edinburgh life even though Andy looks 'queer as fuck'.[40] This friendship
between a 'hulking, muscle-building brute' and a gay dad proposes a far
more fluid set of relations between gay and straight cultures, which does
not simply suggest the assimilation of either position, but which complicates both, provoking both wonder and a wry humour instanced in their
trip to the Botanical Gardens: 'He [Craig] stared at the lilies. It was funny.
He's no queer, perhaps, but I've still got him spending afternoons looking
at flowers.'[41]

Craig's transformation from thuggishness to sympathy suggests the
fluidity of identity within the North, a point stressed by the use of
journeys in Magrs's fiction. The journey, which can be seen as a metaphor
for coming out and the progressivist notions of history which have often
accompanied identity politics, assumes a more ambivalent function in
Magrs's hands.[42] This difference is developed in Andy's juxtaposition of
southern and northern journeys on the London Tube and the Tyneside
Metro:

Whenever I have been in London it surprises me how young and busily energetic all the commuters are. Nervously watching stations notch by. The ladies on the Tyneside Metro system spin their train journeys out. They want to miss their stations on purpose for the fun of going back the way they've been.[43]

Whereas it might be possible to interpret the Metro journeys as signs of the emptiness of life, instead these embody 'the fun of going back', while the stressed London commuters miss the joy of journeying in pursuit of their ends. Indeed, this figure is extended in the journey to Edinburgh which replaces the typical southwards journey to London and liberation for a northwards voyage to enlightenment in a city of hills, sea and light.[44]

This image of Edinburgh is, however, blurred as the city's double nature is stressed. Thus the city of the Scottish enlightenment is also Old Reekie ('This city is filthy. I am sunk into its dirt. It is everywhere and I am included') and even represents degradation through the image of the urine-stained drunk who haunts one of Andy's city dreams.[45] This contradictoriness is also expressed in the city's gay culture. Thus, sitting in a bar, Andy surveys the two visions of gay community offered by the *Pink Paper* and *Boyz*: 'One's full of rape stories and legislation, the other has pictures of soap stars and underwear.'[46] His sexual encounters also range from a teacher who tastes of olives (clearly living in the New Town) to the label-obsessed Cameron.[47] Cameron belongs to the new generation of gay men, e-driven ('he fucks like he dances when he's E'd out of his head. Endlessly and noisily and without satisfaction'), body-fixated and dedicated to sexual and material consumerism.[48] On one hand Cameron's materialism grates, especially when at one point he indignantly reminds Andy his home is a 'private estate' not council owned, yet even this figure for the apparent shallowness of consumerist gay culture is recuperated by how he makes Andy feel 'a dangerously obvious queer'.[49]

The double vision of Edinburgh and its gay cultures pluralises both northernness and gay culture and identity. This reflects the ambivalences of gay identity marked in Andy's earlier conversation with Nanna Jean:

I'm not out to Nanna Jean. Whatever that means. I can't make the phrase sound right in my mouth. That I'm out to anyone is more by luck than design, I suppose. Easier just to be self-evident, no questions asked. But sometimes you want more. You want questions, interest, you want – I suppose – explicit acknowledgement.[50]

This complex response typifies the concern over identity politics which permeates Magrs's fiction. Andy is neither straightforwardly closeted nor simply an out gay man, and his own oscillations between being 'self-evident' and wanting 'explicit acknowledgment' suggest some of the complex personal negotiations involved in gay identities which modern identity politics efface. As Iris Wildthyme, the 'Mrs Orlando' of *Marked For Life*, comments, "'anyway, my being gay is not really the point. I know about gender because I've been a woman and a man, in the course of a terribly long life.'"[51]

Fixed states like fixed topographies are constantly undone in these fictions which celebrate limens, boundaries, doubleness and metamorphoses. Thus even Andy's movement to the city which echoes gay coming out fictions subverts their conception of arriving in a fixed city/state of identity. Instead this ambiguous northern city offers Andy 'autonomy', but also continued transformation and movement:

> You live in that city of yours. It's cold and heaving with busyness and noise. The place where you live is dirty and you never have everything you want … But what freedom you've got, our Andrew! I can hardly believe it. You're in a place where anything can happen. The way you live, you're only ever a few steps from something new.[52]

Not only does this northern, Scottish city reject the southern, English hegemony, offering a more complex understanding of the utopian possibilities of the gay urban experience, importantly this city is not one of arrival and stasis but rather it involves the potential for change and for further journeys: 'you're only ever a few steps from something new'. Unlike popular gay fiction in which the point is to arrive, here the purpose is to travel.

Emerald palaces: towards a northern queer gothic

> Consider the nature of a city. It is a vast repository of time, the discarded times of all the men and women who have lived, worked, dreamed and died in the streets which grow like a wilfully organic thing, unfurl like the petals of a mired rose and yet lack evanescence so entirely that they preserve the past in haphazard layers, so this alley is old while the avenue that runs beside it is newly built but nevertheless has been built over the deep-down, dead-in-the-ground relics of the older, perhaps the original, huddle of alleys which germinated the entire quarter. Dr Hoffman's gigantic generators sent out a series of seismic vibrations which made great cracks in the hitherto immutable surface of the time and space equation.[53]

In Angela Carter's *The Infernal Desire Machines of Doctor Hoffman* the 'obtusely masculine' city transforms from a space of hierarchies and 'determination' into the 'arbitrary realm of dream' where 'complaisant avenues and piazzas were suddenly as fertile in metamorphoses as a magic forest'.[54] This eruption of the fantastic into the mundane equally characterises the fictions of Paul Magrs, as new towns become magic forests and a stuffed leopard from the taxidermist's shop in Darlington roams the dream-streets of Edinburgh. Like Carter, Magrs draws on a extensive range of fairy tales and upon the vocabulary of the fantastic to subvert realism, and in particular the gritty realism associated with northern fiction and film. The style has many affinities not only with Carter but with gothic fiction, a mode especially associated with gay identities.[55] Whereas, as Eve Sedgwick and Patricia Duncker have argued, the trope of the unspeakable and the 'destablisation' of the relation between sex and gender form the dual centres of gothic writing allowing a fictional sexual visibility refused by social norms, Magrs's northern queer gothic uses its fantastic elements, the sense of the 'outlandish', to permit the existence of northern queer spaces and identities outside either the southern place myth or the categories of identity politics.[56] In effect, Magrs redirects Carter's gothic to be more explicitly queer by locating her fairy-tale spaces in the North (echoing, of course, earlier gothic novels such as *Frankenstein*) and emphasising the fluidity of sexual rather than gender identity.

The pervasive influence of fairy tales as expressions of the fantastic, arbitrary dreamworld which suffuses and enchants the North emerges as the leopard-child views Aycliffe as 'something fantastic … [and] magical out of a book, like the Emerald Palace in the Land of Oz'.[57] Similarly, in *Marked For Life* Liz and Iris's house becomes a 'magic circle' which protects the lovers from outside (male) interference and the desire of 'wolves – pencils, clipboards twitching' to define and confine them.[58] This space has existence both in the real world, a cottage which represents refuge for two elderly, single women – half-jokingly seen as a practical solution to the 'problem of single and unwanted pensioners' – yet also a 'magic circle'. This image describes the power of imaginary places, communities created between people, to create a space for themselves, in this case 'a living Georgia O'Keefe exhibition! Cunts everywhere.'[59]

This creation of a magical northern space filled with the fantastic and the 'arbitrary realm of dream' also orders the narrative style and structure of the novels. In part, Magrs defines his writing style in antithesis to other sexual and topographical narratives. In *Could It Be Magic?* Nanna Jean visits Shields museum, a 'Catherine Cookson Country' which consists of 'reconstructions' of 1930s Tyneside.[60] This simulacrum, which has bled the life out of the lived experience, just as Cookson's 'gritty' northern realism has leached the political energy from the Victorian tradition, symbolises not only the total loss of the old ('before modernisation') Tyneside, but the substitution of heritage for heavy industry. The 'reconstructions' in the museum suggest the falseness of this vision of northernness which reduce the history of the region to a washed-out unitary vision which occludes Tyneside's variety. Iris describes, for instance, her recently discovered black relations ('There are all sorts of connections round here') in terms of a reversed mirror image of her white Tyneside kin, bringing forward a part of north-eastern culture which is often ignored by both northern and southern writers.[61]

The arbitrariness of this dreamworld contributes to the shifting identities of both protagonists and places, creating the sense of constant liminality which is fascinating, exciting and disturbing by turns. For example, in *Could It Be Magic?* one of the women sees the tattooed Mark kissing Andy: 'There was a moment of doubt, as if she had seen something entirely fabulous, a made-up animal. And then with a bit more thought, it seemed all too obvious and real.'[62] Elsie's disoriented reaction moving between doubt, the fabulous and the real suggests the ways in which the boundaries continually shift in Magrs's fiction, a point which is developed as Andy, having been impregnated by Mark, develops leopard spots. Andy's spots absorb the magic of Mark's tattoos which themselves appear to come alive, and so his identity shifts as he moves from Newcastle to Edinburgh, becoming more recognisably queer, while beneath his clothes his muscles and spots increase so that he 'no longer felt like his own man'.[63] This gradual metamorphosis, as Andy moves towards leopardhood and back (the spots recede after the birth), suggests the fragility of the boundaries between human/animal, just as Liz the transvestite emphasises the merging of male/female and the narrative technique renders the fiction/reality boundary more permeable.

The creation of this metamorphic world, ruled by fluid continuums of identity and experience, allows Magrs to generate a queer space: strange, distorted and suffused with same-sex desire. This shiftingly queer world is symbolised by the birth of the leopard child, which not only undoes the categories of sex and gender but creates highly self-conscious queer consciousness for both the narrator (Andy) and the reader:

> The conspicuousness I felt walking around with my new child was very like what I feel, now and then, when I think people are giving me second glances and thinking, queer. What a strange and sticky comparison! I don't know

whether I feel better, if it makes queerness more normal, or whether I feel sad, because I feel doubly on show.[64]

The ambivalences of this 'strange and sticky comparison' act to desta-bilise both the situation and the reader's response, aligning notions (parenthood and queerness) which are normally separated. The breakdown of these categories and boundaries generates a sense of complex doubleness which transforms and questions our understand-ings of identity, queering the notions of gay parenting and queerness itself. Significantly, unlike the fairy-tale metamorphoses of Carter's fiction, confined to imaginary realms, these transformations occur in recognisable spaces and places, introducing the potential of the fabulous and the queer throughout our topography, rather than confining it to specialised zones.

The prevalence of dreams woven into the texture of Magrs's fiction marks another important divergence from northern realism (and also Carter's fictional models) through the use of first-person narratives. Confessional and emotional first-person narratives are the centre of both gothic fiction and the gay coming out novel and Magrs uses these forms to criticise the supposed authenticity of northern realism. The multiple, interwoven narrative voices of the novels, like the layered narrative struc-tures of gothic fiction, undermine both the stable authorial voice but also the 'authorised' viewpoint. The layering of 'unreliable' narratives and narrators and the multiplication of perspectives deconstructs the notions of authority and authenticity which underlie both northern and gay fictions. Moreover, these narrative strategies also question the literary conceptions of identity, associated with southern, elite culture, which have shaped gay identity. Magrs deliberately imports a far wider defini-tion of popular culture, drawing on references to comics, soap operas, television shows, rock and pop music, extending Carter's use of popular culture (her novels tend to be restricted to the recuperation of historical popular forms marginalised owing to their gender associations), importing forms marginalised through their class associations. Moreover, the juxtapositions of high and low culture which Magrs relishes takes on a more pointed political purpose when achieved in actual places rather than in fairy tale and fable. Although Magrs's fictions are heavily influenced by Carter's novels, his writings translate the radical potential of her fictions into new areas, producing a queer, northern magic realism which is unsettling and exciting by turns, dense with allusion yet characterised by a deft wit. Just as his academic writing brings out the queer potentials in Carter's writing, his fictions queer the North in novel ways which promise that, as gay fiction develops under a devolved political system, more various voices and a greater range of identities will be given space.

Notes

1 Paul Magrs, *Marked For Life* (London, Chatto and Windus, 1995, repr. Vintage, 1996), pp. 55 and 37. I would like to thank Professors Sue Scott and Richard Wilson for information about Lancaster University and the editors for their perceptive remarks on earlier versions of this chapter.

2 John D'Emilio, 'Capitalism and gay identity' in *Making Trouble: Essays on Gay History, Politics and the University* (London and New York, Routledge, 1992), pp. 3–16, and *Sexual Politics, Sexual Communities: the Making of a Homosexual Minority in the United States, 1940–1970* (Chicago, University of Chicago Press, 1983), pp. 247–8.

3 John Binnie, 'Trading places: consumption, sexuality and the production of queer space' in David Bell and Gillian Valentine (eds), *Mapping Desire: Geographies of Sexualities* (London and New York, Routledge, 1995), pp. 182–99, p. 185, mentions 'bars, discos, special services, newspapers, phone-lines, resorts, urban commercial districts'. See also Lawrence Knopp, 'Sexuality and urban space: a framework for analysis' in *Mapping Desire*, pp. 149–61, esp. p. 158.

4 Paul Hindle, 'Gay communities and gay space in the city', Stephen Whittle (ed.), in *The Margins of the City: Gay Men's Urban Lives* (Aldershot, Ashgate Publishing, 1994), pp. 7–25, p. 11. The queer city is imagined in Susan Golding's 'Sexual manners' from *Pleasure Principles*, cited in Bell and Valentine (eds), *Mapping Desire*, 'Introduction: orientations', pp. 16-17.

5 'Perverscapes' is coined by Bell and Valentine (eds), *Mapping Desire*, p. 16. They describe this new city: 'In the postmodern, postindustrial city, the play of polymorphous decentred exchange in polymorphous decentred landscape makes perfect sense' (p. 17).

6 On this pattern (especially in lesbian fiction) see Kathryn West, 'Get thee to a big city: sexual imaginary and the great gay migration', *Gay and Lesbian Quarterly*, 2 (1995), 253–77.

7 Robert Shields, *Places on the Margin: Alternative Geographies of Modernity* (London and New York, Routledge, 1991), p. 211.

8 For *Marked For Life* see note 1, *Does It Show?* (London, Chatto and Windus, 1997; repr. Vintage, 1997), *Could It Be Magic?* (London, Chatto and Windus, 1998), *Playing Out* (London, Vintage, 1997).

9 *Angela Carter, fiction and the subject at the* fin de siècle (Lancaster University PhD thesis, 1996). The phrase quoted is from 'Boys keep swinging: Angela Carter and the subject of men' in Joseph Bristow and Trev Lynn Broughton

(eds), *The Infernal Desires of Angela Carter: Fiction, Femininity, Feminism* (Harlow, Longman, 1997), p. 186.

10   Bristow and Broughton, 'Introduction', *The Infernal Desires of Angela Carter*, p. 18.

11   Magrs borrows this phrase from Marjory Garber's *Vested Interests* (London and New York, Routledge, 1992).

12   Magrs, 'Boys keep swinging', p. 185.

13   Magrs, *Marked For Life*, p. 176.

14   Magrs, *Could It Be Magic?*, p. 60.

15   *The Winter's Tale*, 4.1, and *Cymbeline*, 2.2.51, in William Shakespeare, *The Complete Works*, ed. Stanley Wells and Gary Taylor (Oxford, Clarendon Press, 1986).

16   Claire Hanson, '"The red dawn breaking over Clapham": Angela Carter and the limits of artifice', *The Infernal Desires of Angela Carter*, pp. 64–5, considers the influence of Foucault.

17   This may in part reflect the intellectual climate of Lancaster University in the 1980s and 1990s where the sociology of space formed an important focus, producing work such as *Places on the Margin: Alternative Geographies of Modernity* (see note 7) and Kevin Hetherington's *Badlands of Modernity: Heterotopia and Social Ordering* (London and New York, Routledge, 1997) which explores Foucauldian geographical concepts central to Magrs. The Department of English where Magrs studied was also heavily invested in critical theory, especially Foucauldian and neo-Foucauldian writings.

18   Magrs, *Could It Be Magic?*, p. 116.

19   *Ibid.*, p. 116.

20   Shields, *Places on the Margin*, pp. 207–51.

21   Magrs, *Does It Show?*, p. 31. Forster also frames Vince's sense of failure and his own limitations, as his father, having read Vince's copy of *Maurice*, awkwardly offers a commercialised soft-porn image as an attempt to broach his son's sexuality (*Does It Show?*, p. 150), connecting Forster with the commercialisation of gay images. In an earlier dream sequence in the same novel Penny is told, 'That was E. M. Forster. This is real life' (p. 102).

22   Magrs, *Could It Be Magic?*, pp. 29 and 57.

23   Magrs, *Could It Be Magic?*, p. 57.

24   Virginia Woolf, 'The novels of E. M. Forster', *Atlantic Monthly*, 115 (1927), 642–8, reprinted in Philip Gardner (ed.), *E. M. Forster: The Critical Heritage* (London, Routledge, 1973), p. 321.

25   Magrs, *Could It Be Magic?*, pp. 142–3.

26   *Ibid.*, p. 9. Significantly, the discourse of educated authority is here attached to an insane male, radically undermining its claims to objectivity.

27   *Ibid.*, pp. 279–80.

28   Aycliffe means 'oak wood' (ac = oak; leah = wood in Old English), or possibly clearing in an oak wood: see Adrian Room, *Dictionary of Place*

Names in the British Isles (London, Bloomsbury Books, 1988). Oak clearings were often Druidic sacred sites. The area's Roman heritage is also stressed as in *Magic*, p. 120.

29 'Nottingham and the mining countryside' cited in Shields, *Places on the Margin*, p. 211–12.

30 Magrs, *Marked For Life*, p. 60.

31 Magrs, *Could It Be Magic?*, pp. 61 and 279, and Virginia Woolf, *Mrs Dalloway*, ed. Claire Tomalin (Oxford, Oxford University Press, 1992), pp. 105–6.

32 Newton Aycliffe is a residential community of some twenty thousand inhabitants built to supply labour first for Royal Ordnance and then for light industry on the nearby industrial estate. It was the first of the County Durham new towns (designated in 1947). See P. Bowden, 'The origins of Newton Aycliffe' in Martin Bulmer (ed.), *Mining and Social Change: Durham County in the Twentieth Century*, (London, Croom Helm, 1978), pp. 202–17, and also 'Newton Aycliffe: the politics of new town development' in John C. Dewdney (ed.), *Durham County and City with Teesside* (Durham, British Association for the Advancement of Science, 1970), pp. 454–63.

33 This trend is most pronounced in the third novel, *Could It Be Magic?*, where the household of disruptive boys imagine themselves as a 'super-team' of 'super-heroes' (p. 60), while Fran also becomes deskilled, ending up cleaning for Fujitsu (p. 280).

34 Magrs, *Could It Be Magic?*, p. 33.

35 *Ibid.*, p. 188.

36 *Could It Be Magic?* alludes to Rosemary and Fred West (p. 184), suggesting how the so-called normative, nuclear family can become a site of horror and abuse.

37 *Marked For Life*, pp. 161 and 163. 'Cold companionable streams' in *Playing Out* is narrated by a Valkyrie.

38 Magrs, *Could It Be Magic?*, p. 250.

39 *Ibid.*, p. 275.

40 *Ibid.*, p. 267.

41 *Ibid.*, p. 269.

42 For instance in *Marked For Life*, p. 150, the snow-bound journey makes the traveller a 'parody of an old-time wayfarer' although the idyllic image of 'falling gently asleep beneath spread branches' is rapidly replaced by the 'disenfranchisement' of the homelessness which menaces everyone: 'It's easy to slip from the orbit of your life.'

43 Magrs, *Could It Be Magic?*, p. 118.

44 *Ibid.*, pp. 255–6.

45 *Ibid.*, p. 271.

46 *Ibid.*, p. 216.

47   *Ibid.*, p. 221. As John Binnie notices, *Boyz* is itself highly ambivalent, 'promoting a self-conscious consumerist ethic among gay men while simultaneously giving advice on how to take control over one's own bodies and make informed choices about life on the scene' ('Trading places', p. 196, see note 3).

48   Magrs, *Could It Be Magic?*, p. 223.

49   *Ibid.*, p. 226.

50   *Ibid.*, p. 116.

51   Magrs, *Marked For Life*, pp. 60 and 159.

52   *Could It Be Magic?*, pp. 288 and 253.

53   Angela Carter, *The Infernal Desire Machines of Doctor Hoffman* (London, Rupert Hart-Davis, 1972; repr. Harmondsworth, Penguin Books, 1982), p. 17.

54   *Ibid.*, pp. 15, 18 and 17.

55   Eve Sedgwick, *Between Men: English Literature and Male Homosocial Desire* (New York, Columbia University Press, 1985), pp. 91–4, and Patricia Duncker, 'Queer gothic: Angela Carter and the lost narratives of sexual subversion', *Critical Survey*, 8 (1996), 58–68, esp. p. 58.

56   Sedgwick, *Between Men*, p. 94, and Duncker, 'Queer gothic', p. 61.

57   Magrs, *Could It Be Magic?*, p. 327.

58   Magrs, *Marked For Life*, p. 52.

59   *Ibid.*, p. 51.

60   Magrs, *Could It Be Magic?*, p. 119.

61   *Ibid.*, p. 121.

62   *Ibid.*, p. 85.

63   *Ibid.*, p. 148.

64   *Ibid.*, pp. 246–7.

Part III

Challenging limits/ crossing boundaries

10

Transgender and les/bi/gay identities

Alan Sinfield

In the metropolitan sex/gender systems of North America and North-western Europe, the years since Stonewall and the women's movement have afforded good opportunity to those who have wanted to be what we have come to recognise as gay and lesbian. We have developed significant institutions, and the beginnings of a legal framework and a climate of opinion where we may express ourselves without too many restraints. But every identity is an exclusion as well as an inclusion. For those who have felt themselves to be engaged with dissident passion but somewhat to one side of the metropolitan identities, gay has been a constraint rather than a liberation. In *Gay and After*, I broached the thought that 'gay' as we have produced it and lived it since 1970 and thereabouts, and in large degree 'lesbian' also, are historical phenomena. They may now be hindering activists and analysts more than they help us.[1]

Shinjuku boys

Even as I was working on those thoughts, issues around transgender[2] were coming into view. Leslie Feinberg in *Stone Butch Blues* and Kate Bornstein in *Gender Outlaw* wrote powerful and successful books based on their experience.[3] Academic studies appeared. And the popular media are following close behind. By early 1999 Polly Toynbee was writing in *Radio Times* (13–19 February) that 'programme after programme seems to be obsessed with people of confused, indeterminate or wrong sex'. She mentions a transsexual prostitute in the BBC1 series *Paddington Green*, a transsexual in Granada's soap opera *Coronation Street* (whose request that hir partnership be blessed by the church was made to coincide with Easter) and a programme in the BBC1 science series, *QED*. 'There is a questioning and a redefining of sex roles going on and these cases are just the most extreme manifestations of a more general and diverse debate', Toynbee avers.

Other television programmes have explored transgender in countries relatively detached from the metropolitan sex/gender system. *Lady Boys*, directed by Jeremy Marre (Channel 4, 1992), is a documentary in an apparent first person about transvestite and transsexual cabaret performers in Thailand. *Midnight Dancers*, directed by Mel Chionglo (Channel 4, 1994), is a violent 'docudrama' about three Filipino brothers, male prostitutes, one of whom takes a transvestite lover. Sometimes such far-flung instances of sexual dissidence have been cited as evidence that we – we metropolitan les/bi/gay people – were always there. They seem to me more intriguing than that. They offer windows on to alternative sex/gender systems, signs of the radically different ways in which people can conceive their subjectivity and focus their desire.

The television film *Shinjuku Boys* is a Twentieth Century Vixen production for BBC TV, 1998, produced and directed by Kim Longinotto and Jano Williams. At Club Marilyn, in Shinjuku, Tokyo, the hosts are all *onnabe*: transgendered people, in varying degrees of female-to-male change, and the customers are all women. The programme focuses on three of the sex workers, Gaish, Kazuki and Tatsu.

In the metropolitan sex/gender model, the immediate assumption is that *onnabe*s and their partners must be positioned as 'lesbians' – women loving and desiring women sexually. That is how I myself tried to read the film when it was shown. However, the whole point for Gaish is that s/he just doesn't feel like a woman. Hir image of a girl 'is really weak and helpless', whereas s/he is 'strong and straightforward'. Tatsu also sees hirself as male, and is having hormone injections. 'You want to keep a bit of the girl in you,' s/he is told by hir hairdresser; 'Most customers say I'm like a man', Tatsu replies; that's what they come to Club Marilyn for. 'Most of the girls I have relationships with say I'm not a woman at all', Gaish reflects.

Gaish insists on a firm distinction between lesbians and *onnabe*s:

> When lesbians have sex – I've never seen it so I don't know – but I've heard that both women take their clothes off. With us, we are the man, we don't regard ourselves as women … My body is not a man's, so I don't want her to see it … Whatever I do, my body can't change – I'll never be a real man. So I don't want to be touched and I don't want to be seen.

Tatsu says: 'For us *onnabe*, when we have sex, we hate to take off our clothes and show our bodies.'

For the *onnabe*s and their customers, gender is prior. There are implications for sexuality, but it is not the category through which they intuitively interpret themselves. Their concern is with the maleness of the *onnabe*. When Gaish goes with 'an ordinary girl', s/he thinks: 'If this girl is letting me do this, then I've fooled her ... I know she's thinking of me as the man and she's the girl. In other words, she has accepted me as a man and I feel relieved.' Don Kulick has observed a comparable attitude among male-to-female *travestis* in Brazil. They choose their macho boyfriends not for sexual fulfilment but because having such a man reassures the *travesti* that s/he is female.[4]

The inappropriateness of slotting such gender preoccupations into metropolitan structures of 'lesbian', 'gay' and 'bisexual' is argued by Evelyn Blackwood. She found that the behaviour and self-concept of Dayan, a *tomboi* woman in West Sumatra, was 'masculine' to the point where s/he couldn't be termed a butch lesbian ('a masculine-acting woman who desired female partners'). 'S/he said s/he felt like a man and wanted to be one. I finally had to admit to myself that tombois were not the Indonesian version of butch. They were men.'[5] Dayan's identity does not derive from sexual object choice; rather, the other way round: s/he 'established a masculine identity before s/he was aware of hir sexual desires'; s/he then 'laid claim to a sexual desire for women'.[6]

In Feinberg's *Stone Butch Blues*, similarly, stone butches are loath to undress and reveal their physical femaleness. Here too, whether such people should be considered as lesbian or as somehow male is an issue. Jess has a dream which 'wasn't about being gay. It was about being a man or a woman'.[7] Generally s/he feels like neither. Theresa, Jess's lover, calls herself a lesbian and urges Jess to join the women's movement – 'You're a woman!' she exclaims. But Jess denies this: '"No I'm not," I yelled back at her. "I'm a he-she. That's different".'[8] Some of the butches seek to ratify their maleness through hormone treatment and surgery. Theresa moves out when Jess decides to embark upon this: '"I'm a femme, Jess. I want to be with a butch ... I don't want to be with a man, Jess. I won't do it".'[9]

The distinction between the butch lesbian and the female-to-male transsexual haunts Sally Munt's splendid collection *Butch/Femme*, which, evidently, started life as an assertion of gendered roles in the face of lesbian feminism, and found itself fighting on the transgender front also.[10] Butches may allude to masculinity or even masquerade as men, most of the contributors say, but their purpose is to pursue their particular ways of being women.

I was always a tomboy, but that didn't stop me knowing I was born female.
(Sally R. Munt, p. 1)

While we were butch, an identification with men would have seemed sordid.
(Sue-Ellen Case, p. 41)

We must dispel the idea that all a butch really wants is to be a man and that a femme is the real woman. A butch is a lesbian woman who moves through the world in a way that is distinct from a man or a femme.
(Jewelle L. Gomez, p. 105)

I don't want to be a man, but I love dressing up in drag.
(Dréd, interviewed by Sarah E. Chinn and Kris Franklin, p. 154)

'Who is more womanly / than the stone butch?'
(Lee Lynch, quoted by Ann Cvetkovich, p. 159)

Heather Findlay chronicles the break-up of her eight-year relationship when Sue becomes John. She is comforted by quotations from *Boots of Leather, Slippers of Gold*, indicating that while butches in the working-class mid-century bar culture cultivated masculinity, 'Yet at the same time they were not men, they were queer'.[11] The issue is whether one sees oneself, *first*, in terms of sexuality or gender.

Sex, sexuality and gender

Alice D. Dreger summarises the story so far: 'Today distinctions are typically drawn between *sex* (which is considered an anatomical category), *gender* (which is thought of as a category of self- and/or social identification), and *sexuality* (a term used to refer to sexual desires and/or acts).'[12] According to ideologies which suppose that pleasing God and continuing the species depend on the exclusive orientation of sexual desire towards reproduction, the three should correspond: men and women should have male and female anatomies and gender identities respectively, and be drawn to each other sexually. Of course, not only do the categories refuse to line up so conveniently; they prove incoherent in themselves.

This is becoming more evident all the time. It is only recently that much academic and political attention has been paid to anatomical gender and 'intersexuality' – approximately, what has been called hermaphroditism. David Valentine and Riki Anne Wilchins tell how surgeons, coming upon infants whose anatomical sex appears mixed or indeterminate, intervene to construct what they regard as more satisfactory gender characteristics. People who have undergone such physical reconstruction are often confused and unhappy. The Intersex Society of North America is demanding that medically unnecessary surgery should be deferred until the child can make an informed decision from within a supportive environment.[13] Even anatomical sex, then, is far from uncomplicated and by no means innocent of ideology.

Gay liberation, by which I mean the reconceptualising of lesbians and gay men, and lately bisexuals, in metropolitan milieux since 1970 or so, has obviously involved a rethinking of large aspects of sexuality. However, it has often been conservative on gender. Part of the claim for the dignity of gay men has taken the form of an assertion that we are masculine really; lesbians have sometimes justified themselves as accomplishing an essence of womanliness. When we have embraced transgender, as in flamboyant effeminacy and purposeful butchness, our deployment of rather narrow stereotypes has sometimes aspired to an aware and hence radical reinflection, but not always. We all know this. What I want to add is that, in the ascendancy of les/bi/gay identities, transgender has often been incorporated as a subcategory of sexual identity, rather than recognised as a kind of gender identity. To be sure, it is frequently noted that transgendered people are not necessarily homosexual. But few commentators have got far beyond remarking that fact.

Even the queer movement, which seized upon transgender as a lever with which to unseat the complacency that was perceived as creeping over lesbian and gay identities, tended to throw the pieces into the air rather than re-articulate them. The anonymous London leaflet 'Queer power now' (1991) proclaims:

> Queers, start speaking for yourself! Queers, Dykes, Fags, Fairies, Arse Bandits, Drag Queens, Trannies, Clubbers, Sluts … Call yourself what you want. Reject all labels. Be all labels. Liberate yourself from the lie that we're all lesbians and gay men. Free yourself from the lie that we're all the same.

Queer theory, inspired by Judith Butler's *Gender Trouble* (1990), embraced the idea that transgender might unsettle heteronormative notions of the naturalness of gender, but then got bogged down in whether it actually works like that (I come back to this in a moment). Overall, gender identity as a force in its own right – linked with sexual identity, but experientially and analytically separate from it – has only recently come into focus.

It has not always been thus. In other times and places it has been the other way round: transgender has been the prior concept, and same-sex passion has been presumed to be a subcategory of it. Consider the mollies of the early eighteenth century, who set up clubs, cross-dressed and took women's names. One contemporary account describes them as 'so far degenerated from all masculine deportment, or manly exercises, that they rather fancy themselves women, imitating all the little vanities that custom has reconciled to the female sex, affecting to speak, walk, tattle, cur[t]sy, cry, scold, and mimic all manner of effeminacy'.[14] This, surely, suggests a subculture organised around gender, not sexuality. For while it is plausible to regard the mollies as forerunners of our camp queen, and they were accused of being sodomitical, there is no sign of the straight-acting partners whom we would expect in the post-Stonewall, gay model.[15] None the less, Alan Bray reads the mollies as 'homosexual': 'There was now a continuing culture to be fixed on and an extension of the area in which homosexuality could be expressed and therefore recognised; clothes, gestures, language, particular buildings and particular public places – all could be identified as having specifically homosexual connotations.'[16] Rictor Norton, who emphasises in his work the continuity of lesbian and gay identities, makes the same elision.[17]

Terry Castle adduces the diaries of Anne Lister, composed between 1817 and 1824, in pursuit of her contention that the lesbian is not a recent invention. Castle may be right, but Lister surely instances dissidence of gender. She and her partners refer to her repeatedly as masculine, a man, gentlemanlike and having manly feelings, and to her feminine partners as Lister's wives and subject to her adulterous approaches. Lister fantasies herself in men's clothes and as having a penis, and models herself on Lord Byron.[18] For Norton, again, this is 'evidence that the lesbian identity existed before 1869'. However, as Judith Halberstam points out, it makes better sense to regard Lister as transgendered.[19] Generally in the nineteenth century, George Chauncey, Jr, has shown, gender was the prior category. 'Investigators classified a woman as an invert because of her aggressive, "masculine" sexual and social behavior, and the fact that her sexual object was homosexual was only the logical corollary of this inversion.'[20]

These arguments have manifest significance for the reading of *The Well of Loneliness* (1928), where Stephen's wish to be a man drives the plot and is allowed to govern the attitude to lesbianism. As Jay Prosser demonstrates, Radclyffe Hall's novel has always been problematic as a foundational lesbian text: 'transgender is *The Well*'s stumbling block, that which must be "worked" if the novel is to [be] made sense of as lesbian'.[21] Of course, Hall is drawing on ideas from the sexologists, who persistently tangle together transgender and homosexual desire. Karl Heinrich Ulrichs puts into circulation the idea of having the soul of a woman enclosed in a male body. Richard von Krafft-Ebing and Havelock Ellis, even while noting that same-sex passion and transsexualism do not necessarily coincide, suggest continually that the gender invert is the most complete type of homosexual. 'Hermaphroditism represents the extreme grade of degenerative homosexuality', Krafft-Ebing declares.[22]

The priority of gender was challenged by Ellis, and then by Freud. David Halperin credits these two with a key discrimination in the development of gay identity: 'That sexual object-choice might be wholly independent of such "secondary" characteristics as masculinity or femininity.'[23] In *Three Essays on the Theory of Sexuality* (1905) Freud dismisses as crude earlier theories of innate inversion, and refuted the anatomical basis they had been claiming. Even a transferral of 'mental qualities, instincts and character traits' cannot be demonstrated, let alone a physiological cross-over.[24] However, Freud cannot entirely resist the thought that gender and object choice might line up, specially in the case of women. Among them, he says, 'the active inverts exhibit masculine characteristics, both physical and mental, with peculiar frequency and look for femininity in their sexual objects – though here again a closer knowledge of the facts might reveal a greater variety'. And in a note added to the *Three Essays* in 1920 Freud posits the existence of two types of male homosexuals, as Sandor Ferenczi had proposed: '"subject homo-erotics", who feel and behave like women, and "object homo-erotics", who are completely masculine and who have merely exchanged a female for a male object'.[25]

So by the mid twentieth century sexuality, defined by object choice, was becoming the prior category. But it had still not entirely escaped from gender. Transgender is becoming the subcategory, only obscurely perceived in itself, returning to disturb the clarity with which sexuality is purportedly described.

The consequent confusion is located by Chauncey in New York in the 1930s. Still men were not divided primarily into 'homosexuals' and 'heterosexuals'. A man displaying a committed feminine manner got called a fairy, but 'the "man" who responded to his solicitations – no matter how often – was not considered abnormal, a "homosexual", so long as he abided by the masculine gender conventions'.[26] Then middle-class men, initially, who identified themselves by sexuality started to call themselves 'queer', as opposed to the fairies who identified by gender attributes; the idea was to assert that you could be queer without being a fairy. However, during the Second World War in the USA, Donald Webster Cory reports, a sailor was still able to assume that 'the stranger who performed fellatio' was 'homosexual', but not 'the man on whom it was performed'. 'The performer was a "fairy". The compliant sailor, not.'[27]

My case, then, is that it is gay liberation that settles decisively upon sexuality, rather than gender, as the prior category in general perception. While our forebears held a confused idea of same-sex passion because they tried to incorporate it into gender identity, we have found it hard to see transgender clearly because we have tried to read it as a subcategory of les/bi/gay identities.

A further question then appears: in gay liberation, who was liberated? Not the kind of gay man whose effeminacy was tantamount to transgender, for he was always visible. Quentin Crisp in *The Naked Civil Servant* (1968) says that people such as he 'must, with every breath they draw, with every step they take, demonstrate that they are feminine'.[28] Crisp was never not-out; continually he is propositioned, harassed and beaten by total strangers. Employers and the army reject him on sight.

Kenneth Marlowe in another popular book of 1968, *The Male Homosexual*, posits the 'effeminate' and the 'masculine' homosexual. The former, 'because of his physical appearance, is sometimes labelled "queer" from the start of his life'. Everyone can see that he's different: his gender behaviour is out of step (it's the same with Stephen in *The Well of Loneliness*). In fact it is paternal rejection of the 'sissy' that makes the boy homosexual: sexuality is consequent upon gender attributes.[29] Meanwhile, 'the masculine homosexual', according to Marlowe, 'is usually referred to as the latent homosexual, the closet queen'.[30] Femininity correlates with conspicuousness, masculinity with self-deception and furtiveness. Todd Butler, recalling New York in 1960, makes a similar distinction: 'He did not look or act gay, which was important for me. It was unusual for somebody to be fully "out" and leading a gay lifestyle to be that butch. Usually, if you met somebody who was gay and butch, they were very uptight, closety types and very, very neurotic.'[31]

In gay liberation, it is lesbians and gays who could pass who gained the option of coming out, because now they were defined fully as homosexual. In other words, sexual orientation became prior, and gender identity was subsumed, more or less uneasily, into it. Transgender demands reconsideration of that model. While gender and sexuality are usually intertwined, either may be experientially and analytically prior, depending on the situation. It is a matter not of adding 'transsexual' to the banner, after 'lesbian', 'gay' and 'bisexual' but of envisaging new modes of categorisation.

The return of essentialism?

The strength of commitment of many transgendered people to the accomplishment of what they experience as their true selves may well raise new doubts about identity and social construction. Saskia E. Wieringa, in an essay on lesbians in Jakarta and Lima, says she has thought of herself as an anti-essentialist – accepting 'that desires are not prediscursive biological or psychological entities arising out of invariate drives'. However, her fieldwork has made her think again. She asks, first, 'how it is that individual women exhibit such levels of rebellion that they prefer to face physical maltreatment, prison, or social ostracism rather than not live their desires? Second, what forces lead to the initial setting up of deviant sexual institutions?'[32]

Such questions about the sources of dissidence have been broached in British cultural studies and in cultural materialism (the Marxist mode of analysis pioneered by Raymond Williams and Stuart Hall).[33] Cultural materialists experienced the failure, by and large, of the revolutionary movements of 1968. They read Louis Althusser's essay, 'Ideology and ideological state apparatuses' (1971), which emphasises 'a reproduction of submission to the ruling ideology for the workers, and a reproduction of the ability to manipulate the ruling ideology correctly for the agents of exploitation and repression'.[34] They asked: if our subjectivities are consti-tuted within a language and social system that is already imbued with oppressive constructs of class, race, gender, and sexuality, then how can we expect to see past that to the idea of a fairer society, let alone struggle to achieve it? As Wieringa says, it is necessary to theorise the scope for dissidence.

While this question is specially pressured in respect of transgendered people, it is not only dissident subjects who manifest extraordinary degrees of tenacity in their determination to confirm that they are who they believe themselves to be. Some people who apprehend themselves as comfortable within the dominant discourse go to extraordinary lengths to assert themselves (for example they mount homophobic attacks).

Blackwood also ponders the sources of dissidence. Our difficulties, she suggests, result from

the conflation of two distinct but interacting processes, gender as subjective experience and gender as cultural category. Viewing gender as a cultural category foregrounds the social structural and ideological processes that make it seem bounded ... Viewing gender as subjective experience exposes all the processes of negotiation, resistance, manipulation, and displacement possible by human subjects.[35]

This argument seems to disclose traces of an older, functionalist kind of anthropology, which was inclined to discover stability in the social systems it described, and of an essentialist humanism which supposes that the individual is the probable, indeed necessary, source of meaning and truth. However, as Blackwood herself amply shows, there is no reason to suppose that 'the social structural and ideological processes' are coherent, unitary and effective; or that individuals, left to themselves, will reliably intuit radical political objectives. Certainly in North-western Europe and North America, gender affords a generous site of conflict, disrupting established institutions (such as the Church of England). Many individuals, conversely, seem trapped in a narrow set of assumptions about who they might be, or become. Fundamentalist Christians in the USA, for instance, seem to have internalised a far more limited notion of their gender potential than that which is available even in 'dominant ideological discourses'.

Dissident potential – I regard this as axiomatic in cultural materialism – derives ultimately not from essential qualities in individuals but from conflict and contradiction which the social order *inevitably generates within itself*, even as it attempts to sustain itself. Despite their power, dominant ideological formations are always, in practice, under pressure, striving to substantiate their claim to superior plausibility in the face of diverse disturbances. Hence Williams's observation, that ideology has always to be *produced*: 'social orders and cultural orders must be seen as being actively made: actively and continuously, or they may quite quickly break down'.[36] This is not to say, of course, that our passions are not individual; on the contrary, it is in the individual subject that they are most entrenched.

Blackwood herself implies such a contradictory and conflicted model of cultural production when she concludes that tomboi identity 'at this point in time is a bricolage, a mix of local, national, and transnational identities'. These offer not just alternative identity-positions but unique clashes and fusions between positions. 'The complexities of their gender identity make it pointless to align tombois with any one category, whether woman, lesbian, or transgendered person.'[37] As Indonesia struggles to accommodate itself to the modernising impetus of an aggressively global capitalism, new identities become available and old ones are undermined.

*Onnabe*s also may be discerned picking their way through an unstable range of identity-positions with considerable virtuosity. It is often alleged that transvestites and transsexuals, in the logic of their commitments, must conform rigidly to gender stereotypes. *Onnabe*s are aware of this: 'It's strange, but if I'm going out with a woman I'm expected to be masculine. There's a pressure not to show any weakness', Kazuki says. However, hir relationship with Kumi, a transsexual cabaret artiste 'who started life as a man' (we see hir introduced as 'the manufactured virgin'), is generating new possibilities. 'I first realised this when I started going out with Kumi: with Kumi I can be dependent sometimes. I can cry, can't I?' Kumi is a good support for the recovery of 'feminine' traits because s/he exhibits them despite having been a man. Kumi cries sometimes as well, Kazuki says, 'and I suddenly see that she's really a woman'. (The pronouns are wild all through *Shinjuku Boys*.)

Tatsu, also, finds that hir relationship with Tomoe, hir female partner, is drawing hir into unaccustomed practices:

> Tomoe was the first one. Until then I'd never let a woman do it to me – when I had sex I didn't take my clothes off. For a woman the feel of your bodies together is important. If she's naked and I'm wearing a T-shirt she can't feel the warmth of my body. But once I'd decided: 'Right, I'll get undressed,' it was easy. She wasn't shocked. I was ashamed to show myself – I always thought a woman would be horrified to see me – I had a complex. But she accepted me as I was.

The *onnabe* prohibition on nakedness wilts before the kind of personal reassurance which we may associate with the companionate couple of metropolitan lesbian feminism. 'It's Tatsu I love, not the fact that he's an *onnabe*', Tomoe declares. But note that she still sees Tatsu as 'he'.

These developments in the practices and self-images of Kazuki and Tatsu take them well beyond the *onnabe* identity required for employ-ment at the Club Marilyn – which, significantly, doesn't like its sex workers to have steady partners. Yet we still cannot simply sort out these people as really lesbians. Their allegiances are too complicated and too distinctive. 'He's a woman who likes women', Kumi says of Kazuki; 'I'm a man who likes men. So we understand each other. On top of that, we're equals, that's why our relationship works.' 'Our relationship is sexless. We don't make love', Kazuki adds, speaking of Kumi as 'she'. 'We just play around with each other and touch breasts and kiss, that kind of thing'.

Cultural materialists generally have come to the conclusion that it is a mistake to try to decide, in the abstract, whether such disturbance of identities is inherently reactionary or progressive. As Prosser remarks, transgender has been accused by some of tending to stabilise the old sex/gender system by insisting on an essential equivalence between gender and anatomy, and celebrated by others as tending to reveal the constructedness of gender categories.[38] In the abstract, there is no deciding. It is a key proposition of cultural materialism that, in itself, nothing is either subversive or contained; the specific historical conditions in which formations, institutions and individuals organise themselves, and are organised by their contexts, must be addressed. Conceptual indeterminacy indicates a site where cultural work is being done, in the lives of individuals in communities and in cultural commentary. The outcome of that work will depend on our efforts and on the conditions in which we make them.

Speaking for myself

I am writing about *Shinjuku Boys* because I was startled and confused by my inability to assimilate the characters into a familiar paradigm. It is in the nature of my project, therefore, that it tends to exoticise the *onnabes*. I am deploying them in a contrast with metropolitan les/bi/gay identities, where I am at home. This may confirm the sense of marginality that non-metropolitan people may feel, and the sense of exile, even from their own bodies, that transgendered people may feel.

The issues that arise from such appropriative reading have been voiced around Jennie Livingston's film about black transvestite and transsexual drag performers, *Paris Is Burning* (1991). bell hooks objects that this film is shot from an unacknowledged and hence naturalised white viewpoint:

> Jennie Livingston approaches her subject matter as an outsider looking in. Since her presence as white woman/lesbian filmmaker is 'absent' from *Paris Is Burning* it is easy for viewers to imagine that they are watching an ethnographic film documenting the life of black gay 'natives' and not recognize that they are watching a work shaped and formed by a perspective and standpoint specific to Livingston.[39]

Ann Cvetkovich has argued, contrariwise, that Livingston's directorial intervention is evident, that the film has particular significance for sexual dissidents, black and white, and that it does make racism, homophobia and economic exploitation visible.[40] Judith Butler suggests that Livingston, by wielding the camera as an erotic instrument, herself assumes the power of the phallus; herself becomes a figurative transsexual. However, Prosser replies that Butler's argument displaces the materiality of transsexuality. It is a penis that these transsexuals want; they are unlikely to acquire the power to claim the phallus.[41]

Shinjuku Boys does seem to allow its subjects space to establish their own realities; they take different attitudes to their situation. Their stories are told mainly through conversations between the principals and interviews to camera with very occasional prompts. Also there are scenes with co-workers and customers, and minimal narration, spoken in English by Shuko Nogochi, a Japanese woman. Probably the net effect of each of these modes is to stake a claim for the reality of the testimony it offers. However, the juxtapositions between them are not smoothed over; they allow the viewer to see that the programme has been put together. What we are not shown is the ownership or management of the club – who is making money here.

Anthropologists have engaged with comparable questions. Of course, they no longer believe that they can observe a strange culture with scientific objectivity. To the contrary, Esther Newton has argued that an erotic dimension should be included in fieldwork narratives and that working with (potential) sexual partners can produce important insights.[42] Blackwood, who describes Dayan as her partner, explains in another essay that her lesbianism has made her specially aware that the anthropologist cannot be neutral. She describes how her sexual relationship 'with an-Other lesbian decentered and displaced me, forcing me to recognize and resist the differences between us'.[43]

All I can do, I believe, is make it plain that my accounts of other people are organised for my purposes; I am speaking for myself. This is not to say that this essay is about to stage my coming out as a transgendered person (though I do think my recognition of the topic is belated). What I have experienced often, though, is *gender disaffection* – a sense of not-belonging when men are being confidently masculine. I suspect this is widespread. A man and a woman to whom I am close each told me recently that their own sense of themselves involves such disaffection. He identifies with women because he experiences himself, habitually, as powerless; she imagines herself as a man because that matches her 'unfeminine' determination to be her own person. Neither intends by this to compromise their identity (as a gay man and a feminist). As transgender people are saying, a more precise and open awareness of gender, sexuality, and the two in combination, may inspire and support new analyses, new identifications.

Notes

1   Alan Sinfield, *Gay and After* (London, Serpent's Tail, 1998).
2   Jay Prosser explains that 'transgender' was used initially to denote a stronger commitment to living as a woman than 'transvestite' or 'cross-dresser', and without the implications for sexuality in 'transsexual'. However, the tendency now is to use 'transgender' in a coalitionary politics, to include all those subjects. In this chapter I do the latter while retaining an emphasis from the former. See Jay Prosser, 'Transgender' in Andy Medhurst and Sally R. Munt (eds), *Lesbian and Gay Studies: a Critical Introduction* (London, Cassell, 1997); Prosser, *Second Skins: the Body Narratives of Transsexuality* (New York, Columbia University Press, 1998), p. 176.
3   Leslie Feinberg, *Stone Butch Blues: a Novel* (Ithaca, NY, Firebrand, 1993); Kate Bornstein, *Gender Outlaw: on Men, Women and the Rest of Us* (New York, Routledge, 1994).
4   Don Kulick, 'A man in the house: the boyfriends of Brazilian *travesti* prostitutes', *Social Text*, 52–3 (1997), 133–60.
5   Evelyn Blackwood, '*Tombois* in West Sumatra: constructing masculinity and erotic desire' in Blackwood and Saskia E. Wieringa (eds), *Female Desires* (New York, Columbia University Press, 1999), p. 186.
6   *Ibid.*, p. 190.
7   Feinberg, *Stone Butch Blues*, p. 143.
8   *Ibid.*, p. 147.
9   *Ibid.*, p. 151.
10   Sally R. Munt (ed.), *Butch/Femme: Inside Lesbian Gender* (London, Cassell, 1998).
11   Heather Findlay, 'Losing Sue' in Munt (ed.), *Butch/Femme*, p. 143; quoting rather freely from Elizabeth Lapovsky Kennedy and Madeline D. Davis, *Boots of Leather, Slippers of Gold: the History of a Lesbian Community* (New York, Routledge, 1993), p. 183.
12   Alice D. Dreger, 'Hermaphrodites in love: the truth of the gonads' in Vernon A. Rosario (ed.), *Science and Homosexualities* (New York, Routledge, 1997), p. 49.
13   David Valentine and Riki Anne Wilchins, 'One percent on the burn chart: gender, genitals, and hermaphrodites with attitude', *Social Text*, 52–3 (1997), 215–22. See also Anne Fausto-Sterling, 'How to build a man', in Rosario (ed.), *Science and Homosexualities*.
14   From Ned Ward, *The History of the London Clubs* (1709), printed in Ian McCormick (ed.), *Secret Sexualities: a Sourcebook of Seventeenth and Eighteenth Century Writing* (London, Routledge, 1977), p. 131.

15 I make this point in Sinfield, *The Wilde Century: Effeminacy, Oscar Wilde and the Queer Moment* (London, Cassell, 1994), chapter 2.

16 Alan Bray, *Homosexuality in Renaissance England*, 2nd edn (London, Gay Men's Press, 1988), p. 92.

17 Rictor Norton, *Mother Clap's Molly House: the Gay Subculture in England 1700–1830* (London, Gay Men's Press, 1992).

18 Terry Castle, *The Apparitional Lesbian: Female Homosexuality and Modern Culture* (New York, Columbia University Press, 1993), chapter 5.

19 Rictor Norton, *The Myth of the Modern Homosexual: Queer History and the Search for Cultural Unity* (London, Cassell, 1997), pp. 196–202; Judith Halberstam, 'Sex debates' in Medhurst and Munt (eds), *Lesbian and Gay Studies*, pp. 330–2.

20 George Chauncey, Jr, 'From sexual inversion to homosexuality: medicine and the changing conceptualization of female deviance', *Salmagundi*, 58–9 (1982–3), 123.

21 Prosser, *Second Skins*, p. 136.

22 Quoted in Sally R. Munt, *Heroic Desire: Lesbian Identity and Cultural Space* (London, Cassell, 1998), p. 62.

23 David M. Halperin, *One Hundred Years of Homosexuality and Other Essays on Greek Love* (New York and London, Routledge, 1990), p. 16. See Sinfield, *The Wilde Century*, chapter 7.

24 Sigmund Freud, *Three Essays on the Theory of Sexuality*, ed. James Strachey (London, Hogarth, 1962), pp. 7–9.

25 *Ibid.*, pp. 11, 13.

26 George Chauncey, *Gay New York: Gender, Urban Culture and the Making of the Gay Male World, 1890–1940* (New York, BasicBooks, 1994), p. 13.

27 Quoted in Donald Webster Cory, *The Homosexual in America* (1951), with a retrospective forward (New York, Arno Press, 1975), p. 188.

28 Quentin Crisp, *The Naked Civil Servant* (New York, Plume, 1977), p. 21.

29 Kenneth Marlowe, *The Male Homosexual* (Los Angeles, Medco, 1968), pp. 12–13. Interestingly, Marlowe's theory of paternal rejection of the sissy boy anticipates Richard A. Isay, *Being Homosexual* (Harmondsworth, Penguin, 1993). Stephen's mother rejects her 'masculine' child in *The Well of Loneliness*.

30 Marlowe, *Male Homosexual*, p. 18.

31 Hall Carpenter Archives and Gay Men's Oral History Group, *Walking After Midnight: Gay Men's Life Stories* (London, Routledge, 1989), p. 87.

32 Saskia E. Wieringa, 'Desiring bodies or defiant cultures: butch–femme lesbians in Jakarta and Lima', in Blackwood and Wieringa (eds), *Female Desires*, pp. 206-7.

33 See Raymond Williams, *Problems in Materialism and Culture* (London, Verso, 1980); Stuart Hall, 'Deviance, politics, and the media' in Henry Abelove, Michèle Aina Barale and David M. Halperin(eds), *The Lesbian and*

Gay Studies Reader (London and New York, Routledge, 1993); John Brannigan, *New Historicism and Cultural Materialism* (London, Macmillan, 1998). The term 'cultural materialism' is used differently by the anthropologist Marvin Harris.

34   Louis Althusser, *Lenin and Philosophy and Other Essays*, trans. Ben Brewster (London, New Left Books, 1971), pp. 127–8. See Alan Sinfield, *Faultlines: Cultural Materialism and the Politics of Dissident Reading* (Oxford, Oxford University Press, 1992), chapter 2.

35   Blackwood, '*Tombois* in West Sumatra', p. 182.

36   Raymond Williams, *Culture* (Glasgow, Fontana, 1981), p. 201.

37   Blackwood, '*Tombois* in West Sumatra', p. 199.

38   Prosser, *Second Skins*, pp. 13-15.

39   bell hooks, *Black Looks: Race and Representation* (Boston, South End Press, 1992), p. 151.

40   Ann Cvetkovich, 'The powers of seeing and being seen: *Truth or Dare* and *Paris Is Burning*' in Jim Collins, Hilary Radner and Ava Preacher Collins (eds), *Film Theory Goes to the Movies* (New York, Routledge, 1993).

41   Judith Butler, *Bodies that Matter: on the Discursive Limits of 'Sex'* (London and New York, Routledge, 1993), chapter 4; Prosser, *Second Skins*, pp. 50–5.

42   Esther Newton, 'My best informant's dress: the erotic equation in fieldwork', *Cultural Anthropology*, 8 (1993), 3–23.

43   Evelyn Blackwood, 'Falling in love with an-Other lesbian: reflections on identity in fieldwork' in Don Kulick and Margaret Willson (eds), *Taboo: Sex, Identity and Erotic Subjectivity in Anthrophological Fieldwork* (London, Routledge, 1995), p. 61.

11

Why RuPaul *worked*:
queer cross-identifying the
mythic black (drag queen) mother

Seth Clark Silberman

O my body, make of me always a man who questions.
                    Frantz Fanon, *Black Skin, White Masks*

For many, RuPaul needs no introduction. And for good reason. When she became a media darling in the United States in 1993, RuPaul/Andre Charles continually introduced herself, and always with perfectly balanced repartee. Her media savvy was confirmed by *the* public approval barometer, *TV Guide*, which instructed us to 'add another leggy looker to the pack of supermodels … who are taking over TV'.[1] This supermodel did not grace *Vogue*'s cover, however. She made the image of a black gay drag queen coiffed in high glamour, tall blond hair and size 14 pumps not only palatable for mainstream audiences but embraceable. With her sashay on to television to promote her hit single 'Supermodel (You Better Work)', her homage to the fashion industry's shutter goddesses, RuPaul went to number 45 on the *Billboard* Hot 100 Singles chart and sold nearly five hundred thousand copies. 'Supermodel' did not, however, work what many suggested, an irrevocable moment heralding 'We're here! We're queer! Buy our music!' RuPaul was unable to duplicate her single success with her first album or with any song from her second (even with her own late-night talk show on VH1 to promote the latter). Her popularity marked no grand societal shift to embrace transgendered individuals; though, as Michael Musto sardonically notes, 'an army of nocturnal cross-dressers continues to step over each other's bound feet in hopes of becoming the next Ru'.[2] But then, of course, to expect sweeping, political transformation from a successfully marketed product reveals a naive understanding of the public's relation to an ideologically and discursively saturated marketplace.

A commodity first and foremost, the smartly designed CD-5 of 'Super-model' makes plain the RuPaul it sells: an image (a toothy shot working her coiled coif, her red Todd Oldham dress and her long, long legs) and a catch phrase ('You better work, bitch!'). What 'Supermodel' sold, however, remains remarkable. Its defining and inspiring moment rests in RuPaul's discursive entry into United States popular culture, the lodging of her pump in the door of the media's public sphere. Her moment still demonstrates the potential populist power of a queer politic best articulated by Teresa de Lauretis in the seminal issue of *differences* she edited, 'Queer theory: lesbian and gay sexualities'. For de Lauretis, queer theory necessarily reconfigures the marginality of homosexuality assumed by recent gay and lesbian civil rights politics. Queer theory envisions same-sexuality as no longer 'marginal with regard to a dominant, stable form of sexuality (heterosexuality) against which it would be defined either by opposition or by homology'; it 'acts as an agency of social process whose mode of functioning is both interactive and yet resistant, both participatory and yet distinct, claiming at once equality and difference, demanding political representation while insisting on its material and historical specificity'.[3] RuPaul furthered this interactive queer dialogue by drawing from the African American cultural tradition of call and response, punctuating her comedic yet pointed commentary with a sermon-like 'Can I get an amen?' She reconfigured what many assumed to be her drag *identity* bound by her body into a social *process* expressed through discourse. By thus equating identity with discourse (*you better work!*), RuPaul resists attempts to position her as other.

The accessibility of black gay drag queen RuPaul, however, was made possible by her transformation into the image of a black woman, an image influenced by centuries of representations of black women as nurturers bound up, as Sheri Parks notes, with 'Western attitudes toward women, caste/class, blackness, and fierce matern[ity]'.[4] During slavery, these images confirmed black women's innate nurturing role; during Reconstruction, they evoked a nostalgia for this peculiar institution in contrast to new representations of violent black men. Since then, they have popped up in US popular culture as mystic shamans. Characters from *Gone with the Wind* to *Ghost* – and is it any coincidence that Hattie McDaniel and Whoopi Goldberg are the only two black women to be 'rewarded' with an Oscar for these 'black mother' roles? – remind us that the black mother is the redeemer, the enabler, the nurturer. She knows secrets and solves contradictions. She understands life, death and beyond. Her mystical powers often enable her to serve as a bridge between black and white communities, often (but not always) in order to provide a happy ending for the narrative's white characters. Both western and Afrocentric creation stories echo her mystical role by describing the mother of the world as black. As Parks illustrates, the mythic black mother

> has been most prominent [in society's mythology] during periods of economic and social unrest, when the status quo conceptualizations of class, gender and race have been threatened as members of the disenfranchised groups pushed for change. Her popularity has peaked during the periods of the Civil War, the Depression, and the Post-Industrial, when she has been used as the mythic figure of transformation and deliverance from chaos back to order. Only she who knows the uncontrollable can conquer it.[5]

RuPaul echoes Parks's assessment, explaining her contemporary significance in *The Los Angeles Times*: 'We're entering the new era of glamour, and actually, I'm heralding it. Glamour is a response to the bleak 80s and a response to the whole Reagan-Bush era. That's why there's a sexy Democrat in the White House, and we're returning to what's fun and loving and … beautiful and full of color.'[6] This 'colorful', successful return to the mythic black mother, then, represents, in W. E. B. DuBois's words, a 'medium through which the two great races were united in America'.[7]

RuPaul uses this medium queerly to combine racial and sexual politics, and humorously to incorporate as many people as possible in her message. During her 8 April 1993 appearance on Black Entertainment Television (BET)'s vanguard music video show, *Video Soul,* she does both, again treating her contemporary significance as a *fait accompli*: 'In the nineties things are really happening. It's a great time to be alive; and I think things are coming to the forefront – you know, people are having to find out how they feel about their sexuality, how they feel about their parents, how they feel about whatever. And, you know, this is one thing people are having to deal with.' Immediately after her serious assessment, she humorously glows with her eyes wide open, first staring at *Video Soul* co-host Donnie Simpson then slowly turning to the camera, 'I'm not going anywhere. I will not be ignored! … Fear of a Drag Planet!' She punctuates her Public Enemy reference with a stage laugh, effectively softening, not retracting, the political significance of what she proclaims. Herein lies the queer practice of RuPaul's media presence: firmly to entrench the political in the jocular in a way that displaces or elides neither. After all, as RuPaul adds, 'every time I bat my eyelashes, it's a political act'.[8]

For *Video Soul*'s largely black audience, however, she delves deeper into 'the medium' of her image: 'you know, in America a black man can't get a hand until he puts on a pair of high heels and a wig!' Or, as she explains a few months before 'Supermodel''s release in black gay magazine *Thing*: 'I'm accessible as a black woman. Our society doesn't know what to do with a black man.'[9] Bringing together the image of the black man with the mythic black mother also illustrates the tensions Frantz Fanon identifies in the absurd residues of colonialism. To borrow from Stuart Hall, RuPaul's moment exposes the 'fixing of the Negro by the fantasmatic binaries of fear and desire which have governed the representation of the black figure in colonial discourse'.[10] These binaries, as her 'Supermodel' interviews reflect, continue to be fuelled by what Fanon perceived: the priority of the genital in relation to the Negro.[11] During every interview she was asked either coyly or directly how she hides her penis. RuPaul's common response that she would write a handbook outlining the ways to 'hide your business' playfully reveals her politic. Not only does it move the anxiety inspired by her 'invisible' penis away from her body and into a narrative, it implies that anyone can 'hide their business' like she does. Yet this discursive manoeuvring has a burden. As Fanon explains, for the disenfranchised 'to speak [with the larger society, it] means to be in position to use a certain syntax, to grasp the morphology of this or that language, but it means above all to assume a culture, to support the weight of a civilization'.[12] For RuPaul, this burden precipitated her public split into a he/she just a year after the height of 'Supermodel' with an August 1994 *Advocate* cover story. Titled 'RuPaul unmasked', the interview and accompanying photographs *sans* wig and couture were meant to release Mr Andre Charles from RuPaul, a caricature which 'left me somewhere between Pee-Wee Herman and Rozalla'.[13] Yet 'RuPaul unmasked' marked Charles in a new way, killing any further 'Super-model' musical aspirations. It identified him visually and verbally as a black gay man, a minoritising label more threatening than the persona RuPaul.

RuPaul's 'unmasking' was a failure. Mr Andre Charles has never been able to doff the alluring spectacle of RuPaul. Even in an April 1999 appearance on Barbara Walters's talkfest *The View*, sporting a suit and tie, RuPaul was still asked the same drag questions he meant to quash. Where RuPaul illustrated that the process of self-identity is a leap into a social narrative that employs seeing as a way of knowing, Charles discarded her queer epistemology for an (earnest) identity politics using a discourse of recovery, a compelling populist narrative except when what is being restored is a confident, self-loving black gay man. By acknowledging this failure I am not necessarily suggesting that Charles's official 'coming out' was a poor personal or political choice; nor am I necessarily indicting the politics of visibility and representation. What I am suggesting is that the primacy of visibility does not in itself overcome alterity; nor does it always achieve the political goals expected of it. As Peggy Phelan argues in *Unmarked: the Politics of Performance*, 'I am not suggesting that continued invisibility is the "proper" political agenda for the disenfranchised, but rather that the binary between the power of visibility and the impotency of invisibility is falsifying. There is real power in remaining unmarked; and there are serious limitations to visual representation as a political goal.'[14] After all, as Phelan rightly quips, 'if representational visibility equals power, then almost-naked young white women should be running Western culture'.[15]

I am arguing here that such a visibility/invisibility dichotomy does not account for the discursive acknowledgement of homosexuality outside contemporary gay identity politics. Such acknowledgement makes possible a queer leverage through an unmarked, but not-hidden presence that can achieve broader political gain in its lack of automatic association with ingrained societal perspectives on homosexuality. Queer presence makes possible queer semiotic play where one can 'cross' boundaries imposed by sexual identification, whether this crossing is acted upon or not. Such a queer cross-identification acknowledges the slippery terrain of sexuality where the fixed-image politics of a gay identity does not.[16] Such queer cross-identifications are already inscribed in so much of our interaction with stars in popular culture. As legendary blues and R&B singer Etta James explains, 'when you're in show business, there are many roles you have to take on. Because you've got women that buy your records; and those women gotta be just as much in love with you as the guys are in love with [female singers]. Or the girls being in love with you as much as they are [in love with] Maxwell or somebody.'[17] Herein lies the potential of de Lauretis's queer theory – not in the sloppy, sarcastic and superficial 'queer readings' scholars use to 'homosexualise' any representation they see fit, a practice which relies on the fixity of a text and its understanding. Queer theory opens possibilities within and through labels, by illuminating latent possibilities within these differences, however fleeting.

I explore here the ways in which RuPaul encourages queer cross-identification both pre- and post-unmasking. Key to both is the archetypal black mother RuPaul uses. Sheri Parks has argued that the black

mother is situated within 'the pivotal and socially explosive categorizations of race, gender, and class/caste [as well as cross-] societally-imposed
and often-dichotomized categorizations of American culture'.[18] RuPaul is
able to refashion the myth of the black mother to work for her because,
like any myth, the myth of the black mother is not fixed. Myth, as Roland
Barthes has illustrated, is the raw material that creates the 'ideas-form'
which shape culture. Myth is 'a mode of signification … not defined by
the object of the message, but by the way in which it utters this message'.[19]
Or, as RuPaul explains: 'It's not what you wear, but *how you wear it!*'
Because of her own success, RuPaul instructs the audience on *Video Soul,*
'if RuPaul can do it … you can write your own ticket.'

Yet how this audience 'writes its own ticket' changes pre- and post-
unmasking. Pre-unmasking she encourages her audience to participate in
an unnamed and queer conscious fantasy. Playing on the expectations
held for the mythic black mother in an *über*-Oprah Winfrey manner,
RuPaul offers her audience drag as a transformative process so they can
nurture themselves. RuPaul fashions herself and the power of drag as an
American Success Story: she proclaims in *Wigstock: the Movie* (1993), a
documentary about the now-defunct annual drag festival in New York:
'When I started out, right here in this neighborhood, they told me I
couldn't make it. They said, wasn't no big black drag queen in the pop
world, and you ain't gonna do it. Well, look at the bitch now!' Outside the
gay and transgendered communities she carefully navigates explicit queer
imagery using *Paris Is Burning* (1991), Jennie Livingston's documentary
of the drag balls in Harlem, as a way both to evoke and to distance herself
from 'authentic' drag queens with whom she shares the stage in *Wigstock.*
Post-unmasking she self-consciously revisits the image she proclaimed
on BET and MTV, redirecting it to a knowing audience. Fuelled by the
recognition that the USA still 'doesn't know what to do with a black [gay]
man', RuPaul's autobiography/how-to manual *Letting It All Hang Out*
(1995) and her appearance on the Don Johnson cop-show vehicle *Nash
Bridges* (CBS) exploit irony and push her populist queer politic further
than before while still employing queer epistemology for social change.
More challenging and thus less accessible to the mass audience 'Supermodel' reached, RuPaul none the less returns to and continues the dialectical vision that sparked her moment.

Her moment began on MTV in the autumn of 1992. Her first introduction to a mass US audience crystallised her transformative, self-help
message. *MTV News* sent reporter Allison Stewart (their only black
reporter) to a New Jersey mall to discuss the phenomenon of RuPaul and

the club success of the just-released 'Supermodel'. And, of course, to do a little shopping. MTV's choice of the mall was intentionally symbolic. Directed at their projected demographic of suburban white youth for whom a mall is a common denominator, it introduced the image of a gargantuan black drag queen singing about the fashion industry. The segment opens and closes with Stewart and RuPaul arriving at and then leaving the mall in a white limousine in order to reinforce RuPaul's 'otherness'. She is not familiar with, nor does she come to, the mall since MTV is bringing her there; and thus she is not part of its community. While MTV's artist profiles are often done either in performance situations (backstage, somewhere around or inside a performing venue or in a recording studio) or somewhere personal (at the artist's house, a favourite hangout), RuPaul's artist profile was filmed in a mall ostensibly because any personal or performance setting would not be as 'accessible'. It's OK to *talk* about her transgendered body – it was on this segment she premiered her line about her height, that she is six foot seven inches 'but with hair, heels, and attitude, honey, I am through the roof!'; it's even OK to make light of the absurdity of RuPaul being in the mall by showing her shopping for size 14 women's shoes to no avail; but to *see* her within the context of the gay or drag communities in which she had been performing for years prior to her Tommy Boy Music contract would 'reveal' too much. Instead, the segment provides images of her transformative powers. Starting with what became, and still is, a RuPaul convention, she instructs willing mall volunteers how to walk and serve attitude, a transformation which serves to unleash the all-powerful queen within their own 'everyday' bodies.

Part of the continued repetition of this transformation is to emphasise the skill of her drag as she explains on *Video Soul*: 'I've been in the business for 11 years but am still learning new tricks. I discovered the push-up bra last year and it *changed my life!*'; or 'Let's face it, in this business you need a shtick. Off-stage I wear jeans and a T-shirt. On stage, I look damn good in a pair of pumps and a blond wig.' Insisting upon her drag as a cultivated and studied performance akin to vaudeville, RuPaul de-emphasises the oft-assumed translation of drag as homosexuality. Mentioning *Paris Is Burning* on *Video Soul* further distances her from the assumptions ascribed to the drag queen. She confesses she 'stole' the title of her album from Octavia St Laurent, an interviewee in the film who admits she wants to become the 'supermodel of the world'.

RuPaul's strategic deferment enabled her to create and address an audience she characterises in *USA Today* as 'mostly young, black and white, kids who've never experienced real glamour and outrageous, unadulterated fun'.[20] On *Video Soul*, she attributes her accessibility to her everydayness as well as to her 'natural' abilities: 'I'm just an ordinary Joe. I just have the unique ability to accessorize.' She echoes her everydayness on her 28 May 1993 appearance on *The Arsenio Hall Show*. Before her live interview, Hall introduces a taped segment of Hall and RuPaul shopping for lingerie. Like her MTV profile, the show uses shopping to demonstrate her 'otherness'. Yet during the segment RuPaul asserts: 'I'm just like anybody else, Arsenio. I put my panty hose on one leg at a time!' When Hall asks, 'What size do you wear?', she replies 'Honey, I wear *queen* size.'

Her linguistic substitutions and deferments may seem at odds with her over-the-top appearance – on *Video Soul* she concedes with a smile to co-host Sheri Carter that people are shocked by her 'and for good reason' – but this juxtaposition shows what Ru *did* learn from *Paris Is Burning* and its subsequent critical acclaim. RuPaul's juxtaposition shows she better understands the pop potential of what Peggy Phelan calls the 'hyper-visibility' of the ball walkers in *Paris Is Burning* than Phelan herself does. For Phelan the ball's 'realness' only emphasises the disenfranchisement of the film's interviewees:

> As one of the informants explains, to be able to look like a business executive is to be able to be a business executive. Within the impoverished logic of appearance, 'opportunity' and 'ability' can be connoted by the way one looks. But at the same time, the walker is *not* a business executive and the odds are that his performance of that job on the runway of the ball will be his only chance to experience it. The performances, then, enact simultaneously the desire to eliminate the distance between ontology and performance – and the reaffirmation of that distance.[21]

The categories of the ball, however, do not suggest a desire to eliminate the distance between ontology and performance, nor do they serve merely to reaffirm that distance. No one in *Paris* ever denies the material realities of being a poor black queen in New York City. No one claims that the balls can change those realities. No one 'confuses' them with reality. Moreover, the same walkers compete in different categories within the film, necessarily upsetting the category-equals-ontology equation Phelan puts forward. What *Paris*'s informants continually affirm – albeit with seemingly contradictory commentary between informants – is that the balls and their categories are a site of conscious fantasy. For one night they can renounce the very real implications race does have for the gap between 'opportunity' and 'ability' in the USA, and the participants can be celebrated for their achievements. Moreover, 'realness' is a leitmotif in US black cultural expression which does not, as Phelan claims, demonstrate the 'impossibility of realizing the[ir] dreams';[22] it affirms community.[23]

Even with this black cultural referent, the possibility of the balls – detached from the real struggles of the ball participants – speaks to many audiences, each writing their own fascination on to their explanation of the film. As Terrence Rafferty explains, 'the material [in the film] is almost too rich, too suggestive. Everything about *Paris Is Burning* signifies so blatantly and so promiscuously that our formations – our neatly paired theses and antitheses – multiply faster than we can keep track of them, and the movie induces a kind of semiotic daze.'[24] RuPaul exploits this kind of daze, wrapping the mythic black mother in a recognisable pop package. She and Monica Lynch, President of Tommy Boy Music who offered RuPaul her historic recording contract, the first – and so far the only – major label contract for a drag queen, crowned the mythic black mother with the signifier of supreme white beauty, a platinum blond wig.

Before signing with Tommy Boy Music, RuPaul was best known for her Starbooty persona, very blaxploitation, very Pam Grier, very Tamara Dobson; but such a look, Lynch must have feared, would be 'too black'. Making RuPaul blond – a look Ru calls 'total glamour, total excess, total Vegas, total total' – was Lynch's way of making RuPaul 'harmless'.[25] RuPaul explains succinctly: 'I'm like Monica's full-size Barbie doll.'[26] As if to model herself for RuPaul's audience, Lynch 'admits to nabbing vicarious thrills through Ru's *über* glamour'.[27] Becoming Lynch's Barbie doll, though, is a means of parodying without succumbing to white beauty standards in much the same way the walkers of *Paris Is Burning* do. Ru's hair, after all, is not just blond but erect. RuPaul's 'total total' acknowledges and mocks the white beauty standards she echoes.

During her 'Supermodel' promotion she similarly acknowledges and displaces questions about sexual identity. To fix her sexual identity would prevent her audience from being able to script whatever is necessary to 'nab vicarious thrills'. The following excerpt from RuPaul's *Video Soul* appearance illustrates how adroitly she negotiates any questions co-hosts Simpson and Carter levy in order to 'fix' her:

Sheri Carter (SC): Now what would you call yourself? If you had to describe yourself, what would you say?

RuPaul (R): My look today is sort of retro – I got my Daisy Dukes on, first of all. I want everybody to know I got my Daisy Dukes on. Did you see my Daisy Dukes?

SC: No I didn't.

R: Well, the Seventies are back with a vengeance, of course. And everybody's wearing Daisy Dukes, like little hot pants.

SC: Oh, OK, well, they would have called them hot pants.

R: Well, we call it – like the song 'I Got My Daisy Dukes on'. So we're featuring Daisy Dukes today. But I am doing a neo-black hooker look today [SC and Donnie Simpson (DS) laugh], which is always fun. When I first started doing drag, you know, I was enamoured – just like Dolly Parton – with hookers. I mean, hookers wear the best clothes, don't they?

DS: [SC and DS laugh] I don't know about that.

R: I think so. I love them. They are the backbone of the American Trade Association [SC and DS laugh]!

SC: I bet there's a lot of politicians that would agree with you [more laughter]. Now, you mentioned that – you said that you are in drag. What does that mean? Does that mean you're gay? Does that mean you really want to be a woman? Or that you just enjoy dressing up as a woman [R laughs as she asks the questions]?

R: I'm laughing because, you know, I've been doing these interviews for a long time now.

SC: Don't they always ask you that, though? Don't they always ask you that?

R: It's the same questions but, you know, it's fine. You know, I don't want to be a woman. Dressing in drag is just that. I mean, everybody is in drag. Any time you step out of the shower and put something on, you're going to get into drag [Turns to DS who looks stunned]. You know what I'm saying? … You're mesmerized by my eye lashes, aren't you [R and DS laugh]?

DS: No, I'm trying to understand this get out of the shower and I'm in drag thing. What do you mean?

R: No, well, you're born naked and the rest is drag.

RuPaul ably questions the assumptions behind what they ask in order to offer the audience familiar context(s) for understanding her – fashion and fads, popular black music, Dolly Parton, even prostitution. She playfully acknowledges the spectacle drag can be when teasing Simpson for staring at her. She caps her navigation with one of what some call her New Age truisms, truisms she repeats with the demeanour of a preacher so that the next time the audience sees her in a television interview they know how to chime in. RuPaul leads her most common sermon on *Video Soul*, asking the viewing audience to place their hands in front of their television sets, then commanding: 'Everybody say love!' She punctuates her call with the following lesson she nabbed from infamous soul singer Millie Jackson: 'It's all about love baby, 'cuz if you don't love yourself, how the hell you gonna love somebody else? Can I get an amen in here?' As *TV*

Guide echoes, 'there's a message behind the makeup, insists the singer. "People ask me, 'Should I call you *he* or *she*?' I say, 'You can call me he, she, or Regis and Kathie Lee.' It's what's *inside* that counts.'"[28]

Even with her queer politic, however, RuPaul's message of love was not always received as openly or as positively as it was on *Video Soul*. Her appearance during MTV's special programming for Spring Break 1993 shows both the tension and the adulation she inspired, as well as how critical RuPaul's charisma was in creating and maintaining her audience. Filmed live in Daytona Beach, Florida, in front of a large audience of college students who had come to party, RuPaul was a guest on the Spring Break edition of 'Chillin' with the Weez', then one of MTV's highest-rated shows starring comedian Pauly Shore. For the interview, Shore dressed in sloppy drag to illustrate, as he later explains to Ru, that while he 'does a chick on his show' he hasn't 'gone the distance' like RuPaul. Throughout Shore's almost hostile interview, he continues to ask, 'what *are* you, a transsexual?' Unfaltered, RuPaul counters, 'it's all about fun', again invoking her preacher demeanour, proclaiming, 'I am a *drag queen*! Can I get an amen in here?' Later in the interview she further asserts: 'I am a big ol' black man wearing women's clothes!'

RuPaul's call and response deflection of the 'fixing' of her identity is what saved her from Shore's assault, and won over the audience, who laughed along with her. As Lynch notes, 'There's something about RuPaul that transcends being a drag queen. People just gravitate towards Ru, regardless of age, race, gender, whatever.'[29] RuPaul elaborates: 'The one thing I do that no one else does better than me is, I communicate somehow. I plug into a frequency that other people understand. When people see me on stage and I'm gorgeous, what they're seeing is a reflection of their own beautiful imagery. When they pick up on my frequency and my rhythm, they go, "Oh, I love that. That's me."'[30]

This recognition through objectification, she claimed at the beginning of the rise of 'Supermodel,' was OK: 'At one point, when I do the thing I do, I know people are looking at me, everyone's staring. But it's not me. It's the "thing" people are looking at. And I can stand outside it.'[31] But keeping that 'thing' separate from herself became taxing. In an intuitive review of *Supermodel of the World*, Vince Aletti prophesied the toll RuPaul's *working* would take:

As a canny, playful critique of gender straitjacketing, drag's the perfect cocktail for the hot and bothered: ambivalence on ice. But drag can be a straitjacket, too; unlike androgyny, which suggests all kinds of possibilities (think Jagger, Bowie, Patti Smith, Boy George, early Prince, early Sylvester, who kept his options open), full drag often seems neutering. At its sassiest and most confrontational, drag's a surprise package; but is it the best of both worlds or an empty box?[32]

For RuPaul, the empty box it became inspired 'RuPaul unmasked' and Charles's desire to come out musically as well. For his second album, then called *Soul Food*, he promised more depth and a touch of autobiography. He even solicited the services of legendary R&B producer Nick Martinelli, who worked with divas Stephanie Mills, Phyllis Hyman and Diana Ross, in order to gain credibility. Martinelli spoke glowingly of legitimising RuPaul as a vocalist: 'I think people are going to be surprised. It's definitely a new RuPaul.'[33] Charles promised to expand upon the 'Disney Ru' of the first album: 'I'm just adding dimension. Fleshing the whole image out. Flapping my wings harder, you know?'[34]

Monica Lynch, however, was not thrilled with Charles's new 'dimension', and subsequently clipped his wings, dropping him from Tommy Boy Music. Though Lynch never publicly commented on the decision, no doubt she was concerned that the new RuPaul would not speak to the masses as well as her *über* black mother image did. Charles's new 'realness' was branded less 'black' and more 'gay'. Soon enough, however, RuPaul picked herself, her wig and her pumps back up and *worked* again. She landed the first spokesmodel contract for MAC cosmetics, an elite line popular for years with celebrities, which decided to use her image when it went 'commercial' with counters at Nordstrom's and other upscale chains. She published *Letting It All Hang Out* with Hyperion Books; headlined a review in Las Vegas; hosted her own video show on VH1, 'RuPaul's party machine', which led to her own late-night talk show, 'The RuPaul show'; and hosted the morning show for New York's WKTU, then New York's leading pop radio station. She landed small roles in major motion pictures including *Crooklyn* (1994), *The Brady Bunch Movie* (1995), *To Wong Foo, Thanks for Everything, Julie Newmar* (1995), *A Mother's Prayer* (out of drag, 1995), *Blue in the Face* (1995) and *Fled* (1996), as well as prime-time television shows, including *Sister Sister*, *All in the House*, *The Crew* and *Nash Bridges*, and a cameo on late-night comedy show *Mad TV*.

Post-unmasking, however, her queer politic could no longer go unnamed. So, as she does with the publication of *Letting It All Hang Out*, she restages the fantasy of the mythic black (drag queen) mother with a vengeance, 'revealing' more of its construction with camp wit. She reiterates the fascination with (what she does with) her penis to a knowing audience. She repositions her own mother as both the primal drag queen and the mythic black mother, the ultimate inspiration she continues to 'channel' when she performs. RuPaul explains that her mother

> was the ultimate inspiration because she was the first drag queen I ever saw. She had the strength of a man and the heart of a woman. She could be as hard as nails, but also sweet and vulnerable – all the things we love about Bette Davis, Joan Crawford, and Diana Ross. To this day when I pull out my sassy persona, it's Ernestine Charles that I am channeling.[35]

With *Letting It All Hang Out* RuPaul reclaims and names the mythic and spiritual role she had cultivated with 'Supermodel': 'A drag queen is like a priest or a spirit familiar. We represent the myths, the duality of the universe.'[36] She reiterates the constant fascination with how she hides her penis by naming the first chapter 'How to tuck', which doubles as her own Ru creation story – this chapter comes even before her standard autobiographical beginning, 'Little Ruru'. The chapter title, and even the book's title, seem to poke fun at the 'delicate balance' Vince Aletti observes in her popularity: 'RuPaul can't take the risk that Dil took in [Neil Jordan's] *The Crying Game* [1992] and dangle the goods in our face; even if the meat is metaphorical, it's sure to upset the delicate balance between subversion and diversion here.'[37] With 'How to tuck', she restages drag as a means of deflecting the captivation with and apprehension towards the penis.

Letting It All Hang Out's jocularity is matched by the daring of her appearance on *Nash Bridges*. While she did not write the part, its explicit evocation of a drag community and of a drag queen's autonomy clearly restages her queer politic. The role is much more radical than other recent black drag queen cameos on hospital dramas *ER* and *Chicago Hope*, whose characters are 'tragic queens', HIV-positive, and dead by the end of the episode. RuPaul's character, Simone (W. E. B.?) DuBois, is the star of the secondary plot line of the 'Javelin catcher' episode where Nash Bridges tracks down an anti-tank weapon stolen from the military. DuBois comes to the precinct in order to report some hate crimes to Bridges's lieutenant. After she is unable to find the assailant in the mug shot books, the lieutenant introduces DuBois to his officers as 'a representative of the gay/lesbian/transgender communities' in order to set up an undercover operation. He explains the hate crimes as follows: 'There's been a rash of beatings on Polk Street. Three transvestite prostitutes have filed reports since January.' DuBois interrupts, 'Excuse me, that's *transgendered sex workers*.' The camera cuts to a close up of her face as she corrects him. (Elsewhere, DuBois repeats the standard 'tell it like it is' caricature she starts her role with, retorting to another transgendered sex worker also searching though mug shot books, 'Child, this ain't no date book. What you think this is, the Love Connection?') Yet her terminological correction of the lieutenant is not punctuated with a laugh track, and the lieutenant earnestly corrects himself – startling stuff for Network television.

The resolution of DuBois's inquiry is no less compromising. Of course, the officer she chooses to help, Evan Cortes, is reluctant to be assigned to the case. But his subsequent cross-dressing is not played for laughs. It is another example of drag as transformative process; it helps him in his relationship with his girlfriend, Stephanie. Fitting Cortes in the right dress, of course, offers ample opportunity for DuBois to shoot one-liners. When Cortes complains that his first outfit is too *Showgirls*, for example, DuBois snaps, 'Please, what do you think you're going to the White House to have tea with Hillary Clinton?' Of course, their banter continues so that DuBois can 'tell him like it is', but her retorts articulate her autonomy. When Cortes again complains that the assignment is not for him, DuBois spouts, 'Let me tell you something. I'm doing this for the girls. I'm not getting paid for this. I'm doing this for the girls. Not for you.' Her resistance to placating Cortes's obvious nervousness here foreshadows what happens later when they go undercover.

The backstory included about Cortes in this episode also contributes to its daring. Just before Cortes is assigned to DuBois, he and his girlfriend try to have sex but he does not perform well. Because of his new assignment, he is not able to have a conciliatory dinner with her as planned. Calling to cancel after trying on dresses for DuBois in the men's bathroom at the precinct – DuBois comes out of a flushing stall to inspect the first one! – he and Stephanie fight. After he catches the assailant later that night, he returns home still in drag to apologise again. His girlfriend, however, suddenly no longer cares that he had to work. She kisses him, explaining that his dress is sexy. The scene ends with the two kissing on her bed, Cortes in drag. While this resolution to Cortes's reticence reduces drag to sexual fetish, it also queers their heterosexual relationship. Not only is the reconciliation of Cortes and his girlfriend not comic, but Cortes unashamedly keeps the 'uniform' after the assignment.

DuBois's role on the show, however, is not simply to transform Cortes. In fact, DuBois does not even assist Cortes undercover as planned because Cortes slanders her. When with a disgusted look and without explanation she walks away down the street, it is her last appearance on the show. Her interaction with the officers is only to fulfil her needs.

Moreover, DuBois's presence on the show is not exoticised or marginalised. When Nash Bridges enters the precinct while DuBois looks at the mug books he casually says, 'good morning ladies'. Even her involvement in the 'secondary' plot line is not entirely removed from the 'primary' one – the man Bridges looks for in connection with the stolen weapon is arrested by Cortes for soliciting, implying the loose boundaries DuBois and the girls' profession has with the rest of the world. Because of these slippery boundaries *Nash Bridges* restores RuPaul's persona, through which self-identity is a leap into a social narrative, and enables any spectator to take part in queer cross-identification even with a post-unmasking understanding of RuPaul. It restages 'Supermodel''s continued contribution to United States popular culture: only by effecting new modes of interaction can cultural politics work. For example, the sea of largely white (presumably heterosexual) college students swishing their hands in the air as RuPaul commanded them to *sashay, shantay!* when she performed 'Supermodel' during MTV's 1993 Spring Break illustrates this process of cross-identification. Their contribution in the call and response of a black gay club directive (*you better work!*) may or may not have revealed for them the semiotic play which might disturb the fixity of their own (sexual, racial) identities. Yet through this ephemeral prance, they – like Cortes – engaged in RuPaul's dialectical vision.

While RuPaul's fame has perhaps faded, the dialogue she sparked continues, for instance, in hip hop, demonstrating the fascination with RuPaul's mythic black (drag queen) mother, even post-unmasking. While The Lox disparage someone for being 'pussy as RuPaul' in Puff Daddy's 'It's all about the Benjamins' (1997), the Notorious BIG proclaim in 'Dreams of fucking an R&B bitch' (1994), 'I fuck RuPaul before I fuck them ugly ass Xscape bitches.' Granted, this is no glowing celebration; but to include Ru within the erotic economy of playful (albeit sexist) fantasies about contemporary R&B singers says something about the tenacity of RuPaul's appeal.

Notes

1   'Same difference', *TV Guide* (26 June 1993), 2.
2   Michael Musto, 'La dolce Musto', *Village Voice* (2 July 1996), 50.
3   Teresa de Lauretis, 'Queer theory: lesbian and gay sexualities: an introduction', *differences*, 3:2 (1991), iii.
4   Sheri Parks, *Lion Mother of the American Soul: the Black Maternal Figure in*

Popular Culture, unpublished manuscript.

5   *Ibid.*

6   Heidi Sigmund, 'Dance music's RuPaul: poised for "world domination"', *The Los Angeles Times* (5 February 1993), F12.

7   W. E. B. DuBois, *The Gift of Black Folk* (Millwood, NY, Kraus-Thompson, 1975), p. 320.

8   Guy Trebay. 'Cross-dresser dreams', *The New Yorker* (22 March 1993), 53.

9   Skinny Vinny, 'RuPaul', *Thing*, 6 (Summer 1992), 28.

10   Stuart Hall, 'The after-life of Frantz Fanon: why Fanon? Why now? Why *Black Skins, White Masks?*' in Alan Read (ed.), *The Fact of Blackness: Frantz Fanon and Visual Representation* (Seattle, Bay Press, 1996), p. 20.

11   See Frantz Fanon, *Black Skin, White Masks*, trans. Charles Lam Markmann (New York, Grove Press, 1967), p. 157.

12   *Ibid.*, pp. 17–18.

13   Jeff Yarbrough, 'RuPaul: the man behind the mask', *The Advocate*, 661/2 (23 August 1994), 66.

14   Peggy Phelan, *Unmarked: the Politics of Performance*, (London and New York, Routledge, 1993), p. 6.

15   *Ibid.*, p. 10.

16   I borrow the term 'cross-identification' from the special edition of *diacritics* Judith Butler and Biddy Martin edited (summer–autumn 1994), where they explain that such crossing may be conceived, on the one hand, as an appropriation, an assimilation or even a territorialisation of another site or position, or it can be understood as a movement beyond the stasis attributed to 'positions' located on a closed map of social power. In this second sense, then, crossing can be a movement that seeks to establish a connection or continuity. It can, of course, also constitute disavowal or defence and do all of this at once (p. 3).

17   Craig Seymour, Interview with Etta James, 12 June 1999.

18   Parks, *Lion Mother.*

19   Roland Barthes, *Mythologies*, trans. Annette Lavers (New York, Hill and Wang, 1972), p. 109.

20   James T. Jones IV, 'RuPaul, "Supermodel" with his own "je ne sashay quoi,"' *USA Today* (30 March 1993), 1.

21   Phelan, *Unmarked*, p. 99.

22   *Ibid.*, p. 94.

23   The 'masquerade' of the balls is not about achieving an 'idealised femininity', about *becoming* a white heterosexual woman. Again, there are numerous categories (butch realness, for one) that do not hold any femininity as an ideal; but even those categories that do feature the mimicking of the look, the adroitness of the walker. Where the 'performances' within the categories do touch on real life, they double as a means of survival. Dorian Corey, one of two elder ball walkers who not only gives the history of the balls but

demonstrates the generational conflicts inscribed in new categories, suggests
that 'femme realness' is when after the ball the contestant can get home on
the subway in one piece, when no one has detected that she is 'really' a he.

24   Terrance Rafferty, 'The current cinema: *realness*', *The New Yorker* (25 March
     1991), 72.
25   Trebay, 'Cross-dresser dreams', p. 49.
26   Michael Musto, 'Musto', *The Village Voice* (24 November 1992), 26.
27   *Ibid.*
28   'Same difference', p. 2.
29   Frank DeCaro. 'Latest supermodel? RuPaul, y'all', *New York Newsday* (1
     December 1992), D5.
30   RuPaul. 'From *Sister to Sister*: confessions, obsessions, revelations and
     proclamations by RuPaul', *Sister 2 Sister*, 5:6 (June 1993), 19.
31   Trebay, 'Cross-dresser dreams', p. 54.
32   Vince Aletti, 'Mr Queen', *The Village Voice* (6 July 1993), 63.
33   Yarbrough, 'RuPaul'.
34   *Ibid.*, p. 67.
35   RuPaul, *Letting It All! Hang Out: an Autobiography* (New York, Hyperion
     Books, 1995), p. 32.
36   Trebay, 'Cross-dresser dreams', p. 50.
37   Aletti, 'Mr Queen', p. 63.

12

Health and safety in the home: Todd Haynes's clinical white world

Glyn Davis

Ten minutes from the end of Todd Haynes's film *Safe* (1996), there is a scene that is indicative of both the text's formal stylistic rigour and its semantic elusiveness. Carol White (Julianne Moore) is being visited by her husband Greg and stepson Rory at the Wrenwood Institute, a commune for individuals with Environmental Illness (EI), an extreme form of chemical sensitivity. Greg and Carol stroll slowly around the Institute's grounds. Greg, dressed in a cerise shirt and khaki slacks, has his arm around Carol's right shoulder; she is dressed entirely in white, carries a small oxygen tank and has her light red hair scraped back from her face, which reveals a large purple lesion on her forehead. The camera is static. In the background, to the left, there is a porcelain igloo, gleaming white. As the couple reach the centre of the frame, Carol coughs, turns and breaks away from Greg, stumbling left. The following exchange occurs:

> Carol: It must be your cologne.
> Greg: I'm not wearing any.
> Carol: Maybe something in your shirt?
> There is a pause; Greg kicks a small stone in frustration.
> Greg: Will you be okay?
> Carol: I'll be fine. It's just for a short time.
> Greg: I know.
> Carol: I'll be fine.

Even at this late stage in the film, we remain unsure of the exact nature and etiology of Carol's illness. Why does she stumble away from Greg? Chemical sensitivity provides a possible explanation, but it is an unsatisfying one; until this point, there has been no suggestion that clothes could be a trigger for Carol. Perhaps it is the union with Greg that is the problem; the rare expressions of affection in *Safe* are cold, empty, clumsy and usually one-sided. Greg's arm around Carol, in a film which focuses on bodily revolt, feels oppressive, restrictive, claustrophobic; it is thus tempting to speculate that Carol's condition is a reaction against compulsory heterosexuality.

This search for meaning is not assisted by the film's dialogue and image composition. Carol's speech throughout is fractured and inarticulate, and peppered with repetitive phrases ('I'm sorry', 'I'm fine/I'll be fine') which are devoid of meaning. In the scene described above, for instance, Carol's frail figure, scarred skin and reliance on breathing apparatus undercut her mellifluous utterances. In contrast to the film's empty use of language, *Safe*'s imagery is replete with suggestions and implications; however, none of these finally provides explanation and coherence. When Carol turns away from Greg, she becomes aligned on the left side of the screen with an igloo. The resultant connection through colour – Carol's surname and clothes, the igloo's gleam – is striking. But why should Carol be so clearly associated with whiteness?

Safe was Haynes's second full-length feature. The first, *Poison* (1991), won the Grand Prize at the Sundance Film Festival, and provoked controversy when America's moral majority discovered that the National Endowment for the Arts had contributed to the film's financing.[1] B. Ruby Rich, in her 1992 *Village Voice* article which identified and labelled 'new queer cinema', acknowledged *Poison* as a progenitor of the movement.[2] Certainly, *Poison* – with its fractured tripartite structure, playful pastiche of generic conventions, and appropriative reworking of gay literary history – rather neatly fitted Rich's definition; since Rich's essay, Haynes has often been labelled as a 'new queer cinema' film-maker.

Unlike *Poison*, *Safe* is not evidently a gay film. However, it does maintain some of the former film's concerns – an interest in our understanding of identity, the power (or lack of it) associated with language – and, like much new queer cinema, it presents a challenge to film form.[3] The plot of *Safe* is relatively simple. The film is set in the San Fernando Valley in 1987. Carol White is an upper-middle-class 'home-maker' who lives in an enormous, immaculately kept house with her husband Greg (whose job remains unspecified), Rory, Greg's ten-year-old son from a previous marriage, and a number of (mostly Hispanic) maids. Carol's day-to-day life consists of aerobics classes, endless lunches with her 'best friend' Linda, minor rose pruning and passing admiring comments on the equally clinical and soulless houses of her social group. Over the first hour of the film, which meticulously details the mundane nature of

Carol's existence, several minor incidents occur. Carol slips while reaching for an address book; she has a coughing fit while caught in heavy traffic; she has a nosebleed at the hair salon; she vomits one morning when her husband hugs her. Carol claims she is 'run down', 'a little stressed out'; she says she has a 'head thing', and 'must have a touch of something'. Her doctor can find nothing wrong with her, and eventually refers her to a psychiatrist. In the meantime, from responding to a leaflet entitled 'Do you smell fumes?', Carol comes into contact with a group of women who have Environmental Illness. Her health gets worse: she has a wheezing fit at a baby shower, which leads a doctor to test her for allergies. Finally, she is hospitalised when she unwittingly walks into a dry cleaner's that is being sprayed with chemicals. While recovering in hospital, Carol learns – from the television – of Wrenwood, and decides to go there.

Wrenwood is run by Peter Dunning, a chemically sensitive man with AIDS, who lives in a large floodlit mansion on a hill above the Institute. Peter preaches a strange 'mixed bag' quasi-New-Age spiritualism – he namechecks environmentalism, multiculturalism and 'holistic study', and offers healing mantras to the Institute's residents ('We are one with the power that created us. We are safe, and all is well in our world'). He also advocates a healing ideology that blames the individual for illness: 'If our immune system is damaged, it is because we allow it to be.' Initially placed in a wood cabin, Carol believes she can smell fumes from the road nearby, and so moves into a porcelain igloo. Wrenwood does not seem to improve Carol's health – the film ends with her scarred, thin figure isolated in a barren bubble.

Safe's storyline unfolds slowly in a linear fashion. Camerawork is mostly static, in long shot, with an occasional very slow zoom. Much of the speech is mundane and fraught with pauses. Many camera shots focus on routinised daily activities for long stretches of time: Carol slowly drinking from a glass of milk; a repeated sequence – once in the dark, once during the day – of the drive up to Greg and Carol's house. Frequently, edits come much later than expected: for example, when Claire (Wrenwood's director) leaves Carol's wood cabin, the camera stays focused on the door for another ten seconds. Richard Dyer has identified a similar editing dynamic at work in the television series *The Jewel in the Crown* (1984); it can be seen also, in an extreme form, in Chantal Akerman's film *Jeanne Dielman, 23 Quai du Commerce, 1080 Bruxelles* (1975). All three texts are concerned with the dreary emptiness of women's lives – *Jewel*, says Dyer, is centrally about '[d]oing nothing, and nothingness itself'[4] – which the makers (writers, directors) want us to experience and acknowledge. The editing style of *Jewel, Jeanne Dielman*, and *Safe*, then, 'suits [their] ruminative nature; it also conveys the tempo of a sluggish, aimless existence'.[5]

Despite its linear plot and slow pacing, *Safe* is a film which, as already mentioned, provides no answers. Even by the film's conclusion, we are not sure why Carol White got sick; as Taubin writes, '[t]there are signs in abundance but no answers or messages'.[6] This means that, in the process of reception, we tend to create our own explanations; as Rayns concedes, the film 'leaves space for radically different audience responses'.[7] It would be possible, for instance, to read the film as being about AIDS: Haynes has stated that all of his films are about illness, because of AIDS;[8] the film is set in the late 1980s, a time when AIDS panic was at a high; there is an exchange between Linda and Carol, following the death of Linda's brother, that intimates AIDS (Carol: 'It, um, wasn't – ?'; Linda: 'No. That's what everyone keeps – . Not at all. 'Cause he wasn't married') while relegating the disease to a subtext; in addition, many new queer cinema films have tackled HIV/AIDS as a topic, either directly or indirectly. And yet *Safe* is clearly not an AIDS metaphor: Peter is identified as having AIDS, and thus the disease 'co-exists [with EI] in the universe of the film';[9] further, EI is now recognised as a 'real' syndrome.[10] And so we search for other possible interpretations, none of which is fully satisfying. Carol herself believes she understands: she is chemically sensitive (despite her doctor's protestation that 'it's not showing up on the tests'), and Wrenwood will help to improve her health. However, none of the residents at Wrenwood – and particularly not Carol – seems to be getting any better. Recovery – of individual Institute inmates, of the film text as a closed form – is impossible. This was always Haynes's intention.[11] In interview, he has acknowledged that his desire with *Safe* was to highlight our need to narrativise and understand both people and illness. As he states:

> the film gives you all these blank spaces to fill in … [and] people create their own sub-story which connects two points that the film refuses to connect for you. And then you get to Wrenwood and you realise that's what this entire institution is based on doing: creating narrative explanations for things that aren't explained and perhaps can never be explained … You get caught doing the same thing Wrenwood does.[12]

This would seem to close off this text from the prospect of analysis. However, there is much more to *Safe* than simply deducing the nature and cause of Carol's illness. In this chapter, I intend to examine the nature of whiteness (and 'race') in *Safe*, taking the film as a symptomatic text: what can it tell us about the social and cultural construction of this identity formation, and how whiteness relates to other key factors such as health, heterosexuality and articulacy? Does the film support, contradict or complicate theoretical understandings of whiteness? It is not my aim, in offering this analysis, to explain away Carol White's malady; rather, I wish to use the film to examine broader theoretical ideas about whiteness. Firstly, I will examine *Safe*'s status as a film about 'race', and explore its use of white symbolism. I will then elucidate the connections Haynes makes between whiteness, health and heterosexuality. Both of these sections will draw substantially on ideas posited by Richard Dyer in his book *White* (1997). Finally, I wish to offer some observations on the status of the white female voice in cinema; in this section, I will be reliant on concepts from the writings of Kaja Silverman, one of the few theorists to consider the intersection of power, subjectivity and the voice in film.

'It doesn't go with anything we have': colour, symbolism and 'race'

Whiteness is clearly a central concern in *Safe*: the film uses colour (and thus evokes associated symbolism) meticulously. In addition, the text problematises 'race' by including a number of non-white characters; their presence would seem to support Toni Morrison's recognition of the 'centrality ... of black representation to the construction of white identity'.[13] These elements – colour, symbolism, skin tone – are intimately bound together: as Dyer states, 'the slippage between the three is ... pervasive [and] ... probably underlie[s] all representation of white people'.[14] Nevertheless, it is worth teasing out each of the three strands, in order to determine the exact nature of their interaction.

The whiteness of Carol's surname binds her intimately to several prominent white items: milk, the igloo, her always pale and usually white clothes (at her second aerobics class, Carol is the only person present not wearing gaudy colours), Peter's house on the hill (which she describes as 'gorgeous'). It also distances her from black items. She is shocked, for instance – 'Oh my God' – when a black sofa is accidentally delivered to her house. Trying to exchange the sofa at the warehouse, she is told that her original order shows black, not teal; Carol claims 'that's impossible, because it doesn't go with anything we have'. Clearly blackness is anathema to Greg and Carol's house and lifestyle.[15]

Of course, white's status as a colour is uncertain: it is conceptualised as both all colours combined, and the absence of colour. White is thus both a colour and colourless, present and absent. This paradox also applies to whiteness as a social and cultural identity: 'white people are both particular and nothing in particular, are both something and non-existent'.[16] Carol White stands as evidence for the simultaneous visibility and invisibility of whiteness: despite her presence within every scene of the narrative, Carol often disappears within the frame. She appears tiny against enormous buildings in long shot (calling at Linda's house; opening her gate for the sofa delivery), or simply – owing to static camerawork, a lack of movement within the frame, and muted colours – is hard to discern (for example, when she speaks to her mother on the telephone).[17] Indeed, Carol's whiteness is often configured as blankness: she rarely displays emotion, concern or interest; we know little of her past (when prompted during Wrenwood therapy, she can't remember a room she had as a child: 'Um, um, um – God, this is, um, I guess there's one I had, was, had, yellow wallpaper, and – '); further, as Haynes intends, Carol is a tabula rasa, a blank slate, on which the audience imposes meaning.

Whiteness as a symbol evokes many interrelated properties: cleanliness, chastity, goodness, purity, virginity, divinity, wholesomeness. Carol's purity is evident – 'I don't take drugs or, or drink … I don't even, um, like coffee very much, um, I'm just a total milkoholic', she tells her doctor, the white milk (and her implied addiction to it) proving her purity. Yet the film details her striving towards a higher, purer ideal – rural, isolated, clean, simple, ascetic – a white ideal which is perhaps never fully attainable, except in death. Carol's relationship towards chastity and virginity is also marked: she is passive and unresponsive in the film's one sex scene, and her 'head thing' keeps her from subsequent sexual engagements. She also has no children of her own, interacts poorly with Rory and is only a peripheral observer at the baby shower. Perhaps most tellingly, during a meal at a restaurant with friends, Carol fails to laugh at a joke about a vibrator; in a stilted silence, she says 'I'm sorry, I don't – '. (This open-ended sentence is typical of the film's suggestive nature: what is it that Carol 'doesn't', exactly?) Sex, it would seem, is not an important or necessary part of Carol's life.

The place of divinity within *Safe* is subtle yet fascinating. Dyer claims that despite the growth of atheism in the West, the Virgin Mary persists as an ideal for women: 'This sets up a dynamic of aspiration … Such striving (which in women must also be passive) is registered in suffering, self-denial and self-control, and also material achievement, if it can be construed as the temporary and partial triumph of mind over matter.'[18] Although Carol is not portrayed as a religious person, this quotation is heavily suggestive. Carol's move to Wrenwood, her abandonment of her materialistic lifestyle and acceptance of a simple asceticism, is a striving not simply for the white ideal of purity but for a divine whiteness. The fact that her illness gets worse – that is, her suffering increases – and that she develops a stigma-like lesion on her forehead all contribute to this observation.

The igloo that Carol ends up in only adds to this argument for a journey towards ideal 'divine' whiteness, as it carries connotations of snow, coldness, barren landscapes, and northern extremes (Dyer states that 'the North is an epitome of the 'high, cold' places that promoted the rigour, cleanliness, piety and enterprise of whiteness'),[19] all of which work against any potential suggestions of Inuit 'colour'. This 'home', so intimately connected to Carol's health and safety, stands in contrast to Peter's large white mansion; here we can identify differently gendered ideals of whiteness. Peter's house, so redolent of the modern mansions Carol has left behind, is an edifice to the power and wealth of white patriarchal masculinity, symbolically placed above the Institute; Carol may admire its beauty, but can only look up to it, and instead seems to prefer her isolated white bubble.

The prevalence of white objects and symbolism throughout *Safe* is overlaid with issues of race and skin colour. Julianne Moore's alabaster skin, a stark contrast to her red hair, is frequently offered up for observation. Early on in the film, an aerobics class member jealously observes that Carol doesn't sweat; this serves to suggest that her skin is not 'right', not 'natural', whilst simultaneously identifying her as an ideal white woman, for only '[n]on-white and sometimes working-class white women are liable to shine [i.e., sweat] rather than glow'.[20] In other words, this sequence, positioned only several minutes into the film, establishes the fragility of whiteness as an artificial, constructed identity based on skin colour: the ideal of white femininity is both perfect and perverse.

At three specific points in *Safe*'s narrative, Carol stares at herself in a mirror: at the hair salon, at the baby shower and in the film's final scene in the igloo. For all three, we are provided with close-up shots and invited, with Carol, to examine her appearance. In all three she looks very ill, her skin 'constantly on the verge of a nervous breakout';[21] at the beautician's, for instance, what should be a moment of beauty is one of horror, for Carol's appearance is that of a corpse in stage make-up, the image composition's flat yellow lighting highlighting her sunken cheeks and dead eyes. Whilst Carol inspects her 'swollen face'[22] in the bathroom during the baby shower, Haynes cuts to the kitchen where one woman asks another, 'Is something wrong with Carol? Her skin looks kind of, –' (note, once again, the presence of an unfinished sentence that misses the all-important descriptor); this sentence highlights how we, Carol and her friends are all aware of her appearance. In only one other scene is Carol's skin subject to intense scrutiny: as the allergy specialism doctor injects an array of potentially hypoallergenic substances into Carol's arm, the camera lingers on her skin, a neatly ordered block of purple welts raised on her marble dermis. We find ourselves siding with the doctor, waiting for a reaction, hoping to understand Carol's ailments. And at the salon, surgery and baby shower, those reactions come in the form of nosebleeds and wheezing fits; it is as if the impermeability of whiteness suggested by Carol's skin breaks down under scrutiny. It is only in the film's final scene that a 'close-up of her no longer triggers a severe and sudden allergic reaction';[23] but by this point the skin has broken down, and the image is dimly lit. Suffering, it would seem, may be an important constituent of whiteness, but if it is physically registered additional components of the identity formation also break down irrevocably.

If Carol's skin is constantly under investigation, Peter draws attention to his. During a meal at Wrenwood, he relates a dream he had in which his arms were covered with 'oozing black sores'. When he looked down again, he realised that they were actually 'beautiful black pansies; … and when I picked them up they turned into beautiful bouquets'. Whilst these sores may be a reference to the skin lesions often associated with AIDS, their significance here lies in their colour: the imagined black sores are not only horrific, but weeping, breaking the immaculate, sealed white skin. That they 'turn into' bright bouquets indicates the stereotypical conceptual links between blackness and 'colour', life and vibrancy; and the antithetical association of whiteness with lack of colour, and death. That this is a man's dream, and the colour blooms from within, yet is separate from, him is not surprising: historically, white men are seen to have darkness – dark drives – within them against which they successfully battle, while '[t]he white woman on the other hand was not supposed to have such drives in the first place'.[24]

Despite Carol's isolation in hyperwhite suburbia, she seems almost colour-blind in relation to skin colour: she interacts in her usual bland fashion with the allergy doctor's black nurse and her Chinese dry cleaner. Even in the more 'multicultural' environment of Wrenwood – where she is met by a black woman – race is not explicitly commented on (or even seemingly recognised) by Carol. It is in quieter moments that Carol's lack of understanding and sensitivity in relation to cultural and ethnic difference is exposed: she clumsily (yet with a lack of self-awareness) asks Fulvia, her head maid, for a glass of milk, then repeats the request in rubbish pidgin Spanish. More tellingly, Rory reads out a graphic school essay assignment at the dinner table, on 'black and Chicano gangs'; the piece mentions stabbings, shootings, rapes, riots and 'limbs being dismembered'. Carol is shocked, asking 'why does it have to be so gory?' Rory tells her 'that's how it really is'. Greg, on the other hand, congratulates Rory: 'Good work, son'. Rory's account may be stereotypical and hyperbolic, but Carol's response is more notable for betraying her naiveté: not only does she live in multiracial Los Angeles but her house is also full of noise pollution – what Haynes beautifully describes as 'vacuum cleaners and Spanish television and Lite-FM'[25] – which must surely include some news. This interaction with Rory also provides a gendered contrast with an exchange at the baby shower, at which Carol tells a little girl drawing a princess that her picture is 'very realistic'. Greg praises Rory, just as Carol praises the girl: appropriate role behaviour is approved of by the correctly gendered adult. The young male's 'realism' is black, violent and savage, while that of the young female is dreamlike, rarefied, pretty; again, masculinity is more 'coloured' than femininity. With the comparison effected by these scenes, Haynes subtly undermines the perceived neutrality/invisibility of whiteness, by indicating how racial identities are connected to – and as constructed as – socially transmitted gender roles.

'Nobody has a fucking headache every night of the fucking week': whiteness, heterosexuality and illness

The culturally constructed forms of whiteness, then, are different for men and women. As already noted, men have a relationship to colour that women must not have; as *Safe* subtly suggests, adults raise children into gendered conformity with these differential ideals.

The ideals of white womanhood are notably paradoxical; like the Virgin Mary, white women are expected to be both pure, beautiful virgins and perfect mothers. As the comments on chastity and virginity made above suggest, Carol only really fits one of these roles, for her status as a mother is tarnished. She interacts poorly with children and mothers: at the baby shower, while Carol's social group scoff cake and flaunt their swollen stomachs, she hides in the bathroom, staring at her swollen face. When, shortly after emerging, she has a wheezing fit, it is unclear whether this was provoked by the cake, a child who sat on her knee, the baby

shower in total or some other indiscernible factor. Carol may be excluded
from the mothering role, yet *Safe* hardly paints maternity in a positive
light. Carol's friends are, I suspect purposefully, remarkably similar to the
Stepford Wives; their near-identical hair and clothing, which render them
essentially interchangeable, foster a subtle, sinister echo of the earlier text.
The sole purpose for the lives of these women, Haynes seems to imply, is
to serve as receptacles for their husbands; they clearly have nothing better
to do, and lack even the most rudimentary of skills ('Did you wrap that
yourself?' asks Carol; 'Are you kidding?', replies her friend, 'I'm not that
creative'). The primary aim of white women is to produce and raise white
children; for the white race, writes Dyer, '[t]hey guarantee its reproduction, even while not succeeding to its highest heights'.[26]

Thus it is that heterosexuality is intimately connected with whiteness.
A connection between the two might be expected, as within western
culture both occupy the privileged position of normativity. However, the
most important link is that heterosexual reproduction is a necessity for
maintaining the white race; and within this connection are imbricated
ideal gender roles. As Dyer puts it, '[r]ace and gender are ineluctably
intertwined, through the primacy of heterosexuality in reproducing the
former and defining the latter'.[27] The white women at the baby shower are
empty, subjugated vessels, whose only 'work' entails perpetuating a
particular racial lineage. This conjunction of race, gender roles and
heterosexuality is also signalled – although in an ironic manner – by
Safe's opening sex scene between Carol and Greg. Bathed in a cold blue
light, Carol lies passive, still and unemotional as her husband grunts and
grinds away on top of her; in the centre of the frame, Carol's wedding ring
shines white. The heterosexual union, whiteness and gendered
active/passive roles are signalled and linked; the irony is Carol's absence
(her vacant stare, lack of passion, and failure to interact with Greg) from
this forged connection, immediately suggesting her failure to fulfil the
role of ideal white woman.

Carol's inability to relate 'properly' to heterosexuality complicates her
relationship to her whiteness; she may pursue a path of purity and cleanliness, but her inadequacies as mother and lover prevent her attainment
of full social white womanhood. Is it possible that this structuring
absence – sex and children – can be replaced by an alternative; namely,
illness? That is, could illness round out Carol's white identity, serving as
a substitute for that which she lacks or is unable to provide? Such an
argument would necessitate a reconfiguration of illness as a positive
force. Doane[28] has illustrated how, in 'medical discourse' melodramas of

the 1940s, women characters who were not fulfilling 'correct', socially acceptable feminine roles would develop illnesses. The problematic relationship to femininity that these women experienced often centred around sex; women who were frigid or overzealous in the bedroom exhibited the worst symptoms. Figures of patriarchy – doctors, psychiatrists and 'good men' like Rock Hudson – would enter the narrative and either bring the woman back into line … or let her die.

In *Safe*, figures of patriarchy also try to cure Carol. It is Greg's 'well-meaning, paternalistic embrace'[29] that first sends Carol to the doctor. All of the doctors she sees are male; when her regular doctor recommends that she sees a psychiatrist, he hands the card to Greg, rather than Carol. In one notable scene, Carol is caught wandering in her garden at night by police who mistake her for a burglar. On her re-entering the house, Greg is up on the balcony, looking down at her: 'Carol is literally caught in the middle between private and public spheres, between the male enforcers of law and order and the male head of the household – between men who impose their own worlds upon her.'[30] Even after her move to Wrenwood, Carol is still under the gaze and control of a man, Peter, who wishes to explain and cure her ailments.

It is necessary to pause at this critical juncture for clarification. *Safe* could be seen to suggest, in a manner that follows the diegetic outline of 1940s melodramas, that Carol's illness (and seeming failure to recover) is due to her inability to fulfil her feminine role. However, the film's failure to provide adequate resolution and account for all possible signification present in the text means that this (finally unsatisfactory) explanation, like all others, is only one among many. Further, Haynes is fully aware of the tried-and-tested narrative tropes he is drawing on; the fact that he at times explicitly positions us with the representatives of patriarchy – with the doctor testing Carol's arm for allergic reactions, for instance – informs the knowing audience that they are being directly led, and makes them aware that they, like the doctors, are trying to explain away Carol's condition.

The alternative is perhaps to read illness not as a symptom of failure but as a positive force. Elizabeth Grosz has argued lucidly for a reconceptualisation of desire as an intensity and innervation; opposing the genealogy of thought that runs from Plato through Hegel to Freud, and which conceptualises desire as a lack, she draws on Spinoza, Deleuze and Guattari to reconfigure the concept as 'the force of positive production, the energy that creates things'.[31] I'd like to suggest a similar (partial) rethinking for illness, which is usually theorised as an aberration, a monstrosity, evidence for personal lack. Certainly, the notion of illness may immediately evoke associated feelings of discomfort, the need to return to full health; yet in certain situations, it is possible that illness could be a positive force, a catalyst, a stabiliser. In *Safe*, Carol's ailments may be non-recoverable, but she does not seem unhappy. Haynes has said that 'the illness in *Safe* is the best thing that happens to her' and that 'the illness and its chaos is where hope lies in the film'.[32] Carol's symptoms give her something to talk about; at lunch with Linda, she babbles away about her newfound chemical sensitivity in a cheery but rather incoherent manner. It is also the onset of illness that provokes her move to Wrenwood; it would seem that her recognition of the instability of her body makes her see the transience of identity generally, and thus how easy it can be to change. At Wrenwood, 'the secluded atmosphere of the camp allow[s] her … to fully embrace her illness'.[33] If we reconfigure illness as a positivity, then *Safe*'s narrative thrust becomes one of enlightenment. Carol does not recover by the end of the film because she does not want to. When Peter tries to get her to engage in a group therapy discussion, she politely declines by shaking her head: she may be unable to join in, or she may simply not want to heal.

I have already suggested that Carol's move to the cleaner, purer Wrenwood, plus her slowly escalating illness, may be a striving towards a divine whiteness that embraces suffering. Wrenwood may offer to Carol the opportunity for one type of complete whiteness, in contrast to that available – or rather, required – by the San Fernando Valley. Divine whiteness recognises the sanctity of the spirit or soul against the dirty, material body. As Dyer states: 'What makes whites special is the light within, though modern man must struggle to see, let alone regain this. This light, which is white, is dirtied ('stained') by blood, passion, movement, which is to say, isn't it, life.'[34] That is to say, the recognition of divine whiteness is rare, its attainment rarer; further, true divinity can be attained only in death, which whites – through their 'lack of colour' – already have a special affinity with. By the close of *Safe*, Carol is very close to literal and symbolic death. Any seemingly meaningful affective ties have been virtually severed, and the materiality of her southern California lifestyle renounced. In addition, her body is starting to decompose, and her oxygen tank is trundled around behind her like a life support machine. Dyer has argued that the desert in Westerns (a very white genre) signifies death. At Wrenwood, the desert is doubly present: literally, in terms of the location of the Institute outside Albuquerque, New Mexico, but it is also semiotically implied by the igloo's evocation of barren tundra.

In the final scene of the film, Carol locks herself into her porcelain bubble at night. She sits on the bed, and breathes in oxygen through a mask. She then walks to her mirror and, after a pause, says slowly, 'I love you. (Cough). I love you. I really love you. I love you.' After another pause, the film cuts to black. Unlike the film's other close-ups on Carol's face, in this final shot we cannot see the mirror; we only see her, not what she sees. Perhaps her path towards white divinity through suffering is at an end, and in the mirror she is able to see her white spirit reflected; Carol's proclamation of love, which is admittedly tentative and wavering, may be for her a recognition of God, the holy white spirit, within herself. The weak flesh has served its purpose, and is appropriately poorly lit; the cut to black thus signifies the death of Carol's physical form and her simultaneous attainment of white nirvana.

'The words are just the way to get to what's true': whiteness, femininity and articulacy

'The soundtrack has had a curious theoretical history', wrote Silverman in 1988, a history in which it has been '[n]otoriously passed over in favour of the image'.[35] Sound is a vital component in *Safe*'s texture and structure; this is especially true of the voice. In this final section, I would like to turn to a consideration of the film's use of speech and language, and how these interrelate with discourses of gender and whiteness marshalled by the text.

For Silverman, there is a fundamental structural difference in film's use of gendered voices: 'classic cinema', she argues, 'holds the female voice and body insistently to the interior of the diegesis, while relegating the male subject to a position of *apparent* discursive exteriority by identifying him with mastering speech, vision, or hearing'.[36] In other words, women tend to be trapped within and controlled by narrative, produced by discourse, whilst men are in charge of discourse and thus aligned with power, authority and, ultimately, the cinematic apparatus itself. Power, language and gender are, therefore, interlinked: 'whereas the male subject has privileges conferred upon him by his relationship to discourse, the female subject is defined as insufficient through hers'.[37] This is not to say that women are incapable of producing speech; however, it is the case that they tend to be associated with unreliable, thwarted or acquiescent language.[38]

A central concern of Silverman's is the synchronisation of the body with speech in cinema: that is, film's depiction – and thus assertion – of the 'correct' alignment between material subject and vocal properties. For women, this synchronisation is imposed more strongly; men's voices, on the other hand, can be removed from their bodies and the narrative with greater ease, so that they may speak 'from an anonymous and transcendental vantage, "over" the narrative'.[39] Women's synchronisation ties them into diegetic (and visual) film space; narrative construction then serves, via several mechanisms – limiting the physical space female characters inhabit, for instance – to emphasise and reinforce female interiority.

Safe is certainly not 'classic cinema', yet it provides examples of many of Silverman's points. The relationship of men and women to language within the film is markedly different. Most of the men, as already noted, are representatives of patriarchy; generally, they tend to talk in full sentences, and use their voices to reassure and relate information. Peter's voice, for instance, is calm, measured, controlled; he speaks with authority, clarity and precision. In contrast, the women communicate in brief, fragmented sentences: key words are often omitted, and interactions are disrupted by uncomfortable, empty silences.

If Carol's pidgin Spanish is poor, her English is no better. However, it is notable that, as the narrative of Safe progresses and Carol's illness escalates, so her articulacy increases. She is stimulated and excited by her symptoms, which provokes her into utilising longer sentences. This progression climaxes in a clumsy, rather meaningless speech Carol gives at Wrenwood on her birthday; a speech, moreover, which intimates that illness made her recognise the form and stagnant nature of her Valley life ('I couldn't have done it without you … It's just that I really hated myself before I came here and, um, so I'm trying to see myself hopefully, um, more as I am …'). Thus, as Carol follows her trajectory towards a purer, whiter lifestyle – which involves stepping away from a 'correct' heterosexual female role – her articulacy increases.

Two of the film's sequences are rare in that they use a voice-over, delivered by Carol; their placement within the narrative, the images that accompany them and their relation to prominent male characters make them worthy of sustained analysis. In the first, Carol sits in bed, writing a letter to the EI group, after picking up their 'Do you smell fumes?' leaflet. The soundtrack presents us with Carol's disembodied voice, reading her letter, as the camera slowly pans along the surface of a dressing table on which there are a large variety of framed photographs of Greg, Carol and Rory (separate or in combination). We are thus presented visually with signifiers of family, and family fracture, accompanied aurally by an internal monologue that 'makes audible what is ostensibly inaudible, transforming the private into the public'.[40] The voice-over is almost shocking: it is the first time that we access Carol's subjectivity, and it is the first occasion on which we are provided with (admittedly unimportant) information about Carol's history – that she had asthma as a child. In the middle of writing the letter, she is interrupted by Greg entering the bedroom; the voice-over stops, and the film's clinically detached objectivity is immediately reinstated. 'What are you doing?' asks Greg, the simple inquiry marked, perhaps, by an accusatory tone: what is a *woman* doing, using language to express herself clearly? After a pause, Carol replies: 'I was writing this, um. I don't know. Oh God, what is this? … Where am I? Right now?' Carol's developing illness has motivated her to try to take control of language and write a letter; Greg's interruption causes embarrassment and trauma. She is so disoriented – as are we – by her fleeting control of articulation that she seems momentarily to lose her placing in time and space.

Later in the film, Carol writes a second letter, this time to Greg and Rory. As the missive's dull platitudes unfold, we see several images of Carol alone, walking around the grounds of the Institute, ending with a shot of her on the veranda of her wooden shack as she completes the letter. Again, Carol's voice has been privileged by the soundtrack; on this occasion, it is paired – almost synchronised – with images of her body. Further, this time she completes the letter. As she finishes writing, Peter appears, and asks Carol how she is getting on at the Institute. 'I'm just still learning, um, you know, the words', she says; 'Oh. Well', replies Peter, 'the words are just the way to get to what's true.' Peter's statement is a redundant one, as *Safe* clearly demonstrates the instability and meaninglessness of language; further, Peter's 'truth' is a sham, as the Institute is clearly not toxin-free, non-profit-making or even therapeutically successful. However, Carol is clearly learning how to use language. Indeed, as her articulacy increases, so does her utilisation of speech just for herself: one night at Wrenwood, she stands in the dark on her stoop and sings quietly to herself in a thin, reedy voice, 'Forever and ever … sweet love shone'. (These words may pre-empt the final scene of the film, in which Carol again speaks to herself; that sequence, as argued above, also mobilises concepts of love, shining whiteness and spiritual – eternal – nirvana, present in these song lyrics.) In addition, Carol learns to control the power of enunciation: at the outdoor group therapy session, she refuses to contribute to discussion.

Despite her increased abilities with language, Carol's voice remains the same: a little too high and unstable. Julianne Moore has discussed her performance of Carol's vocal qualities: 'I would put question marks at the end of the sentence all the time – that way she never makes a statement; it makes her very unsure and very undefined. I also went above my own chords, because I wanted the sensation of her voice not being connected at all to her body.'[41] Although Wrenwood takes Carol away from hetero-sexuality and femininity, her 'too high' voice sounds persistently hyper-feminine. Silverman has argued that the low and husky voices of Dietrich and Bacall codify their speech as masculine, 'so that the voice seems to exceed the gender of the body from which it proceeds. That excess confers upon it a privileged status vis-à-vis both language and sexuality.'[42] In other words, if a woman's speech is masculine, it carries more power; thus Carol's increased articulacy throughout *Safe* is undercut by her overly high female tones. It is destabilised further by the points Moore outlines above: the lack of definitive statements, and the unnerving disparity between the body and the voice, a disparity that interrupts cinema's desire for synchronisation.[43]

As spectators, we also embrace such synchronisation. Heath has argued that 'the regime of sound as voice in cinema' – by which he means diegetic synchronised sound – is 'the "safe" place'.[44] In other words, classic cinema's conventionalised use of sound sutures us into a safe viewing and listening position. Following this criterion, *Safe* is not a 'safe' film to experience: not only does it highlight the meaningless nature of language, but Carol's mismatched voice and body centre the film on a point of uncertainty. No matter how hard the narrative and image composition attempt to confine Carol to interiority – by, for instance, moving her from mansion to small igloo[45] – she is not recuperable through such mecha-nisms owing to her increased whiteness, advanced linguistic skills and, perhaps most importantly, the text's ultimate inability to rationalise her illness. As the film ends, with Carol staring both into her igloo's mirror and directly at us, she is facing the chaos of incomprehension, and ('I love you') embracing it.

It would perhaps be foolish (if not impossible) to endeavour to provide a neat conclusion to a chapter examining a film which evades semantic closure. *Safe* is a fascinating and important film to examine, yet it prevents any attempt at a definitive analysis. I have focused here on its complex depiction of 'race', because *Safe* does for whiteness what *Poison* did for homosexuality: that is, it explores the cultural discourses surrounding an identity formation, and tests their boundaries through tales of marginalised individuals. In doing so, Haynes not only exposes the links between major identity formations, indicating how they cannot be examined or represented in isolation, but also demonstrates how 'queer' film-makers can extend their concerns into new areas; areas which may complicate the separatist divisions erected and maintained by many. If Carol White learns from her illness to disregard fixity and embrace chaos and transience, perhaps *Safe*'s main message to its audience is to defy the prescriptive and categorical.

Notes

1 See Justin Wyatt's *Cinetek: Poison* (Trowbridge, Flick Books, 1998) for an account of the film's controversial reception.
2 B. Ruby Rich, 'New queer cinema', *Sight and Sound*, 2:5 (1992), 30–34.
2 'People define gay cinema solely by content: if there are gay characters in it, it's a gay film … I think that's really simplistic. Heterosexuality to me is a structure as much as it is a content' (Haynes in Justin Wyatt, 'Cinematic/ sexual transgression: an interview with Todd Haynes', *Film Quarterly*, 46:3 (1993), 8).
4 Richard Dyer, *White* (London: Routledge, 1997), p. 187.
5 *Ibid.*, p. 202.
6 Amy Taubin, 'Nowhere to hide', *Sight and Sound*, 6:5 (1996), 32.
7 Tony Rayns, review of *Safe*, *Sight and Sound*, 6:5 (1996), 59.
8 Taubin, 'Nowhere'.
9 Haynes, interviewed by Oren Moverman, 'And all is well in our world – making *Safe*: Todd Haynes, Julianne Moore and Christine Vachon' in John Boorman and Walter Donohue (eds), *Projections 5: Film-makers on Film-making* (London: Faber and Faber, 1996), p. 213.
10 For a journalistic account of people with EI, see Robert Ashton, 'The clean team', *Guardian Weekend* (14 June 1997), 44–9; for an alternative fictional character, see The Bubble Man in the television series *Northern Exposure*.
11 Such indeterminacy was evident in the script: 'for every single scene, with every simple reaction, Todd has built in an emotional reason and a physical reason for what Carol is experiencing. You don't really know what has made her sick' (Julianne Moore in Moverman, 'And all is well', p. 224).
12 Moverman, 'And all is well', p. 202.
13 Dyer, *White*, p. 13.
14 *Ibid.*, p. 63.
15 The following observation remains anecdotal, but I feel is worth making: *Safe* seems to me to leave a white memory trace. On re-watching the film, it is surprising, then, how much of the film is blue. Almost all of the first half of the film – doctors' surgeries, Carol and Greg's house, the baby shower, the 'vibrator' restaurant sequence – is shot in different shades of cold blue;

perhaps the chilling form of this blueness, without life or warmth, indicates the deadness of Carol's white existence.

16   Dyer, *White*, p. 47.
17   Julianne Moore lost so much weight for the role that she began to experience symptoms of anorexia. 'I wanted to look like someone who is disappearing', she said, 'which would create a sense of a person's body betraying them' (in Moverman, 'And all is well', p. 220).
18   Dyer, *White*, p. 17.
19   *Ibid.*, p. 118.
20   *Ibid.*, p. 122.
21   Roy Grundmann, 'How clean was my valley: Todd Haynes's *Safe*', *Cineaste*, 21:4 (1995), 23.
22   *Ibid.*
23   *Ibid.*, p. 25.
24   Dyer, *White*, p. 28.
25   Taubin, 'Nowhere', p. 34.
26   Dyer, *White*, p. 29.
27   *Ibid.*, p. 30.
28   Mary Ann Doane, *The Desire to Desire: the Woman's Film of the 1940s* (London: Macmillan, 1987).
29   Grundmann, 'How clean', p23.
30   *Ibid.*
31   Elizabeth Grosz, 'Refiguring lesbian desire' in Laura Doan (ed.), *The Lesbian Postmodern* (New York: Columbia University Press, 1994), p. 75.
32   Taubin, 'Nowhere', p. 33.
33   Grundmann, 'How clean', p. 25.
34   Dyer, *White*, p. 207.
35   Kaja Silverman, *The Acoustic Mirror: the Female Voice in Psychoanalysis and Cinema* (Bloomington and Indianapolis: Indiana University Press, 1988), p. 42.
36   *Ibid.*, p. ix.
37   Kaja Silverman, 'Dis-embodying the female voice' in Mary Ann Doane, Patricia Mellencamp and Linda Williams (eds), *Re-vision: Essays in Feminist Film Criticism* (AFI Monograph Series, Frederick, MD. University Publications of America, Inc., 1984), p. 131.
38   *Ibid.*, p. 132.
39   *Ibid.*, p. 133.
40   Silverman, *The Acoustic Mirror*, p. 53.
41   Moverman, 'And all is well', p. 219.
42   Silverman, *The Acoustic Mirror*, p. 61.
43   And yet, complicating this argument still further, Silverman argues that a move away from synchronisation is a move towards masculine power.
44   Stephen Heath, *Questions of Cinema* (Bloomington: Indiana University

Press, 1981), p. 55.

45 Silverman has written that 'Hollywood usually obliges only woman to display the stigmata of diegetic interiority' (*The Acoustic Mirror*, p. 71); it is thus tempting to see Carol's visible lesion as a result of the narrative's attempt to control and understand her.

13

Being seen: 'the lesbian' in British television drama

Lizzie Thynne

In the 1980s the slogan 'lesbians are everywhere', scrawled across advertising billboards featuring women, was a response to the lack of representations of lesbians in the contemporary media. The slogan fulfilled two roles: it appropriated the image of the woman to a lesbian reading and it left the trace of an invisible but ubiquitous gang who were defacing hoardings across the country. The invisible hand could surreptitiously subvert dominant meanings while keeping her own identity hidden. By the late 1990s, however, 'the lesbian' had achieved an unprecedented degree of visibility in popular culture, making regular appearances on television, in the cinema, in magazines and in advertising.[1] No self-respecting British soap is now without a lesbian character (with the notable exception of *Coronation Street*) and female couples are used to advertise goods from Kronenbourg beer to Peugeot cars and sunglasses. The tables have apparently been turned, with the outlaw being herself appropriated to a wide range of representations, and, while not often centre stage, at least no longer marking the boundaries of the bizarre.

In this chapter, I focus particularly on recent examples of television drama output in order to explore the limitations of this new inclusivity. I see the proliferation of images not as the sign of a revolution in the social power held by lesbians but as serving particular ends in the television economy and the wider consumer market. I examine a spate of 'quality' dramas (*Playing the Field*, BBC1, 1998, 1999; *Close Relations*, BBC1, 1998; and *Real Women* BBC1, 1998) centred on groups of women to discover what ideological function the now obligatory 'lesbian' character fulfils in relation to the heterosexual love interest around which the plots continue to revolve. I contrast the way in which lesbian characters are still featured predominantly in narratives around the difficulties of coming out or social acceptance with the wider field of gay representation opened up by the recent Channel 4 series *Queer As Folk* (Red Productions, 1999) in which the characters' homosexuality is taken for granted and the gay 'lifestyle' was used as a selling point.

Women like us

The post-9pm drama series has traditionally been addressed, like the more popular mid-evening soaps, to a female audience. Both the series and the single play, unlike the soap, assume a greater proportion of upmarket viewers, who are interested in 'adult' drama reflecting contemporary social concerns in a more complex way than in the soaps. In particular, these series are designed to deliver the kind of women viewers – young, middle class and urban – attracted to images of 'strong women' as developed in the US context in series like *Cagney and Lacey*, *Kate and Allie* and *LA Law*. As Sasha Torres notes, these are the women 'whom advertisers particularly covet, the collation of feminism with consumerism means that feminist audiences "count" for programmers in the way that few other minority groups do'.[2] The female groups on which the British series concentrate indicate this appeal to women and to a popular feminism: a group of northern prostitutes (*Band of Gold*), a women's football team (*Playing the Field*), sisters (*Close Relations*), schoolfriends (*Real Women*). The latter three series were all first broadcast on BBC1 in 1998 and were part of new controller, Peter Salmon's, campaign to 'de-bloke' the 'laddish culture' of his channel which, he claimed, was 'too reliant on Dawn French, Caroline Quentin and Pauline Quirke'[3] (i.e., presumably, did not feature enough women apart from a handful of female stars). The series all feature lesbian characters in a belated catching-up with the soaps on the part of liberal drama commissioners.

Playing the Field[4] takes place in the former mining town of Castleford, where it is the women who are now the main breadwinners as well as forming the local football team; in *Close Relations*, Stephen has lost his publishing job to his lover Prudence (Amanda Redman) and has to take manual work as a builder employed by her father. Men's economic redundancy potentially weakens women's ties to them and leaves the way open for a strengthening of their relations with other women. This is the scenario envisaged in *Playing the Field*, where the women's football team, albeit under male management, fosters the alliances and support the women offer each other in a gesture towards feminist utopia. Within this utopia, the lesbian character would seem to function in a similar way to that of the character of Marilyn, the out-of-the-closet nurse practitioner, in the US prime-time series *Heartbeat*. Torres, in her discussion of this series, highlights the contradictory ways in which mainstream US television represents lesbianism by 'an alternating appeal, following Eve Kosofsky Sedgwick, to universalizing and minoritizing definitions of lesbian identity':[5] in the former definition, lesbianism is part of a continuum of bonds shared by all women; in the latter, 'the lesbian' is queer in the sense of being the only site of homosexuality in a particular text. She notes: 'even as Marilyn and the lesbian characters who occasionally appear on *Kate and Allie*, *The Golden Girls* and *LA Law* signify "feminism" they also ease the ideological threat of such feminist programs by localizing the homosexuality which might otherwise pervade those homosocial spaces'.[6]

In the British series, the boundary between heterosexuality and homosexuality needs to be policed not so much because the action is located entirely within a female environment but because of the visible crises in the women's relationships with men, men whose power is already undermined by the decline in their economic status. The storylines of *Playing the Field* and *Close Relations*, despite the apparent centrality of the female group, focus as much on the women's relationships with men as with each other and the narratives of their conflicts with male partners form the main dramatic interest of the series and take up the most screen time. In *Playing the Field*, Diane's husband, Rick, has had an affair with his sister-in-law, Geraldine, and is racked by doubt as to whether he is the father of her baby. When Diane discovers this she confronts him and throws him out of the house. When he comes back to apologise, there is an emblematic scene between them. Diane is unrepentant, and during their row on the doorstep she shouts at him: 'you can fuck off altogether as far as I'm concerned because I'm thinking of becoming a lesbian'. As she says this she exchanges glances with the lesbian couple, Gabi and Angie, who happen to be passing the house at that moment. The sequence is overdetermined: there is no narrative reason for the appearance of the lesbians – instead the shots of them symbolically reinforce Diane's threat to Rick, which has, however, little probability of being actually realised. Similarly, Geraldine and her husband, Dave, fight over her affair with Rick, his brother. Geraldine asserts she had the affair because Dave no longer wanted to have sex with her. Dave has become impotent because he is undermined by Geraldine's more powerful position as the main breadwinner. This conflict over a woman's power in a heterosexual relationship is contrasted with the scenes of Gabi's first orgasm in bed with Angie, the lesbian character, who is also Gabi's first woman lover. Gabi confesses she has always faked it with men. In *Real Women*, Karen and her woman lover of a few months, Chris, having made love before the sequence begins, lie on the living room floor recalling the noises they made when they first slept together at a conference. In all these dramas, the lesbian sex is always part of an initiation involving one who has never slept with a woman or is in her first gay relationship. As such it is always thrilling, always new – the idealised other of the conflict-ridden power imbalances of heterosex.

In *Close Relations*, set in north London, the principal characters are the three Hammond sisters and their parents. The roller-coaster breakdown of relationships and recouplings in this family presents such an unstable world as to undermine its claim to be realist in its narrative and charac-terisation – here it seems anything could happen, at times tipping the series over into farce. After a heart attack, Dad (Keith Barron), having previously been overtly racist, falls in love with his black nurse half his age; Prudence, who's having an affair with a married man, Stephen, gets given his job and is seduced by his wife; Mum (Sheila Hancock) crashes into a man's car after Dad has left her and immediately starts an affair with him; Lou discovers her husband has had an eight-year affair and mortgaged their house for his lover's business; Lou's sixteen-year-old daughter, Imogen, gets pregnant by the serial adulterer blacksmith; Maddy falls in love with egocentric careerist writer Erin and has her first lesbian affair only to find herself becoming a put-upon housewife. In this context, where the series seems determined to exploit the theme of the crisis in the traditional family to allow the maximum number of sex scenes as each new couple get it together, the lesbianism is both one among the many sexual adventures yet also different. On the one hand, Maddy's newly found sexuality creates ripples amongst her sisters, Prudence and Lou, bringing them closer to a possibility they have not themselves explored and apparently offering an alternative to the prevar-ications they experience at the hands of men – Prudence's lover, Stephen, is still attached to his marriage and children; Lou has been unknowingly betrayed by her husband despite the façade of a successful marriage. Lou is tidying her children's bedroom when Prudence calls her to tell her about Maddy's coming out; when she returns to the housework after the call she comments: 'I wish I was a lesbian and there'd be no children and no horrible, horrible mess.' Lesbianism is constructed as allowing a freer lifestyle than the constraints of marriage. On the other hand, the character identified as 'lesbian' is attributed with the conventional signifiers which accompany the term: political correctness, dowdiness and a bad haircut. The 'dyke' becomes the negative signifier of this excessive feminism; she is politically correct, unstylish and unattractive. The character of Maddy in *Close Relations* is given all these traits – ginger-haired, baggy-trousered, she even wears a cheesecloth blouse, the *non plus ultra* of 1970s bad taste. She is the unappealing counterpart to the 'normal' femininity represented by her sisters, Prudence and Louise.

This series is designed to appeal to a wide female audience of predominantly heterosexual female viewers – it is 'women's-feet-up-after-supper-and-the-kids-are-in-bed television'.[7] As such it is at pains not to alienate the presumed sensibilities of its audience. It does this through reiterating the distinction between different definitions of lesbianism found elsewhere in the women-orientated media. As Sue O'Sullivan comments in her discussion of women's magazines, 'The persona of the lesbian overburdened with politics is not seductive for [the "normal" heterosexual housewife]; lesbianism as part of a newly discovered interest in diversity – of identities and sexual acts – is'.[8] O'Sullivan wittily analyses media attempts to demarcate 'lesbianism as a major political statement' from 'sex acts between women as part of a trendy smorgasbord of sexual possibilities'.[9] The detachment of lesbianism from what is perceived an excessive feminist politics is a necessary strategy in appropriating the appeal of female nonconformity for the marketing of a range of products from clothes to television programmes.[10]

In *Close Relations*, the opposition between lesbianism as defined by a narrow identity politics and sex between women as a pleasurable activity, regardless of identity, is articulated through the contrasting stories of Maddy and Prudence, the blonde, sensuous counterpart to her sister. First Maddy and then Prudence have sex with another woman. Maddy's first night of passion with Erin is presented as a coming home, a discovery of her true identity. For Prudence it is a thrilling one-off with her lover – Stephen's wife, Kaatya – in which Stephen is also a participant. The latter scene draws on existing pornographic conventions, which mark it as conventional male fantasy. Prudence is curious to meet Kaatya, and she goes with Stephen to have dinner with her. Kaatya, who only appears in this scene, is an exotic Dutch woman, an uninhibited redhead, in the mould of the lesbian vampire (the most commonly featured lesbian figure in fiction) who proceeds to seduce Prudence. The seduction takes place with a blazing fire in the background as Stephen looks on drunkenly from the sofa. As in pornography, the scene lacks substantial realist motivation but we are supposed to believe this is Kaatya's manipulative way of getting Stephen back. It also, significantly, takes place as a man watches, and when Kaatya takes Pru upstairs to bed Stephen is there too, invited to take part in a threesome. Sex between women is shown as not just something 'lesbians' do but as something which can result from the eruption of desire between characters defined as heterosexual. The fact that both sisters – one marked as heterosexual and the other lesbian – discover the joys of Sapphic sex would appear to undermine the binary opposition between heterosexuality and homosexuality making this quite a queer family. However, the pornographic conventions within which the scene operates place the women's sexual encounter within the familiar framework of male voyeurism.

The last drama from 1998 I wish to discuss is *Real Women*, another series purporting to be grounded in the way 'we' live now. More comedic in tone than *Playing the Field* and *Close Relations*, it is also the most 'feel-good' in its affirmation of enduring bonds of friendship between women. The utopian premise this time presents a group of thirty-something north London ex-schoolfriends from a working-class background who have remained chums for over twenty years despite their changing fortunes. While this female group includes a closeted lesbian school-teacher, Karen, who lives with her university lecturer girlfriend, Chris, its diversity does not extend to race. Although over one-third of the popula-tion in its actual location is black, all the characters, even secondary ones, are white. Black women, never mind black lesbians, still appear to be invisible to British television as significant consumers whose interest might be addressed. This lack of diversity reinforces the impression that the modish addition of lesbian characters to this type of drama is not born out of any newly discovered egalitarianism; rather it provides further opportunity for the deployment of (white) women as sexual spectacle, albeit within the framework of a serious realist drama where such spectacle can be justified in terms of its supposed narrative integrity. The absence of black faces is also undoubtedly because the series features an array of well-known character actresses, most of whom are well-known television stars and bankable names – Pauline Quirke (*Birds of a Feather*, BBC1), Michelle Collins (*Eastenders*,BBC1), Frances Barber (*Sammie and Rosie Get Laid*, dir. Stephen Frears), Gwyneth Strong (*Only Fools and Horses*, BBC1) Lesley Manville (*High Hopes* and *Secrets and Lies*, dir. Mike Leigh). With the possible exception of Cathy Tyson, there are no black actresses who have been able to win this television star status.

The series quite clearly establishes the importance of the ideal (white)

female community in the opening section – a black-and-white sequence
of teenage schoolgirls frolicking in the playground and being
photographed by one of their number. In the next sequence, the key girls
from this sequence, now grown women, are linked as this same photo is
revealed in each one's house and we are introduced to the tensions of
their present-day lives. The girls' school is conventionally the site of
lesbian desire in cinematic representations from *Maidens in Uniform* (dir.
Leontine Sagan, Germany, 1931) onwards, but none of the women in this
series – except for the poor closeted gay girl, Karen – seems to have
come across lesbianism. The fact that the series is set in north London –
where, again, this 'minority' has a very visible presence and established
subculture – is not allowed to disturb the conventional narrative placing
of 'the lesbian' in a story of 'coming out' to her straight friends. While
these friends struggle with issues of infertility, abortion, career versus
family, being trapped in a stale relationship, fears of growing old and
being left alone, Karen's problems are centred entirely on how to reveal
her sexuality to her mates. While 'the lesbian' is increasingly becoming
'ordinary' in the sense of regularly appearing in these women's dramas
and soaps, being part of the female world envisioned, her role is nearly
always confined to signifying this one kind of otherness. In that sense,
despite her ordinariness she remains extraordinary, outside the usual
concerns of female experience. She is not a 'real woman' is the sense the
others are. Within the terms of adult femininity, as defined by these
dramas, she is condemned to a perpetual adolescence. Once her secret is
revealed, she has no story, since her story is just her sexuality. This was the
fate of the Ellen character after the 'Puppy' ('Coming out') episode, first
transmitted in the UK in April 1998, the same year as the dramas under
discussion. Ellen's naming of herself as gay marked the death of the series.
This was not only because the network decided it was no longer 'family
viewing' but because of the logic of its own narrative. The programme
seemed caught in a double bind between making humour out of the
absurdity of reducing someone to their sexuality and being itself unable
to do anything other than make gags about gayness.

Queer As Folk

Queer As Folk, transmitted in February/March 1999, in many ways marks
a major shift in the representation of homosexuality on prime-time
British television, prefigured only by the dramatisation of Armistead
Maupin's *Tales of the City*. Set in contemporary Manchester, it follows the

story of three gay men and in particular fifteen-year-old Nathan's infatu-
ation with the older Stuart, with whom he first has sex. It is one of the first
mainstream dramas to take the characters' sexuality as given – the storylines do not revolve around 'coming out' to a straight world but instead
are focused on the men's relationships with each other, as friends and
lovers. In this final section, I want to make some comparison between this
and the women-centred dramas already discussed and look at how the
gay lifestyle as represented in *Queer As Folk* is used to signify modernity
and freedom.

The series played an important role in the attempt to rebrand Channel
4 and provides an interesting example of how 'gay' is being extensively
reconstructed in some sections of the popular media as no longer a
despised identity but a sexy, glamorous one. Michael Jackson, Chief
Executive of Channel 4, highlighted the series as central to his vision of 4
as the 'channel of modern culture', portraying 'the experience of living
now'.[11] Channel 4's statutory remit to show programming catering for
minority audiences has, many critics have argued, until now resulted in
dull, worthy programming – programmes which address issues, are
educational but lack style and wide appeal – reflecting a long-standing
debate within both radical cinema and television about education versus
pleasure and entertainment. What is seen as the didactic approach is now
rejected in favour of a more crossover address – programmes which
focus on gay 'lifestyle' rather than identity politics and can appeal to a
diverse audience. 'In the past', comments Jackson, 'this subject would have
been handled in a self-conscious manner. But in *Queer as Folk*, there are
no issues, only emotions, unsympathetic gay characters and shockingly
no safe sex message.'[12]

Both male and female homosexuality may be used as a draw for
audiences, as Michael Bronski comments: 'when gay sensibility is used as
a sales pitch, the strategy is that gay images imply distinction and nonconformity, granting straight consumers a longed-for place outside the
humdrum mainstream'.[13] Gay male sexuality, though, has the advantage
of being unencumbered by the politics of feminism and is already associated with stylish clubs and music, available for consumption by the
young and hip audiences that the channel covets. Unlike ITV the
audience of which is older, it doesn't worry about the 'old ladies' who
might switch off. The realist portrayal of sex between women is already
so heavily coded as pornographic for a straight audience, or as asexual
because of its rejection of conventional femininity and/or the lack of a
penis, that it presents some problems in terms of consumption. Gay

men's sexuality is more easily appropriated as pleasurable and provides a daring spectacle with which Jackson can establish Channel 4 as the rebel channel in opposition to the plethora of more restrained, paternalist or 'safe' channels, none of which, he claims would have broadcast this series.

The presenter announced the first episode as featuring sex with a capital S – a far cry from the conventional warnings about scenes that may be offensive to some viewers. The high-profile poster campaign for the series featuring the three attractive young leads embracing each other with the strap line 'How much fun can three lads have together?' also promised risqué sex. A warning about the use of 'strong language' prefaced the last episode. By then it had also lost £2 million of sponsorship from Beck's Beer, suggesting that although the programme's queerness could be utilised to re-define the channel's brand as an innovator it could not function simply as a vehicle for marketing lifestyle goods such as Beck's. The consumerist discourse which defines gayness as an attractive, hedonist designer lifestyle is still at odds with the moral discourse on homosexuality even though the people who articulate that discourse are themselves now a minority. Only a hundred complaints were received about the series compared to 1,554 received about the transmission of Martin Scorsese's *The Last Temptation of Christ* in 1995. Most of the complaints about *Queer As Folk* were received 'not from viewers who objected to gay sex on television but from gays who objected to the portrayal of homosexuals as heartless flesh-eaters'.[14]

From a marketing point of view it is not of great consequence to Channel 4 if a minority is offended, whether because of identity politics or moral disapproval. On the contrary, it has courted a reputation for controversy in sexual matters and relished the dubbing of the previous chief executive, Michael Grade, as the 'pornographer-in-chief' by *The Daily Mail*. Since the advent of digital television and the arrival of many more channels, the ability to attract this kind of publicity is an even more important asset. Channel 4's audience may be relatively small (around a ten per cent share) but the kind of viewer profile it has is extremely attractive to advertisers – a high proportion of the sought-after sixteen-to-thirty-four-year-olds, especially in the higher socio-economic groups. The protagonist of *Queer As Folk*, Stuart, is a sexy rogue who lives in a fashionable loft, works in PR, has a four-wheel drive, clubs and fucks the night away – he leads the quintessential young, single, affluent lifestyle, which many of the targeted audience aspire to. The series both celebrates and critiques this 'party' lifestyle. Vince and Nathan show up Stuart's shallow egocentricity, but the memorable images from the series are from those sequences where men watch other men in the charged erotic atmosphere of the club: Vince and pals watching Stuart dancing with two men he's picked up before taking them home; Vince and his lover enviously admiring the beautiful fifteen-year-old Nathan strutting his stuff.

Where, then does this leave 'the lesbian'? Still, in *Queer As Folk*, on the margins of the narrative as a kind of unattractive counterpart to the fun-loving boys. The lesbian couple, Romey and Lisa, who are bringing up the child, Alfie, that Romey has conceived by Stuart, are known half-ironically to the other characters, both straight and gay, as 'the lesbians'. Romey signifies the opposite to Stuart's fecklessness, since she is responsible, politically conscious and maternal – not values which are endorsed by the series' ideology. As the repository of political correctness, she is determined to marry a black friend, Lance, to save him from being deported, prompting retaliation from Lisa and Stuart who see Lance as a threat. In focusing on Stuart's inadequacy as 'the father', the narrative completely sidelines the role of Romey's partner as a co-parent, reiterating the conservative notion of parenthood as primarily involving the biological parents. Lisa apparently does not see Alfie as her child even though she is living with him and caring for him. Instead, she is jealous and resentful of Stuart and Lance. As secondary characters, 'the lesbians' are inevitably drawn in relatively simple shorthand but it is disappointing to see that even in this overtly gay series they still represent the relatively unattractive 'other' in relation to the gay protagonists.

Male sexuality remains the norm against which female sexuality, whether it be straight or queer, is defined. While for mainstream television, both male and female homosexualities present novel additions to the potentially hackneyed tale of boy meets girl, the terms in which our otherness is defined are still bound by gender. A truly queer dynamic would destabilise definitions of both gender and sexuality, problematising the ways in which the one is constructed within and in relation to the other; such a dynamic would, however, make perversity less easily consumable by the crossover audience which prime-time television schedulers seek. To enter into popular representation is to be subject to specific and limiting definitions. We are not, as Robyn Weigman puts it, able to 'wend our way back to the moment prior to commodity production'[15] and therefore the recirculation of our diverse sexualities into marketable packages is the price of visibility. 'The lesbian' in this genre has not been a sign that significantly destabilises the meaning of heterosexuality since she is either negatively framed as the bearer of unfashionable politics, caught in a struggle for social acceptance or represents the perpetual thrill of initiation. While, on the one hand, it would be a pleasure to see the complexity of lesbian subcultures represented in television drama, on the other, greater inclusion alone would not prevent our more radical potential being reduced to a set of saleable attributes, re-marking and expanding the boundaries of heterosexuality.

Notes

1   A number of articles have discussed the 1990s phenomenon of lesbian visibility in the mainstream media, in particular Diane Hamer and Belinda Budge (eds), *The Good, the Bad and the Ugly: Popular Culture's Romance with Lesbianism* (London, Pandora, 1994), and Louise Allen, *The Lesbian Idol: Martina, kd and the Consumption of Lesbian Masculinity* (London, Cassell, 1997).

2   Sasha Torres, 'Television/feminism: *Heartbeat* and primetime lesbianism' in Henry Abelove, Michèle Aina Barale and David M. Halperin (eds), *The Lesbian and Gay Studies Reader* (London and New York, Routledge, 1993), p. 178.

3   Peter Salmon quoted in *Gay Times* (April 1998), 91.

4   A second series of *Playing the Field* was broadcast in 1999. My discussion alludes to both series. Both *Playing the Field* and *Band of Gold* were written by Kay Mellor.

5   Torres, 'Television/feminism', p. 176.

6   *Ibid*, p. 179.

7   *The Sunday Times* (24 May 1998), 31

8   Sue O'Sullivan, 'Girls who kiss girls and who cares?' in Hamer and Budge (eds), *The Good, the Bad and the Ugly*, p. 89.

9   *Ibid.*, p. 78.

10 See Danae Clark's discussion of capitalism's restyling of lesbian self-repre-sentation into the trendy and chic in her 'Commodity lesbianism' in Abelove *et al.* (eds) *Lesbian and Gay Studies Reader*, pp. 186–201.

11 Michael Jackson, 'Four the record', *Media Guardian* (5 July 1999), 2.

12 *Ibid.*, p. 3.

13 Michael Bronski, *Culture Clash: the Making of Gay Sensibility* (Boston, South End Press, 1984), p. 187; quoted in Clark 'Commodity lesbianism', p. 197.

14 Mary Braid and John Walsh, 'So what's your complaint? waste of money; sexual deviant; bully; drug pusher; hamster molester', *The Independent*, Q2 (24 March 1999), 169.

15 Robyn Weigman, 'Introduction: mapping the lesbian postmodern' in Laura Doan (ed.), *The Lesbian Postmodern* (New York, Columbia University Press, 1994).

Part IV

Desire: in future

14

Too hot for Yale?

Jonathan Dollimore

It was a memorable and scary class. I knew that if I could not control an escalating argument between two students, then not just that one class but the entire course might be wrecked for the rest of the term.

Class warfare

The course in question was part of the Sexual Dissidence programme at the University of Sussex. It attracted some notoriety for being the first of its kind in the country. You can imagine the scene: right-wing Members of Parliament proclaiming loudly that the University should at least be shut down, and preferably bombed as well (I do not exaggerate). The tabloid press agreed, but also conjured up lurid fantasies of *what* exactly we did on such a course.

It's characteristic of academics to get highly indignant about this kind of publicity – and not a little self-righteous as well. In truth it did us little harm. It was so ludicrous that informed opinion had to mobilise in our support. But it did lead some students to assume that an in-your-face radical stance on homosexuality was a guarantee that one would complete the course successfully. The argument that blew up in the class that day involved one such student, a young gay man who was insisting that homosexuality was a revolutionary force in western culture, with the power to entirely subvert its heterosexual underpinning. And a good thing too: he disliked that culture and wanted sexual dissidence to be the spearhead of all the forces that would overthrow it. The other student, also gay, insisted that this was wishful thinking: homosexuality could exist comfortably alongside heterosexuality and it was only a residual outmoded prejudice that led some people to think otherwise. Education could and would change all this. And part of this process of education involved gay people showing straight people that we really were not that different. More to the point, he insisted that the course that had brought us together in that class should be a part of this rational, reformist programme and *not* the platform for the self-deluding revolutionary rhetoric being advanced by the radical student.

The battle lines were drawn up. Silence fell and each deferred to me – or rather looked menacingly my way, implicitly demanding support. I needed to buy time. I could try 'good lord, is that the time' and break for a coffee, or I could resort to the no less diversionary tactic of asking the views of some other, so far silent, student. I opted for the latter: 'Jeremy, what do you think?' This was his reply: 'I feel excluded and oppressed by this discussion. It completely ignores bisexuality, and I am bisexual.' Suddenly a new battle line was mapped on to the existing one, and for a moment the revolutionary and the reformist students suspended combat. As out gay men they each distrusted the bisexual, not least because they regarded him as sitting on the fence, unable to make up his mind, avoiding commitment because lacking the courage. 'Good lord', I exclaimed, 'is that the time …' Angry silence on all sides; nobody moved. The day was saved only by a mobile telephone going off in the satchel of the radical student, who hastily left the room to take the call while the rest of us did indeed go for coffee.

I helped devise that course on Sexual Dissidence, and at times like that I half-wished I had not. It could be impossible to teach, and not just because of clashing personalities. Something much more significant was implicated in that three-way stand-off that day, something which made the presence of such a course as worthwhile as it was difficult to teach. Unbeknown to them, those two gay students were re-enacting one of the most fundamental antagonisms within the politics of sexual dissidence over the past century. As for Jeremy, little did he realise that in just a few years bisexuality would cease to be regarded as the dishonest third option. Marjorie Garber's much-discussed 1995 book *Vice Versa: Bisexuality and the Eroticism of Everday Life* consolidated bisexuality's return as a viable and progressive sexuality. Meanwhile in the academy, a new bisexual politics, increasingly influential in Britain and the USA, would be claiming this to be the quintessentially postmodern sexuality – mobile, unfixed and subversive of all existing sexual identities, including the gay one.[1]

If one central objective of that course was to get students to engage with the longer history of such arguments, one central difficulty it encountered was that students were already so embroiled in the arguments that the effort of historical understanding seemed, to them, to be beside the point. We encountered that strange but familiar position in debates about modern sexuality: if recent history has profoundly changed the ways we think about sexuality, it has also led us to experience it in ways which seem to have little if anything to do with history.

Too hot for Yale

Let's for a moment stay with that stand-off between the radical and the reformist gay students. The argument not only remains with us but has if anything become more conflicted now that the so-called Sex Wars and the Culture Wars have been mapped onto each other. Consider the front cover of the American paper *The Village Voice* for 29 July 1997. It proclaims: 'It's here, it's queer, [and] It's too hot for Yale'. The sub-heading reads: 'Gay studies spawns a radical theory of desire'. The story is about how Yale is apparently trying to play down its earlier reputation as a centre for gay studies, declining an offer of several million dollars from Larry Kramer for a full-time professor of gay studies on the grounds that this was not yet a proven academic discipline. This was met with loud charges of homophobia. Though I have no brief for Yale University, scepticism is justified here. Not because homophobia doesn't exist, but on the contrary because it does exist, and to an extent which gives plausibility even to false claims about it. But it is also the case that, as lesbian and gay studies have become increasingly fashionable in the US academic marketplace, claims are made on its behalf which are sufficiently spurious to give at least a degree of credence to the Yale scepticism about it. And this *Village Voice* article is a prime instance of what I mean. I don't want to dwell on yet another squabble in the US academy – they are as tedious as they are frequent – but this one does focus a problem fundamental to education, and in particular the project of a compelling cultural critique. Bluntly, I believe that much sexual radicalism today is not radical at all but tendentious posturing. Further, this is symptomatic of the way that much radical critique is ineffectual because it has become academic, metropolitan and professionalised. If I'm especially critical of the US academy this is because it's there that the problem is most obvious, and because that academy increasingly partakes of the general cultural imperialism of the USA.

Leo Bersani has criticised the lack of self-criticism in the lesbian and gay community. The reason for that lack is partly a fear of the academic thought police, who brand as homophobic any criticism of gay self-promotion, thereby confirming the point about homophobia made a moment ago. But, more understandably, it is also because such criticism is felt to betray the gay cause and give ammunition to the enemy. But, says Bersani, 'we have enough freedom, even enough power, to stop feeling like traitors if we cease to betray our intelligence for the sake of the cause, and if ... we admit to having told a few lies about ourselves (and others)'.[2] Bersani is to be admired for the way he's prepared to take on the gay thought police, and also some no less censorious feminists, lesbian and otherwise. His writing is important for the way it takes issue with the comfortable and sometimes spurious radicalism that some (mostly US-based) gay academics currently propagate. He mentions in passing speaking at a lesbian and gay conference about gay men's love of the cock, only to be reproached by a lesbian colleague for having given a talk which 'marginalised women'. I've no idea which conference this was, but I can guess at its kind. It aspires to be the most radical of occasions while being at heart deeply conformist, tyrannised by the punitiveness of a certain kind of academic sexual politics which listens only for the opportunity to castigate the speaker for exclusions which, allegedly, obliterate the significance of anything directly said. This of course encourages speakers to spend so long covering their arse against any suggestion of racism, phobia, imperialism, class bias etc. etc., that they have little of significance to say anyway. Instead they tell the audience what it wants to hear in the desperate hope of becoming its favourites, or at least avoiding the dreaded reproach of discrimination-by-ommision. The complainant at this conference recalls those who have been so resentful that Eve Kosofsky Sedgwick hasn't spent as much time talking about lesbians as about gay men, sometimes with the implication that this is a deeply damaging, even conspiratorial, exclusion. In practice, the reverse is the case: the very success of Sedgwick's project actually helps create a space for someone else to do what she hasn't; her omissions became others' opportunities.

Returning to that *Village Voice* article, we learn that this radical theory of desire that's too hot for Yale has been spawned not by gay studies but by something rather more recent called queer theory. The major strands of queer theory took off in part as a reaction to lesbian and gay studies because the latter were deemed not radical enough. Queer theory has been very influential in academic, intellectual and metropolitan circles in the last few years. It's difficult to define exactly. Certainly the author of this article, Richard Goldstein, had great difficulty doing so. After he had heroically struggled through the language of the major queer texts, the most famous of which, Judith Butler's *Gender Trouble*, he calls 'as dense as a black hole', the only radical agenda he can derive from them is that – wait for it – nothing is really fixed and we are or should be free to be and do what we want. And Goldstein is actually sympathetic.

To be fair, queer theory also celebrates sexual perversions, although it's hardly original in doing so. Fetishism is quite high on its agenda and also what is sometimes called part-object sexuality. If a lesbian or gay man is foolish enough to be overheard saying something incredibly old-fashioned like 'I am attracted by the person rather than their superficial attributes', they are likely to be met with howls of derision by queer theorists. For them, such humanist sentimentality is a huge sexual turn-off. They have great sympathy with the fetishist who famously declared that he was in love with the foot but had to settle for the whole person. This is of course a quintessentially postmodern anecdote because, depending on whom you tell it to, you can substitute bits of anatomy as you wish. Erring on the side of caution here, I settle for the foot. In truth, my own erotic sympathies, not to mention my ironic ones, tend in the direction of this anecdote. To the extent that the English can be said to be European (and some of us are trying), I'm proud to learn from the decadent traditions of the old world. But that's hardly the point – or if it is, it's only to the extent that queer theorists are often oblivious to the history which has anticipated them.

But there's an important sense in which queers were right about a certain kind of gay/lesbian activist of the 1980s whose radicalism was steeped in a petty-bourgeois ethic; for all the ostensible radicalism, at heart he or she could accept their own homosexuality, and certainly other people's, only if it was respectable and self-policing, and represented to themselves and others in positive images. Their indignation at homophobia was genuine and justified, but was also intensified by, and helped to conceal, anxieties about aspects of homosexual behaviour by which they felt threatened or disgusted. Their counterparts today are those gays who want homsexuality to be simultaneously subversive and politically correct.

Something comparable to the queer challenge to gay happened with feminism at least a decade ago. Some feminists imagined a unified movement around the so-called homosexual continuum – roughly, the idea of being 'women-identified' without the lesbian sex. This was rather wickedly caricatured by the lesbian activist Pat Califia when she said:

> After the wimmin's revolution, sex will consist of wimmin holding hands, taking their shirts off and dancing in a circle. Then we will all fall asleep at exactly the same moment. If we didn't all fall asleep something else might

happen – something male-identified, objectifying, pornographic, noisy, undignified. Something like an orgasm.[3]

More recently Julie Burchill, in her *Absolute Filth: an A to Z of Sex*, tells us that orgasm is 'The point, the whole point and nothing but the point of having sex in the first place. If what you want is cuddling, buy a puppy' (entry for 'Orgasm'). Califia has been leading a campaign to put sex back into lesbianism, whereas Burchill is here apparently speaking for everyone.

To a degree, queer theory is just the latest instance of this pleasurable strategy of upsetting the prescriptive agenda of the previously fashionable radical movements by promoting the sexual practices they ignore or exclude. Califia has especially recommended sado-masochism. And in the name of sexual libertarianism this strategy of upsetting the new normative agendas seems to me to be not only pleasurable but productive. But as the grounds for claiming a radical new theory of desire? I think not. Often I see little more than a libertarianism which dovetails fairly conveniently with the consumerist aesthetic of the well-heeled and well-insulated metropolitan.[4]

On a more intellectual level, queer rehearses a familiar postmodern move whereby it rejects not just the old religious idea of the soul (barely remembered anyway) but also the modernist secular soul-substitutes. So, for instance, even the idea of having a comparatively fixed sexual identity is rejected as too soul-like. Some queer writers will even say it is a form of self-oppression for gay people to claim or assume such an identity. This is particularly exasperating for those who came to gay consciousness believing it was a form of self-oppression *not* to make such a claim. So today the radical agenda is less a question of what one is than of what one does: 'Queers, start speaking for yourself! … Call yourself what you want. Reject all labels. Be all labels. Liberate yourself from the lie that we're all lesbians and gay men … Queer is not about gay or lesbian – it's about sex!'[5] The following anecdote, apochryphal or not, perfectly queers the relation between sexual identity and sexual behaviour. An American student eventually gets to meet a cult writer in the US lesbian S/M scene whom she admires greatly. The writer asks the student what kind of person she sleeps with. The student, grateful of the opportunity to do so, eagerly announces that she too is lesbian:

> Writer, surprised: Are you telling me you mean you don't fuck men?
> Student: Definitely not. Like I said, I'm lesbian. Like you.
> Writer (after reflective pause): You mean you don't even fuck gay men?

Student: Well no – I mean they're still men, aren't they?
Writer (after further pause): Well, you sound like a pretty straight dyke to
   me.

The beauty of insisting on sexual practices rather than identity is that
anyone can now be queer. It's a very democratic form of radicalism. Carol
Queen writes: 'Heterosexual behaviour does not always equal straight.
When I strap on a dildo and fuck my male partner, we are engaging in
"heterosexual" behaviour but I can tell you it feels altogether *queer*, and
I'm sure my grandmother and Jesse Helms would say the same.'[6] Actually
I doubt if 'queer' would be the first word which sprang to the lips of
Granny and Jesse, and certainly not 'queer' as it has been refashioned by
postmodernism. But you never know, and I certainly don't want to be
patronising – at least not to Granny. But the real issue here is whether
such sexual practices can ever be inherently radical. To imagine they are
is to be closer in thought to Granny and Jessie than Queen realises: after
all, to regard a sexual practice as inherently radical is really just the
obverse of regarding it as inherently evil or, indeed, as inherently normal.

One thing we learn from the history of dissidence is that the subversiveness of a dissident culture derives in part from the force which resists
it. That means there is a severe and violent dialectic between the two. In
a rather trivial sense this is apparent from Queen's claim: somehow the
'queering' of that particular sexual practice required, if not the actual
presence of Granny and Jessie, then certainly their imagined disapproval.
The transgression has to be regarded, discussed, known about in order to
be transgressive. Which is one reason why today sexual transgression is
talked about so much. But as we talk up our transgressions, let's never
forget that historically the working out of this dialectic has involved the
murder, mutilation and incarceration of sexual dissidents. I repeat: the
subversiveness of a dissident culture derives in part from the force which
resists it. Hence that violent dialectic and all the broken people left in its
wake.

But maybe I'm becoming too serious and missing the new queer insistence on the importance of pleasure for the dissident agenda. I would
indeed hate to be associated with the puritanical attitude which used to
say that nothing pleasurable could be radical, and that politically effective
action had to painful. If it wasn't hurting either the activists or those they
were trying to change, it wasn't working. Depending on its size, maybe
that couple with their dildo were upholding the puritan tradition after
all. Of course there's nothing wrong in principle wih the new insistence

on mixing politics and pleasure. The error is to pretend that, because it's pleasurable, sexy and shocking, it's subverting patriarchy, heterosexuality, masculinity and whatever else we don't like. It's an obvious point, but it seemingly needs saying: pleasure, sex and shock are neither necessary nor sufficient conditions for radical political effect. To want them to be so, corresponds to a more general move today whereby the undoubted truth that sexuality is political through and through, has allowed many to delude themselves into believing that sexuality is the only political focus worthy of attention. This is a development which goes hand in hand with an increasingly naive notion of the political, and very probably an abdication of the political.

Radical versus reformist sexual politics

And that in turn has left contemporary sexual politics caught in a real contradiction between what I earlier described as the radical and the reformist agendas, as epitomised in the stand-off between those two students. The radical position represents gay people – sorry: queers and dykes – as disturbing, disruptive, anarchic, ludic and more. They express the militant, radical, subversive difference of queer desire, especially when seeking to deliberately pervert heterosexuality, *à la* Queen, the dildo and her partner. Queer radicals welcome the idea that there remains something residually daemonic about homosexual desire; it is why they think or hope it can never be accommodated within an existing respectable sexual order. But it is also the reason why it cannot be tamed by respectable self-representations by gay people themselves.

What does daemonic mean here? I'll return to this; for now let it refer to that something in sexual desire which cannot be socialised. The more we try to contain and control sexuality the more likely some part of it will escape or resist control, and probably return to disrupt, and maybe even subvert whatever or whoever is trying to control it. Of course sex radicals tame and rework the daemonic in various ways, one of which is especially relevant here: they tend to represent themselves as personally immune to the subversiveness of desire. It's an immunity which comes with being radical, since to be radical is not to be repressed and, via a simplification of Freud, it is only the repressed who can be fucked over by desire. In other words, sexual radicals are the agents of the disruptiveness of desire but rarely, if ever, its victims. But they are of course victims of social discrimination against their desire – Jessie and Granny – rather than the desire itself. But the tone of much radicalism suggests otherwise: often supercilious, it is also anxious, defended and sometimes paranoid. Eve Kosofsky Sedgwick has just written a perceptive and, I hope, influential piece on paranoia in the US academy and beyond. One hesitates to agree, however, with Sedgwick's claim – she is writing in 1997 – that 'to theorize out of anything *but* a paranoid critical stance has come to seem naive, pious, or complaisant'.[7] Sedgwick is speaking specifically of gay and queer theory, although she gives the paranoia in question a certain intellectual pedigree by alluding to its origins in the so-called 'hermeneutics of suspicion' in philosophers and analysts like Marx, Freud and Nietzsche. In fact, US queer theorists would probably be less paranoid if they paid more not less attention to such writers. I suspect their problem has more to do with the professional in-fighting in the US academy, in which, it seems, the higher you go and the more powerful you become, the greater the paranoia. That Sedgwick is herself assuming that frame of reference is suggested not only by her actual examples of paranoid writing but by her need to state the obvious rather defensively: 'To be other than paranoid ... does *not*, in itself, entail a denial of the reality or gravity of enmity or oppression.'[8] Obviously not, and in the context of the writing of gay historians and gay theorists one could cite the outstanding non-paranoid writings of, among others, Dennis Altman, Jeffrey Weeks and Alan Sinfield. Such work also indicates that, contrary to what Sedgwick implies, the critical strategy of seeking to expose a concealed truth is not an intrinsically paranoid activity. Nor should it be assumed to be definitively modern, given its origins in the fundamental distinction between appearance and reality as it evolved in diverse areas of human thought including philosophy, theology and astronomy to mention only some of the oldest.

In complete contrast to the radicals, the reformists emphasise the sanity of homosexual identity and they tend to do so in non-paranoid ways. They deem negative attitudes to homosexuality to be irrational: in a more enlightened, non-homophobic culture, homosexuality would be accepted. What is required is not full-scale radical social change so much as the elimination of outmoded prejudice. This reformist position is by no means necessarily a conservative one, but its conservative wing is conveniently reflected in the title of recent books: Bruce Bawer's *A Place at the Table* and Andrew Sullivan's *Virtually Normal*.

In that seminar of mine, the radical and the reformist positions were represented in the stand-off between those two students. But most queer theorists, especialy those in the US academy, seemingly want it both ways. This compromised position is starkly apparent in the way we have witnessed such academics keen to out-queer each other on the conference circuit with ever more provocative papers, only then to become self-rightously indignant when the right-wing press responds exactly as anyone could have predicted. The radical agenda is in the deliberate provocation; the reformist agenda in the indignation at the response provoked. To some of these academics it seems unthinkable that sexual dissidence may have a price in terms of professional status. But why not, if, as they claim, sexual dissidence really is a form of political dissidence? Where else would such dissidence be free of risk? Some of the anger of sexual radicals against contemporary society is justified. But in the academy, and in the disputes which spill over from the academy into the public domain, anger is also manufactured; the academically ambitious, and that includes sexual politicians within the academy, notoriously empower themselves through indignation.

Moreover, they have been known to keep themselves empowered by controlling who is allowed to be dissident. We sometimes speak of pushing back 'the frontiers of knowledge'. Of course it's misleading to speak of knowledge as if it is a geographical, territorial strategy of expansion. And yet the professionalisation of the US academy keeps this way of speaking half-applicable because its knowledge-frontier moves all the time but in predictable, limited and controlled directions. Those actually on the frontier – i.e., in the prestigious university departments – are rather few and highly influential in deciding who else might come up alongside. One consequence of the professionalisation of knowledge is that its frontiers are policed even as they are unfolded. And again, that is nowhere more apparent than in the patronage system of the academy. In certain respects nothing has been more conformist in recent years than the academic output of a younger generation of 'radical' US scholars whose careers are dependent upon the approval of the 'stars' who control the field. Simon Jarvis observes the double bind on the queer-theory student: the need to be transgressive is acted out within an academic regime which encourages 'cowed tutelage'.[9]

The problem has become serious enough for some to question whether the academy is any longer the right place for dissident social critique. The scholar and Palestinian activist Edward Said has more than once criticised a professionalising attitude to ideas in our universities which leads to theory being taught 'so as to make the student believe he or she can become a Marxist, a feminist, an Afrocentrist, or a deconstructionist with about the same effort and commitment required in choosing items from a menu'.[10] Said's metaphor makes clear the consumerist dimension to this. (One wonders if 'queer' might now be added to the menu.) And this points to another, equally important dimension of the problem, and one which goes beyond the university.

More than ever before, movements like postmodernism and queer theory are hugely influential in the humanities departments of universities, but equally thrive in a larger metropolitan context. This was forcefully brought home to me in a very different context – in South Africa, at a conference on post-colonialism. African delegates spoke critically of what they called metropolitan theory – that is, theories of post-colonialism originating not just within the major western cities but within centres of western capital. It was felt not just that these theories were inapplicable to the African context but that they misrepresented it in ways which seemed almost like a new colonisation or at least a form of intellectual imperialism. What made the resentment of those South Africans so acute was that they had to work through a double bind: the theory which mispresented the African reality was also the theory which had helped make the conference possible and given some visibility to the issues. Again, a dialectic not dissimilar to the one I remarked earlier, violent in a very different way, and by which real politics proceed. Some of the US speakers at this conference were especially resented because they seemed to regard the South African context as like any other: just somewhere else to take the same old academic road show with its radical pretensions, and a thoroughly conservative US-centred focus.

For all its cosmopolitan affect, much metropolitan thought thrives on a new parochialism – that self-absorbed, inward-looking and relatively insulated existence which has always, to a greater or lesser degree, characterised academic life and which now, albeit very differently, is also a feature of intellectual, urban avant-garde culture. Which means that, even as this theory gestures towards cultural difference, it remains insulated from it. The geographies of some modern cities epitomise this of course, with privileged and the deprived tightly juxtaposed yet still effectively segregated. Increasingly, cultural and intellectual life in the metropolis partakes of this situation of segregated juxtapositions. Diverse cultural networks criss-cross with each other yet individually remain insulated from the greater complexity to which they belong. Of course interaction does occur, but it is often regulated by the sophisticated communications characteristic of advanced capitalism, communications which, in many ways, have only refined the more traditional kinds of segregation based on class and race.

Queer theory is quintessentially metropolitan and, at its worst, little more than intellectual style politics (for which there should be a place in every fallen world). Its claim to a poised and perfect radicalism reflects the influence of a facile postmodernism, the kind which competes to be be on the forward edge of our own contemporary moment, and from there clamours to announce a profound new insight into the here and now, telling us that today radical change is in the air while knowing that tomorrow it will all change again and anxious to be in on the diagnosis when it does. Postmodernism of this kind partakes of what I call wishful theory: a preconceived view of the world is elaborated by mixing and matching bits and pieces of diverse theories. If anything in 'reality' offers resistance, splice in or jump-cut to another theory better suited to erasing the difficulty.

To escape the limitations of the contemporary, cultural theory needs the longer perspective of the history of thought. With such a perspective we can see that the oscillation between the radical and the reformist positions in sexual politics doesn't have to be simple hypocrisy. Many sexual dissidents, just like many other radicals, have experienced this ambivalent wish to be outside and inside at the same time. (As so often, the actual life of Oscar Wilde, not to mention his writing, epitomises the conflict in fascinating ways.) Indeed, this very ambivalence is sympto-matic of one of the great formative disputes about sexual desire – especially deviant desire – in western culture: is such desire really inher-ently radical, dangerous and disruptive – daemonic – or does it become so, if at all, only when thwarted and distorted by repressive social arrange-ments?

The reformist position tends to align with the second view, and in doing so inherits the great rationalist legacy of the Enlightenment, for which the problem is indeed not sexual desire so much as the society which distorts and persecutes it; if only desire could be freed from super-stition, discrimination and other irrational constraints, we would be happier as individuals and society would be better for it. By contrast, the radical view inherits a much older idea of desire as inherently dangerous and always potentially disruptive. This is the dominant view in western culture. We associate it mainly with Christianity, but it goes back before that: the Greeks were very clear about the disruptive potential of excessive desire, and it continues right up to Freud's claim that there will for ever always remain a fundamental struggle between the demands of instinct and those of civilisation. The conservative response to this struggle is to side with civilisation against desire: social cohesion requires desire to be controlled, harnessed, restrained and, in so far as is possible, educated. The radical response is to side with desire against civilisation; it seeks to

liberate repressed desire and use its energies to revolutionise the way
we live.

And yet the radical view remains indebted to the conservative view that
it breaks away from. We seem unable to conceptualise momentous
cultural development except in terms of radical breaks. Postmodernism
especially has been obsessed with going beyond, with rapid transition, the
moment of complete change. But we should recognise too what I can
only call, with deliberate awkwardness, radical continuity. By this I don't
mean tradition – that slow, more or less conscious process of selective
development. Rather it refers to the way something can seemingly
disappear, yet actually be mutating in the form of its (apparent) opposite
or successor. In other words, the two things are strangely complicit, the
radical break both disguising and facilitating the radical continuity. For
example, sexual radicals are typically stridently anti-religious. They reject
the idea of original sin, and even the modern (diluted) Christian distrust
of sexual desire. They even break with the secular philosophies which
succeed Christianity, for instance psychoanalysis, to the extent that such
philosophies regard the repression of desire as inevitable and necessary to
some degree. But the indebtedness of sexual radicalism to religion
remains apparent in the way it imagines sexuality as a powerful force.
Only now it is the medium not of evil but of freedom; liberated desire has
the potential to overthrow the unjust society which represses the individual and everything else truly human. This depends on the secularisation
of the soul: our freedom comes to be identified with our spiritual capacities as unique mortal individuals but also, increasingly, our capacities as
rational, civilised beings; and unfreedom is associated more with social
existence: man is born free but everywhere is in chains. The religious
antecedents are also apparent in the sexual radical's idea of sexual desire
being an identity, the source of an authentic selfhood for which we must
be prepared to fight and suffer. A spiritual conception of the self has been
appropriated for a sexual politics and St Augustine doubtless turns in his
grave. And let him: he of all should know that culture evolves through
such audacious appropriations.

We've already seen that queer sexual radicals are embarrassed by the
religious implications of this sense of desire as the basis of authentic
identity; not for them any suggestion of inward essence. But they are
suspicious too of the idea of desire as an energy or force because that
smacks of another kind of essentialism almost as bad as religion:
'biologism'. So what exactly is left of the radical agenda? It's a good
question: the very things which once made desire disruptive have been

systematically (or not) deconstructed, while the wish to keep it disruptive has, if anything, increased. One move is to mask the problem with ever more sophisticated theoretical analysis – hence the difficulties of our *Village Voice* journalist and many others struggling to get to grips with what queer theorists really mean.

For these and other reasons, the reformist position is gaining ground against the radical. Let's for a moment imagine that it wins the future. Its advocates successfully persuade the majority that hitherto demonised practices like homosexuality are more or less compatible with society as it is; they present no threat, for example, to the family, which that same majority are now happy to see evolve into new and diverse forms. Homosexuality is at last integrated as an option, no more remarkable than say, those married heterosexuals who choose to have no children or four. Others in this tradition will go further, seeking even wider reforms, yet with the same insistence that sexual behaviour is in itself unremark-able; what precisely one does, and the gender of the person with whom one does it, is not the issue; what matters are the relationships, and most especially the power relationships, that obtain within human sexuality. Consent, agreement, responsibilty and above all equality before the law will be of paramount importance.

Let's imagine further that the reformist has a completely free run into the next century and manages to demystify human sexuality finally and fully. Looking back, people then will marvel at the ever-increasing signif-icance of sexuality through the nineteenth and twentieth centuries; the way it became a surrogate religion, even, or rather especially, in the most apparently secular and progressive areas of life. Current queer theory, and the rediscovery of bisexuality as quintessentially postmodern, if remem-bered at all, will seem equally bizarre. And yet, the norm will surely be bisexuality. Not in the sense that most people will be having partners of both sexes. Rather, bisexuality will be the unremarkable, unprescriptive norm, and those people who happen to cohabit predominantly or exclu-sively with a person or persons of the one sex will not stand out as such, any more than those who do otherwise will stand out for whatever they do.

This will mean that, a century from now, our own obsessive binary division between hetero and homosexual will be considered one of the most bizarre things about us. But there will be other kinds of dominant clasification. In the context of AIDS, penetrative sex has taken on new significance as a sexual behaviour. It may even be that in future a 'straight' pair and a 'gay' pair doing penetrative sex might be classified as more alike than (e.g.) one gay pair doing penetrative sex and another gay pair not. Likewise with gay and straight people practising auto-eroticism rather than inter-personal eroticism.

The return of the daemonic?

No matter how successful it might be, this enlightened agenda for sexuality could never have a completely free run across the next century. Culture just doesn't evolve like that; it never develops without conflict and resistance. But where will the challenge come from? I do not think it will come from either the radical view of sexual dissidence, so influential in the last half-century, or from the conservative attitudes which it repudiated.

I think a challenge may come from a mutation of a conception of sexual desire which preceded both the conservative and the radical political agendas and from which they both borrowed, often unawares. I mean a vision of sexual desire as daemonic. Hitherto I've considered this only in relation to its tamed counterpart in sexual radicalism. In fact it is expressed much more powerfully in some of the great mythic oppositions of western culture: the Greek one between Apollo and Dionysus, the Renaissance ones between Reason and Passion, Culture and Nature, and most recently Freud's account of human history as the unending antagonism between civilisation and instinct. In each of these far-reaching mythic oppositions, desire is obviously a life-force: it is the Dionysiac, Passion, Nature, instinct, or drive. But it is untamed, unsocialised and at heart non-human. Its amoral core becomes the more potentially of the human as a result of human attempts to tame it. As Georges Bataille put it: 'eroticism is an insane world whose depths, far beyond its ethereal forms, are infernal'.[11] More fundamentally still, this is a life-force indifferent to life itself. What this means, as Bataille insisted in this book and others, is that the life force is also, and indifferently so, a force of death, dissolution and destruction. Eros and Thanatos are not enemies like God and Satan; they cleave together, each indifferent to the other. This is the heart of the pre- or non-Christian idea of the daemonic. Christian theology disavows this earlier realisation of 'nature's' indifferent binding of death into life, by replacing it with the more reassuring enmity of God and Satan (the translation of the daemonic into the demonic). Of course the earlier realisation influences that theology; one has only to recall the widely held belief from ancient times through to the Renaissance and beyond that ejaculation literally shortens the life of the male. This is what the Renaissance poet John Donne meant when he wrote: 'profusely blind / We kill ourselves, to propagate our kind'.[12] Donne, half-inside the religious taming of nature's indifferent binding of death and life, translates the daemonic into the satanic, and blames Eve for bringing death into desire. This is from the same poem, just a few lines before: 'that first marriage was our funeral: / One woman at one blow, then killed us all, / And singly, one by one, they kill us now'. Undoubtedly misogyny has a lot to do with patriarchy, but it is one of the delusions of a progressive sexual politics to believe this is the beginning and end of the matter. Misogyny connects with some of our civilisation's most fundamental disavowals.

In the myth of Eden it was Eve's transgressive desire which brought death into the world. The Christian body is imprisoned between desire and death not least because sexual desire ruins, torments and destroys us with the experience of lack. To be in its grip is to be radically unfree. Just to desire is to begin to die. How heroic then of later radicals to make sexuality the source of human liberation! What magnificent hubris! How the old Gods must laugh! But if we hear in that cruel laughter just a hint of desire, we will not be mistaken: if it was our hubris which made the gods punish us humans, it was also what made them fall in love with us. I just wrote that to desire is to begin to die. The Christian God, unlike his predecessors, does not desire. He is complete, wanting and lacking nothing. He absolutely does not desire because to desire is an imperfection and a limitation inseparable from mortality. Being perfect, the Christian God doesn't desire, but then he doesn't laugh, either.

The pioneer Christian theologians believed that the creation of true civilisation in a fallen world requires the repression of a large measure of human instinct. But they also half-knew what Freud would later formulate in psychoanalytic terms, namely that the more developed the civilisation, the more it becomes vulnerable to the return of what it necessarily has to exclude, forget, and repress. And via both Freud and another of those ironic and hubristic twists which mark the tortuous history of thought, this realisation helps to radicalise sexuality in the work of those like Norman O. Brown, Wilhelm Reich and Herbert Marcuse.

Such writers seize on the idea of the return of the repressed. The crucial point here is that what is repressed is never eliminated; it can never simply be expelled either from the individual psyche or the social order. Rather, it remains inside both, always threatening to destabilise them. Every individual experiences the struggle to a greater or lesser degree: instinct, the id and the unconscious are always there to wreck whatever precarious equilibrium is achieved by the ego. But the sexual radicals argued that this force, instead of wrecking the individual through repression, might be liberated and turned against the society doing the repression. It's a remarkable turnabout: now sexuality is not the reason we are radically unfree, but the impetus for a radical vision of freedom. From torment, guilt and death comes sexual liberation. Perhaps it is not surprising that this reversal involved a taming of desire which amounted to a new kind of repression. Sexual radicalism wanted desire to subvert some things but definitely not others; it had to destroy the old order but serve the new. The hope was that liberated desire would, as it were, civilise itself. But it is unwise to rely upon desire to discriminate between good and bad social orders, and the very radicalism which made so much of the idea of the return of the repressed would soon encounter the return of its own repressed.

Progressive and secularist theories of desire have struggled to displace the Christian, forgetting the daemonic which preceded both. From the daemonic perspective desire cannot be regarded as delinquent only when denied an outlet. Such a 'wild oats' account disastrously fails to recognise that this is a force at best indifferent to civilisation and probably inimical to it. The return of this repressed has the potential to disintegrate any individual and any society.

Whenever the radical and the reformist visions of desire become disorganised by their own repressions, the daemonic becomes half-visible again and constitutes an obscure challenge to both. In crucial respects of course it has never not been visible. The artistic imagination has always been fascinated by the daemonic, especially in terms of erotic risk, and the erotic encounter with death. A recent collection of short fiction is called *High Risk: Writings on Sex, Death and Subversion*. It claims its contributors to be on 'the cutting edge of literature'[13]. It is more likely that most of them are catching up. Some eighty-five years ago Thomas Mann was writing more insightfully about sex, death and subversion in *Death in Venice*. Thirty-five years after that he gave epic expression to the same theme in his important but now neglected novel *Dr Faustus*. Mann made a daemonic, erotic encounter with disease and death the focus of a history of Europe in the first half of the twentieth century. It seemed, say twenty years ago, unthinkable that anyone might do the same for the first half of the twenty-first century. Now, again, it has become thinkable.

The daemonic is being hesitantly revived by some queer theorists, most of whom are vague about its history. One queer slogan a couple of years back was 'put the homo back into homicide'. But its most controversial recent intellectual advocate has to be Camille Paglia, and she is very aware of its cultural history. I'm referring mainly to her influential book *Sexual Personae*, first published in 1990. Paglia resurrects the idea of human history as a struggle between the Apollonian and the Dionysian. The truth of the Dionysian is not to be found in the earth's surface but in its bowels, and if we have a deep revulsion from slime, it is because it's what we came from. The essence of nature is what Paglia calls the 'chthonian', that is, 'the blind, grinding of subterranean force, the long slow suck, the murk and ooze'. All culture, including aesthetics and science, is built on the repression or evasion of the fact that we begin in a primal melting pot where the life force in also a force of dissolution and death:

> Everything is melting in nature ... An apple tree laden with fruit: how peaceful, how picturesque. But remove the rosy filter of humanism from our gaze and look again. See nature spurning and frothing, its mad spermatic bubbles endlessly spilling out and smashing in that inhuman round of waste, rot, and carnage ... Nature is the seething excess of being.[14]

Human culture is a massive and necessary defence against this nature. But our sexuality still partakes of it. Which is why sex is unfree, inhumane, compulsive and aggressive, characterised by a 'daemonic instability'.[15] In sex we are caught up in a 'backward movement towards primeval dissolution'; sex threatens annihilation. This is why, says Paglia, so many men turn away or flee after sex: 'they have sensed the annihilation of the daemonic'.[16] She believes a perfectly humane, guilt-free eroticism to be impossible.

To hear academics and others dismissing Paglia as a fascist or merely a spokeswoman of the new right, is to know they are on the defensive.[17] Paglia may already be an embarrassing victim of her own success; she is certainly an American celebrity, which is almost the same thing. One good reason for her success is that Paglia polemically restates, often crudely, occasionally brilliantly, some of the most powerful myths of western culture, myths which both the reformist and the radical attitudes to sexual dissidence have tried to forget. Of course it remains open to question as to whether those myths articulate profound truths or pernicious mystifications. But they persist in the cultural memory, and they return because the realities they articulate or mystify remain intractable. I believe, against Paglia, that the daemonic is not pure nature returning to blast culture apart, but the return of a repressed cultural history so inextricably bound up with nature it is impossible anymore to distinguish between the two.[18] And even if it were possible to tell them apart, I suspect the most recalcitrant kind of desire might be more socialised than 'natural'. I could put this differently, in the form of a familiar paradox which artists have explored, for example Thomas Mann in *Death in Venice* and Joseph Conrad in *Heart of Darkness*: only the highly civilised can become truly daemonic. Put yet another way, it is when we believe we have comfortably and completely superseded the past that it returns to haunt us and it does so not from the past but from within the present; older ways of thinking and feeling emerge precisely from within the discourses which we thought had superseded them. That is a situation I earlier described in terms of the radical continuity. It is the reason why I advocate an intellectal history over the pseudo-radicalism of a postmodernism forever claiming that the present has made a radical and irreversible break with the past, and that we cannot ever really know the past anyway.

In the very same month that the *Village Voice* article appeared, Michelangelo Signorile wrote a rather more disturbing and controversial piece for the magazine *Out*.[19] He drew attention to the growing numbers of people having unsafe sex in contexts in which the risk of HIV infection is high. According to Signorile, these people are not being merely careless; on the contrary, they are deliberately eroticising the risk factor. High-risk unprotected sex is called 'barebacking'. He further identifies a trend toward eroticising the HIV virus itself, in fantasy and in actual practice. Signorile writes this article because he fears this tendency may be widespread, and growing. It connects with the culture of drug use. The explanation that drugs make us sexually careless is not the complete story. The encounter with risk and danger is sometimes more deliberate, more calculated than any rational approach to either sexuality or drugs wants, or can afford, to allow. 'Barebacking' is not obviously widespread, but it has attracted much attention since Signorile's article, and also has its own website ('xtremesex'). In one of the more thoughtful recent articles devoted to it, Celia Farber concludes that barebacking is a powerful reminder that sex is never safe.[20] At the very least it confirms what we always knew: the daemonic experience of desire continues to circulate in fantasy, and in ways which are making even the queerest of postmodern radicals pause for thought as they encounter the past they thought they had escaped.

Notes

1   I've expressed scepticism about this elsewhere – see 'Bisexuality and wishful theory', *Textual Practice*, 10:3 (1996), 523–39.

2   Leo Bersani, *Homos* (Cambridge, Mass., Harvard University Press, 1995), p. 53.
3   Pat Califia, 'Unravelling the sexual fringe', cited from Lynda Hart's challenging study *Between the Body and the Flesh: Performing Sadomasochism* (New York, Columbia University Press, 1998), p. 49.
4   Donald Morton argues at length that queer values correspond all too neatly with modern capitalism; see his 'Queerity and ludic sado-masochism: compulsory consumption and the emerging post-al queer' in Donald Morton *et al.* (eds), *Post-ality: Marxism and Postmodernism*, Transformation, 1 (Washington, Maisonneuve Press, 1995), pp. 185–215.
5   Anonymous London leaflet, 'Queer power now' (1991); cited from Alan Sinfield's *Gay and After* (London, Serpent's Tail, 1998), p. 8, itself the most thoughtful account of the recent challenges to the gay identity.
6   Carol A. Queen, 'Strangers at home: bisexuals in the queer movement', *Outlook*, 16 (1992), 33; cited here from Elizabeth Wilson's provocative and recommended article, 'Is transgression transgressive?' in Joseph Bristow (ed.), *Activating Theory: Lesbian, Gay, Bisexual Politics* (London, Lawrence and Wishart, 1993), p. 113.
7   Eve Kosofsky Sedgwick, 'Paranoid reading and reparative reading; or, you're so paranoid, you probably think this introduction is about you' in Sedgwick (ed.), *Novel Gazing: Queer Reading in Fiction* (Durham and London, Duke University Press, 1997), p. 5.
8   *Ibid.*, p. 7
9   Simon Jarvis, 'Reflections in the golden bowl', *TLS* (8 May 1998), 25.
10 Edward Said, *Culture and Imperialism* (London, Chatto and Windus, 1993), p. 389.
11 Georges Bataille, *The Tears of Eros* (San Francisco, City Lights, 1988), p. 69.
12 John Donne, 'An anatomy of the world' in *The Complete English Poems*, (Harmondsworth, Penguin, 1971), p. 273.
13 A. Scholder and I. Silverberg (eds), *High Risk 2: Writings on Sex, Death and Subversion* (London, Serpent's Tail, 1994).
14 Camille Paglia, *Sexual Personae: Art and Decadence from Nefertiti to Emily Dickinson* (Harmondsworth, Penguin, 1992), pp. 1–6, 41–2.
15 *Ibid.*, p. 13.
16 *Ibid.*, pp. 4–5. Male sexuality is especially insecure, always haunted by the prospect of failure and humiliation ('a flop is a flop'), and even when successful is inherently mutable, going from erection through orgasm to detumescence: 'Men enter in triumph but withdraw in decrepitude. The sex act cruelly mimics history's decline and fall.' Which also means that male sexuality is inherently manic-depressive (p. 20).
17 See, for example, Elizabeth Wilson, 'Is transgression transgressive', p. 114, and bell hooks, *Outlaw Culture: Resisting Representations* (London and New York, Routledge, 1994), chapter 7, 'Camille Paglia: "black" pagan or white

Coloniser?'.

18   Paglia subscribes to a binary antagonism between nature and culture which is reductive of both: 'Moral codes are always obstructive, relative and man-made. Yet they have been of enormous profit to civilisation. They *are* civilisation. Without them, we are invaded by the chaotic barbarism of sex, nature's tyranny, turning day into night and love into obsession and lust' (*Sexual Personae*, p. 131).

19   Michelangelo Signorile, 'Bareback and reckless', *Out* (July 1997), 36–8; see also Michael Warner, 'Why gay men are having risky sex', *Voice* (31 January 1995), 33–6, and Celai Farber, 'Unprotected', *Continuum*, 5:5 (1999), 62–3.

20   Farber, 'Unprotected', p. 63.

Index

Note: 'n' after a page reference indicates a note number on that page.

freedom
  sexual 33, 43, 58
  spiritual 58
Frenchness 84–5, 86, 87
Frenesí see Bardem, Miguel, Albacete,
  Alfonso and David Menkes, *Más
  que amor frenesí*
Freud, Sigmund 72, 90, 225, 228, 229
  *Three Essays on the Theory of
  Sexuality* 156
Frye, Ellen
  The Other Sappho 14–15
'Fucking Faggot' 117
functionalism 159
Fuss, Diana 18

Gaish 151-2
Galford, Ellen
  The Fires of Bride 16
  Moll Cutpurse: Her True History
  17–18
Gallop, Jane 71
Garber, Marjorie
  *Vice Versa: Bisexuality and the
  Eroticism of Everyday Life* 215
Garcia Serrano and Juan Luis Iborra
  Amor de hombre 96, 99, 102–3, 108,
  109
gay rights 42, 43, 103
Gay Village 130
gay/lesbian activism 218
gender 61, 69, 122, 152, 153–4, 191,
  195–6
  disaffection 162
  identity 121, 154
  instability 75, 108
  performativity 121
genealogy
  erotic 14
  lesbian 12–13
ghosts 16
glamour 168
Goldberg, Whoopi 167

The Golden Girls 204
Goldstein, Richard 217–18
Grade, Michael 210
Greeks 225, 228
Grosz, Elizabeth 5, 193
'grunge' 113

Halberstam, Judith 155
Hall, Arsenio 173
Hall, Radclyffe
  The Well of Loneliness 155–6, 157
Hall, Stuart 158
Halperin, David 156
Hampstead Heath 58
hauntings 16
Hayes, Penny
  The Long Trail 21
Haynes, Todd
  Poison 184, 198
  Safe 7, 183 -99
Heath, Stephen 198
herbalism 55, 59
hermaphroditism 153, 156
heroism
  lesbian 19
heterosex 205
heterosexism 21, 50, 56, 108, 109
heterosexuality 22, 69, 72, 75, 100,
  101, 120–1, 184, 192, 209, 214
Heterosoc 52, 58
*High Risk: Writings on Sex, Death and
  Subversion* 230
Higson, Andrew 56
hindsight 77
history 4–5, 22, 23, 30–2, 216
  black 31
  lesbian 12–13, 19, 20, 24
HIV 84, 86, 88, 232
Hollinghurst, Alan 5, 131
  The Folding Star
  The Spell
  The Swimming Pool Library
home 71